*Sociology
and
School
Knowledge*

# Sociology and School Knowledge

CURRICULUM THEORY, RESEARCH AND POLITICS

## GEOFF WHITTY

METHUEN · LONDON

First published in 1985 by
Methuen & Co. Ltd
11 New Fetter Lane,
London EC4P 4EE

Photoset in Great Britain by
Nene Phototypesetters Ltd,
Northampton
and printed by Richard Clay,
The Chaucer Press,
Bungay, Suffolk

*British Library Cataloguing in
Publication Data*

Whitty, Geoff
Sociology and school knowledge:
curriculum theory, research and politics.
1. Education – Great Britain – Curricula
I. Title
370.19'0941      LB1564.G7

ISBN 0–416–36960–X
ISBN 0–416–36970–7 Pbk

*For Alison and Patrick*

# Contents

# Acknowledgements

I am grateful to Basil Bernstein, Brian Davies and Michael Young for first alerting me to the possibilities inherent in a sociological approach to the school curriculum in lectures they gave at the University of London Institute of Education in the late 1960s and early 1970s. I should also like to thank John Eggleston for first suggesting that I should write this book back in 1978. I will always be indebted to my various collaborators over the years, namely Michael Young, Denis Gleeson, Madeleine Arnot and Richard Bowe, who will no doubt recognize their parts in the genesis and development of many of the ideas expressed in this book. Similarly, my conversations and correspondence with Jean Anyon, Michael Apple, John Beck, Bob Connell, James Donald, Henry Giroux, Andy Hargreaves, Richard Smith and Valerie Walkerdine have been especially helpful to me. However, for the ways in which their contributions have been put to use in this particular volume, I must assume full responsibility. My greatest debt is to my colleagues and students at the University of Bath, the University of Wisconsin-Madison and the University of London who, sometimes consciously, often unconsciously, have helped me to clarify my academic and political priorities. Finally, I would like to thank Marilyn Toft for helping me with the preparation of the manuscript and for so cheerfully accepting the fact that living with me has also involved living with this project.

Acknowledgement is due to Falmer Press, Croom Helm, the Open University Press and Pluto Press for permission to use material that has appeared in different form in various of their publications. It has been substantially revised before inclusion here.

# Introduction

I begin this book with a brief excursion into my own biography, because I believe it will help to explain why I initially set out to explore the sociology of the school curriculum and why I am still doing so when many others have abandoned the field for other interests. I suppose I have been fascinated with the idea that the curriculum could be different from the way it is, in terms of its content and its form, ever since my final term as a pupil at one of London's direct grant grammar schools. For most of my career there in the late 1950s and early 1960s, I doubt if I ever asked myself, let alone anyone else, why I was studying the particular assortment of subjects presented to me or why the content of those subjects was constituted in the particular way it was. That is not to say for one moment that I was uncritical of the education I was getting, but my criticisms focused almost exclusively on the way I was being taught particular subjects rather than on the value and purpose of the grammar school curriculum and its particular content. Only in my final term, when I read E. H. Carr's *What Is History?* (Carr 1961) did I even begin to glimpse the idea that school knowledge was a selection from a much vaster range of possible knowledge and that its content might be socially determined.

Whether or not the interest in historiography that this engendered in me helped me to gain a scholarship to one of our élite universities, I did not find much evidence within that institution that the questioning of the status of received knowledge was an activity exactly encouraged among undergraduate students. Indeed, I was able to muster a respectable degree by regurgitating facts in tripos examinations as if they were god-given and incontrovertible. Yet this was not because I had lost interest in questioning their status as knowledge, it was rather that the lack of intellectual stimulation within the courses on offer led me to devote my time to other activities. As this was by now the mid-1960s, such activities not surprisingly included radical student politics. Far from it being an escape from intellectual work, this provided me with by far the most exciting intellectual experience of my time at Cambridge – listening to Perry Anderson present an early version of his paper 'Components of a national culture' (P. Anderson 1968) to the Alternative University organized by the student left. That paper convinced me of the need to expose the social basis of knowledge not just to those in the relatively privileged context of higher education but to those who, as things were, never glimpsed what one of the new sociologists of education was later to term 'the open human possibilities of creating new knowledge structures and their modes of transmission' (Esland 1971).

It was the development of these interests that gave me the then rather rare privilege of finding the postgraduate certificate in education year the most rewarding academic experience that I had had to date. I found myself at the Institute of Education in London just when the prevailing assumptions of philosophers about what was worthwhile knowledge were beginning to be exposed to critical scrutiny by sociologists. The lectures of Basil Bernstein seemed to cut through so much of the mystifications of the philosophers and helped me to see the curriculum as it existed as but one of a number of possibilities but one whose form served particular social functions. At the same time, my experiences of trying to teach the traditional grammar school curriculum to working-class boys in a Paddington comprehensive school while on teaching practice made me realize that that curriculum was often meaningless to those exposed to it. This led me to sympathize with a claim I came across from another sociologist writing in the first issue of the *Journal of Curriculum Studies* that: 'there is a profound sense in which compulsory education over the past century has been essentially senseless. The curriculum to which educationists have ascribed a variety of subtle motives has been a structure of activity designed to fill the time' (Musgrove 1969).

Emerging into the teaching profession in the late 1960s, I was, like so many others at that time, fired with an enthusiasm to change things. To change not only the experience of schooling for my pupils, but also to use those changes to foster changes in consciousness that would ultimately transform society. Such was my belief in this sort of possibility that I virtually abandoned much of my involvement in broader political activities to foster change through education. Teaching firstly in a traditional grammar school that was reluctant to admit that it was in the process of becoming comprehensive and then in a progressive comprehensive struggling to espouse quite different ideals (Daunt 1975), I increasingly recognized the naivety of my aspirations. Change, even in a relatively favourable environment, was neither easy nor predictable in its consequences. I did not abandon my commitment to change but felt determined to understand more of the sociological work that I had come across in my year at the Institute of Education, so that I could have a more realistic idea of both the possibilities and the problems of radical educational change.

I returned to the Institute to explore these issues and found, to my astonishment, that the theories being espoused by sociologists about the 'open human possibilities' were, if anything, even more naive than my own. The first phase of the 'new sociology of education' was at its height but none the less stimulating for its over-optimistic excesses. I returned to some of the texts that I had come across as a student activist in the 1960s and sought to make the connections between them and the newer literature to which I was now being exposed. The product of this was a dissertation, part of which was published as an article entitled 'Sociology and the problem of radical educational change – notes towards a reconceptualization of the new sociology of education' (Whitty 1974). This warned sociologists not to romanticize the possibilities of radical change in and through the school curriculum especially in absence of broader attacks on the prevailing 'culture of positivism'. I suggested that, important as the politics of everyday life undoubtedly were, an over-emphasis upon them could lead to a neglect of the significance of 'Politics with a big P'. I concluded that a sociology of the curriculum that was more adequate both theoretically and politically might emerge if more notice was taken of some of the relevant Marxist literature.

Little was I to know that this was exactly what would happen to the field in the very near future, though not I suspect as a result of my own strictures. What came about was a volte-face in the sociology of education and an espousal of forms of Marxism that seemed to deny the 'open human possibilities' for change and suggest that everyday pro-fessional processes merely sustained broader structures of oppression whose origins lay elsewhere. All possibilities for radical work within schools seemed for a time to be ruled out by the theoretical fiat of this new phase in the sociology of education.

Despite the frustrations that this alternation between extreme pos-itions engendered, I held on to the idea that sociological study of the curriculum would yield important insights into opportunities for radical practice in and around the educational arena and, in my work over the past ten years or so, I have constantly returned to this issue. This present book brings together some of this work in a substantially revised form and is divided into two sections. The first section opens with an attempt to trace the theoretical and empirical developments in the sociology of education and related areas that are pertinent to my concerns. It then tries to suggest ways in which a sociology of the curriculum could develop closer links with pedagogical and political practice in a manner that would make it more relevant to those engaged in developing radical approaches to educational policy and practice. The second section contains some of my own attempts to understand contemporary developments in the curriculum field by interrogating them critically with sociological theories about the nature of schooling. The book concludes with an assessment of the issues these studies throw up for the Labour movement in contemporary Britain.

It should be clear that my own biography and my own particular interests in the sociology of the curriculum are not necessarily typical of all those people who work or have worked in the field. This is what gives my own work its particular orientation and also what explains why I have chosen to discuss only a limited range of literature in this book rather than trying to provide exhaustive coverage of the field. There are also other limitations that are less justifiable, though the main one, the over-emphasis on the secondary school curriculum at the expense of that of primary or further education, is itself at least partially explicable in terms of my own career. I hope nevertheless that the more general arguments of the book will prove of interest and value well beyond the rather limited group of people who have followed a career path similar to my own.

# Part One

## From theory and research to policy and practice

# 1

## Sociological approaches to the school curriculum

The sociology of education in Britain is generally regarded as having gone through a paradigm shift in the late 1960s and early 1970s. A supposed 'new direction' in the sociology of education was seen to emerge from the work of Basil Bernstein and Michael F. D. Young and their colleagues and students at the Institute of Education in London. This shift, but also the lack of a single-minded adoption of any one of a number of possible lines of development, was symbolized in the sub-title of the first major publication by this group – *Knowledge and Control: New Directions for the Sociology of Education* (Young 1971a). In so far as there was anything that had a coherent claim to be termed a 'new sociology of education' (Gorbutt 1972), its approach was one that sought to make problematic that which had hitherto been taken for granted in education (Young 1971b). As, at least initially, many of the writers associated with these developments chose to make the nature of school knowledge one of their central problems (Esland 1971; Keddie 1971), this period is often seen as opening up for the first time the possibility of a genuinely sociological approach to the study of the school curriculum. As early as 1970 Young defined the central project of the group associated with him as an attempt to relate the 'principles of selection and organization that underlie curricula to their institutional and interactional setting in schools and classrooms and to the wider social structure' (Young 1971b). This fairly ambitious and catholic definition of the task of a sociology of the curriculum is worth bearing in mind throughout our exploration of the way in which different elements of the formulation received emphasis at different times during the following decade, as different figures in its somewhat eclectic intellectual heritage of phenomenologists, interactionists and Marxists gained ascendancy.

There are some who seem to regard the whole of the 1970s as something of an eccentric interlude in the history of the sociology of education. For some observers, the period that was dominated by the so-called 'new sociology of education' and its various phenomenological and neo-Marxist derivatives diverted a generation of sociologists of education from the central concerns and tasks of the discipline. Some of these same observers have seen in the publication of a new book by one of the founding fathers of British sociology of education (Halsey *et al.* 1980), and in the work of the latest generation of writers in this field (Demaine 1981), evidence that the 1980s have brought a return to the older orthodoxies in the field (St John-Brooks 1980). However, I want to suggest that, despite its many shortcomings, the work of the 1970s has not been entirely at odds with the mainstream concerns of the discipline and that its legacy is of continuing value to contemporary sociologists, curriculum theorists, policy-makers and teachers, even if this is in ways that were not generally grasped at the time. The book therefore begins with an attempt to trace the various ways in which sociologists have sought to conceptualize the relationship between curricula and their institutional and societal contexts over the past fifteen or so years.

## The emergence of the 'new' sociology of education

In some ways at least, the emphasis on the newness of the new sociology of education is misleading. Certainly, leaving aside the work of Mannheim (who seems to have been neglected by old- and new-style sociologists of education alike), the idea that the curriculum should be seen as a social invention, reflecting conscious or unconscious cultural choices that accorded with the values and beliefs of dominant groups, was not a central one in British sociology of education prior to that date. Nor were the sociology of knowledge and phenomenology perspectives that figured in the work of the major practitioners in the field such as Halsey and Floud. On the other hand, Banks (1974) has pointed out that sociological analysis of the curriculum was not entirely lacking in the traditional sociology of education, as could be seen in the work of Cotgrove (1958) and Musgrave (1967) on technical education. Nevertheless, these features of the work of Young and his collaborators were those which received most initial attention and there was thus a tendency for its advocates to emphasize its refreshing 'newness' and its adversaries to point to its idiosyncracies. Yet, at the same time, it is important to insist that there is a sense in which the new sociology of education constituted a development of, rather than a break with, the dominant tradition in the

British sociology of education since its emergence as a major field of study in the 1950s, a tradition largely concerned with the under-achievement of working-class children in school. I want to suggest that an important influence in the subsequent development of British sociology of education was this same concern emerging in new, and politically more radical, guises. Indeed, as will be seen, much of the history of the sociology of education in Britain since the late 1960s was, in part at least, the product of an interplay between this dominant political concern and successive fashions within academic sociology.

I shall therefore briefly try to locate the so-called new sociology of education within the history of British sociology of education more generally. The dominant theoretical paradigm adopted by British sociologists of education in the 1950s and 1960s was that of structural-functionalism though it was rarely made explicit. However, the research tradition was also strongly influenced by a commitment to a version of Fabian socialism and social engineering via education. Like the policy-makers with whom they became associated, British sociologists in the twenty years after the Second World War were largely concerned with the problem of increasing access to schooling rather than with examining the nature of the education which they sought to distribute more widely. Their interest focused upon the consistent tendency for the children of manual workers to receive less schooling and achieve less success at each of the successive educational hurdles than the children of professional and managerial workers. In most of these studies of working-class failure (Silver 1973) there was a confident assumption that what we took for granted as education was a 'good' in itself and that it was in the interests of both individuals and the national economy that they should receive more of it. Much the same assumption seemed to be made about the social mobility that education was presumed to encourage. The variety of statistical studies produced during the 1950s and early 1960s made it clear, however, that the tripartite system of education was failing to increase significantly the number of upwardly mobile working-class children, and it was hoped that sociologists would be able to explain working-class failure and thus provide a basis for policies that would produce the equality of opportunity which the earlier reforms had failed to achieve.

Given this basic orientation, sociologists began to examine in more detail the relationship between social class and educational performance. Their initial work sought to explain the phenomenon of school failure by reference to the cultural features of working-class life (Craft 1970), though the concept of culture they employed was a heavily loaded one and the methodologies they employed were hardly able to grasp the nature of this culture in the way recent approaches to cultural studies have sought to do. The general orientation was one in which working-class culture was characterized as creating a 'deficit' in the child that would have to be remedied before he or she could hope to succeed at school (Keddie 1973). So long as the nature of education was taken for granted, home background was seen as the key variable in the production of educational success and failure. The response of policy-makers was to pursue two related strategies, which involved broadening access to schooling and developing ways of counteracting the influence of class culture upon school achievement. The introduction of comprehensive education, RoSLA, 'compensatory education' programmes and the extension of nursery education may all be seen, in some respects at least, as examples of such strategies. Clearly the organizational structure of schooling did itself come under a certain amount of critical scrutiny, and indeed underwent successive changes, but these were generally designed to increase the penetration of an education, the nature of which continued to be taken for granted.

However, as one organizational innovation followed another, and the correlations between social class background and school achievement remained remarkably consistent over time, in both Britain and the USA, the validity of the assumption that the major problems for working-class pupils were those of home background and of access to schooling was increasingly called into question. Studies began to home in on the school as a site of interaction between home culture and school culture. Some of these studies were more micro-sociological in orientation and attempted to grasp how a pupil's experience of school produced success and failure. In some ways Colin Lacey's book, *Hightown Grammar* (Lacey 1970), supports his own view that it stood (along with David Hargreaves's *Social Relations in a Secondary School* (Hargreaves 1967)) at a crossroads between the old and the new sociologies of education. Yet, although Lacey's book proposed a change from streaming to mixed-ability teaching, it did not even entertain the notion that the nature of the central activities of schooling might be altered and it ended with a suggestion that working-class children should be helped to adapt to schooling – by appointing social workers to those whose home backgrounds seemed most likely to create problems. Even Hargreaves only raised the possibility of redefining the nature of education in one of his concluding remarks and it was far from clear what he meant by it. Yet these two studies were exceptional in placing any emphasis at all on the process of schooling as an explanatory variable.

Thus, the tendency of sociologists to treat the curriculum as outside the scope of their enquiries persisted even within those studies that began to look more critically at the institutions of schooling. Young made the comment about sociological studies of public schools that 'one can read them and hardly be aware that considerable periods of pupils' time are taken up, and presumably their consciousness is developed, by what they do in classrooms, laboratories and libraries and by the kinds of courses made available to them' (Young 1973a). This was more widely applicable to studies of other kinds of schools as well. Young also suggested that the neglect of curriculum issues by sociologists until the late 1960s might well be explained by the difficulty of conceiving of alternatives when 'the organization of knowledge implicit in our own curricula is so much part of our taken-for-granted world' (Young 1971b). It was only with the failure of those policies that attempted to tackle the less deeply embedded features of education, and only when a broader movement for curriculum change had already developed, that the nature of what working-class pupils were failing at began to be given serious attention by sociologists of education. Warwick (1974) goes so far as to suggest that some of their work in this field was explicitly intended to provide theoretical support for the growing 'movement for a progressive curriculum based in the concept of integration'.

It is therefore interesting to notice that, writing as long ago as 1961 and before many of the successive organizational innovations had been introduced into the British educational system, Raymond Williams, in *The Long Revolution*, made the following comment in the course of a perceptive analysis of the development of English education:

> Attention has been concentrated, by critics in the public educator tradition, on the organization of secondary education to the point where a common general education of a genuinely secondary kind, will be available to all. The detailed proposals for this are interesting and many successful experiments have already been undertaken. Yet it remains true that the crucial question, in any such programme, is that of curriculum and teaching method, and it is difficult to feel that the present grammar-school curriculum, or its partial imitation and local extension by the secondary modern school, is of such a kind that the problem is merely one of distributing it more widely. An educational curriculum as we have seen again and again in past periods, expresses a compromise between an inherited selection of interests and the emphasis of new interests. At varying points in history, even this compromise may be long delayed, and it will often be muddled. The fact about our present curriculum is that it was essentially created by the nineteenth century, following some eighteenth-century models, and retaining elements of the medieval curriculum near its centre. A case can be made for every item in it, yet its omissions are startling.
>
> (Williams 1965: 171–2)

It is perhaps significant that during the period of organizational reforms in the 1950s and 1960s, only those like Williams on the political left and Bantock on the right, were arguing that 'the basic educational dilemma of our time is a cultural one and affects the nature of the meanings to be transmitted by the schools' (Bantock 1973). Meanwhile the radical and libertarian movement in education in the USA, and subsequently the deschoolers (Illich 1971; Reimer 1972), were also becoming known in Britain by the early 1970s and posing, from a different perspective again, critical questions about the role of schooling in social control. What is interesting about Williams, Bantock, and the radical educators is that they were all working outside the broad arena of consensus politics in which educational policies were formulated and in which most of the leading British sociologists of education were located (CCCS 1981).

By the late 1960s and early 1970s the social democratic consensus was already beginning to fall apart and the notion that state policy would serve to reduce significantly social inequalities and bring in a fair and just society by gradualist means (the classic dream of the Fabian socialists in Britain) was increasingly being called into question. It was also, of course, the tail-end of the period of 'flower power' and the philosophy of doing your own thing and creating your own realities. The so-called crisis of western sociology (Gouldner 1972) and the 'discovery' of a new brand of phenomenologically informed sociological theory (Filmer *et al.* 1972) were not unconnected with these trends. Yet the enthusiastic way in which phenomenology, and some of the ideas of American radical educators, were taken on board within the new sociology of education was not merely the result of fashion. It also stemmed from a belief that they offered both analytic and practical tools for tackling the very same issue of working-class school failure which earlier (and apparently discredited) perspectives and policies had failed to overcome.

It was at this time that a number of established sociologists of education were also turning their attention to the social basis of the selection, organization and distribution of knowledge in the school curriculum. In the paper entitled 'On the curriculum', first circulated in 1969, Bernstein suggested a way of conceptualizing the school curriculum which made clear that:

> there is nothing intrinsic about how educational time is used, or the status of the various contents or the relation between the contents. I am emphasizing the social nature of the system of choices from which emerges a constellation called a curriculum.          (Bernstein 1977b: 80)

This exploratory paper, from which much of Bernstein's subsequent work developed, illustrates the way in which the content of the curriculum, and its social organization, were no longer being taken for granted. At about the same time Musgrove was suggesting that sociologists might fruitfully begin to:

> examine subjects both within the school and in the nation at large

as social systems sustained by communication networks, material endowments and ideologies. Within a school and within the wider society subjects are communities of people, competing and collaborating with one another, defining and defending their boundaries, demanding allegiance from their members and conferring a sense of identity upon them. . . . Even innovation which appears to be essentially intellectual in character can be usefully examined as the outcome of social interaction and the elaboration of new roles within the organization.                                     (Musgrove 1968: 101)

Similarly, Musgrave (1973) has claimed that a recognition of the centrality of the curriculum came to him on a walk in Bristol in the autumn of 1968.

Nevertheless, it was probably only in 1971, with the publication of *Knowledge and Control* (Young 1971a), that the importance of the school curriculum as an area of sociological study came to be widely recognized, although the particular approaches the book espoused made it the centre of a considerable amount of political and academic controversy (see e.g. Bernbaum 1977; Best 1976; Flew 1976; Simon 1974). For Young and his collaborators, the sociology of education was 'no longer to be conceived as an area of enquiry distinct from the sociology of knowledge' (Young 1971b). Gorbutt characterized the new 'interpretive' paradigm in the following way:

The sociology of knowledge occupies a central place within interpretive sociology in contrast to its place as a fringe specialism within the normative paradigm. The work of Berger and Luckmann [1967] argues for the recognition of the social origin of all ideas. Knowledge at all levels, common sense, theoretical and scientific thereby becomes thoroughly relativized and the possibility of absolute knowledge is denied. Whereas Marx and Mannheim, key figures in the sociology of knowledge, asserted that some knowledge can be free from social bias, Berger and Luckmann argue that all knowledge is socially constructed and ideological. Truth and objectivity are human products.

                                                    (Gorbutt 1972: 6–7)

Gorbutt suggested that this approach had particularly significant implications for the study of three related areas; educational knowledge, the categories of educators and classroom interaction. In the following extract he spelt out some of the implications for the study of educational knowledge:

The relativization of educational knowledge is implicit and explicit in several of the contributions to Michael F. D. Young's book *Knowledge and Control*. . . . As Young points out 'Treating "what we know" as problematic, in order that it becomes the object of enquiry, rather than as a given, is difficult and perhaps nowhere more so than in education. The out-thereness of the content of what is taught, whether it be as subjects, forms of enquiry, topics or ways of knowing, is very much part of the educator's taken for granted world.' . . . It is not surprising that treating knowledge in this way has excited more than a ripple of interest, particularly amongst philosophers of education, for the worthwhileness of particular educational activities can no longer be justified in absolute terms once the social basis of such justification is recognized. The apparent self-evident justification for education into particular forms of knowledge is laid bare as an ideological statement. The process through which particular curricula are institutionalized and justified becomes open to sociological examination. Thus for example, the social assumptions underlying compensatory education, meaningful curricula for non-academic school leavers and mathematics for all can become the object of enquiry. We are forced into an often uncomfortable re-examination of the content and underlying assumptions of the curriculum at all levels.          (Gorbutt 1972: 7–8)

As Gorbutt implied, these ideas generated a lively debate between sociologists and philosophers. Philosophers were often critical of what they saw as a lack of clarity in the arguments of the sociologists and, in so far as their position did seem clear, of the theory of knowledge (or epistemological stance) implicit in work in this field. In particular, some philosophers (e.g. Pring 1972) were critical of those approaches to the sociology of knowledge that seemed to suggest that reality is '*nothing but* a social construction' or that 'all knowledge is relative' and 'criteria of validity and truth . . . are . . . open to socio-historical relativization'. I do not propose to explore in any detail the debate between sociologists and philosophers on this issue, since I do not believe that the significance of a sociological approach to school knowledge is entirely dependent upon the resolution of questions about the ultimate status of our knowledge of the world – were that, indeed, even possible. While such questions are by no means unimportant, my own view is that, if sociologists have been correct to stray into the field of epistemology, traditionally the preserve of the philosophers, they have been less wise in deserting some of the territory more conventionally that of the sociologist.

Even if it were the case, as philosophers would argue, that there were some features of knowledge not subject to relativization in any conceivable circumstances, there would clearly be others that varied in differing socio-historical circumstances. Certainly there are aspects of the way in which *school* knowledge is constructed, selected, organized, represented and distributed that are by no means absolute or beyond the realm of social action for change. To a certain extent, relativization may therefore be viewed not as a statement of an epistemological position, but as a useful procedural device for subverting our taken-for-granted assumptions about the seemingly absolute status of the knowledge which has come to be institutionalized in the school curriculum. A statement, to which Young subscribed, explicitly stated that a commitment to 'calling into question "what might be taken as education" indicates not a move to relativism, but an engagement in, and an invitation to the reader to engage in, the ongoing construction and exploration of what is to be questioned, or what is to be taken as problematic' (Beck *et al.* 1976). The issue of the ultimate status of knowledge was thus, by implication, left in abeyance.

It is therefore not of overwhelming significance whether Young was making a fundamental epistemological point about the validity of different types of knowledge, when he told us that the new sociology of education began by:

> rejecting the assumption of any superiority of educational or 'academic' knowledge over the everyday commonsense knowledge available to people as being in the world. There is no doubt that teachers' practices – lecturing, syllabus construction, examining, writing textbooks, etc. – are predicated on just the assumption of the superiority of academic knowledge that is being called into question.
>
> (Young 1973b: 214)

Whatever the thinking behind this statement, a rejection or suspension of prevailing assumptions is an important prerequisite for the asking of sociological questions about the school curriculum. It was, however, clear that most of the proponents of such an approach to the sociology of education were, in a much fuller sense, critical of the assumptions embedded in prevailing conceptions of the curriculum and of their social consequences; the analytic procedures they chose to adopt were, of course, related to that stance. Thus, for some of the new sociologists of education, it was not just that the newer sociological perspectives seemed more theoretically adequate than the earlier ones, they also seemed to offer up an enticingly simple route to social change. If the prevailing definitions of education were class-biased, they were also (along with the rest of social reality) socially constructed and hence could be reconstructed. If, as was argued, reality was the product of consciousness, then teachers could be brought to an awareness of the significance of their assumptions and everyday activities and thus to change them in ways that would benefit working-class pupils (Gorbutt 1972). There was therefore a practical, as well as an analytic, purpose in the new sociology of education, just as there had been a policy orientation in its earlier manifestations.

I am not suggesting that this was true of all the articles in *Knowledge and Control* (Young 1971a) (and indeed the book's richness lies partly in the fact that it combines a number of contradictory elements), but it is certainly one way of reading some parts of the work of Young, Esland and Keddie. It is even clearer in the work of those who attempted to popularize their ideas, as well as being a major focus of criticism of the whole new directions movement. This practical purpose underlying the critical analysis of school curricula and classroom interaction was perhaps clearest in the work of Gorbutt, who suggested in the article already quoted (Gorbutt 1972), that the reflection upon and unmasking of taken-for-granted assumptions about the nature of schooling should become an integral feature of the life of every school or college, a process that would revitalize them and 'possibly fulfil the promise of education for all'. Though others, such as Esland (1971), saw prevailing definitions of schooling as more firmly embedded in teacher consciousness, there still seemed to be a prevailing belief that the point of change was via professional processes. Hence there was little incentive to pursue the analysis into a study of the structural location of schooling, and what schools were for, particularly if social structure was something that could be dissolved through a change of consciousness on the part of those who sustained it. Even Eggleston (1975) pointed to the problems a radicalized teaching force alone could pose for social control and he seemed to regard its emergence as by no means beyond the realms of possibility.

This orientation to educational and social change was typical of the early phases of the new sociology of education. It was based upon a particular interpretation of phenomenological sociology symbolized in the first course in Sociology of Education to be produced by the Open University (OU). This was *School and Society*, written in the early 1970s and dominated in terms of theory by the contributions of Esland and Dale. The theoretical emphasis was very much on the role of teacher consciousness and professional process in defining reality in the classroom, in sustaining prevailing conceptions of schooling, and hence in perpetuating or challenging social inequalities. While there was already an awareness of the more structural approaches of Althusser (1971), Bernstein (1971) and Bourdieu (1971a, 1971b), they were either marginalized or interpreted in such a way as to fit a phenomenological problematic. Before going on to consider why the heyday of such an approach to the sociology of the curriculum was so shortlived, I shall comment briefly on the strengths and limitations of the sort of empirical work generated by this first phase of the new sociology of education.

## Early explorations

In *Knowledge and Control*, Young (1971b) stated that, 'we have virtually no theoretical perspectives or research to suggest explanations of how curricula, which are no less social inventions than political parties or new towns, arise, persist and change, and what the interests and values involved might be.' I suggested earlier that one of the reasons for the sociological interest in the school curriculum was to be found in the failure of more conventional sociological analyses of education to explain adequately why working-class pupils fail at school. The analysis of the nature of school knowledge was therefore never limited to a task of philosophical critique even though, in debates with philosophers, this point was sometimes obscured. The concern was to explore the possibility that there was some contingent relationship between prevailing definitions of school knowledge and the broader social structure. The intention was to establish, and indeed expose, the 'interests and values' implicated in prevailing curricular arrangements, usually with a view to changing them.

In the early and mid-1970s, the new sociology of education therefore embarked upon a programme of empirical research to explore the nature and functions of the 'overt and covert knowledge found within school settings' (Apple and King 1977). Shortlived as this experience was, and limited though the empirical fruits of the new sociology of education are often claimed to be, a whole range of studies by students at the Institute of Education did begin to rectify the lack of research on the values and interests embedded in the curriculum that had been noted by Young at the beginning of the decade (Young 1971b). Despite the limitations of these studies, some of them, such as that by Vulliamy (1972) about school music, demonstrated both the character and the potential utility of empirical work in this genre.

The major thrust of Vulliamy's study was to suggest that what was usually defined as music in school constituted but a small element of what might conceivably be regarded as musical activity. He argued that the assumptions that allowed music educators to define out whole areas of musical experience as 'not serious' served the interests of a particular social group. He further implied that, in regarding classical and avant-garde music as legitimate content for the school curriculum, whilst excluding the sort of music likely to be more meaningful to the majority of pupils, schools were guilty of an *unjustifiable* cultural bias. This resulted in many pupils 'switching off' from school music. In the following extract from a later account of some traditional features of music teaching in a particular school, he identified a further aspect of the process that ensured that only a small proportion of pupils would be a success at classroom music as the school defined it, and went on to suggest that only certain types of pupils tended to be selected for extra-curricular musical activities at this school:

> The prevailing definition of 'What counts as Music' in the school with its emphasis on musical literacy, the provision of information about

music, and the teaching of musical theory (all of which were strongly emphasized at 'A' or 'O' level and to a lesser extent CSE) makes the 'discipline' of music not unlike other 'academic' disciplines with their emphasis on literacy, abstract theory and so on. It was not surprising to find, therefore, that the music teachers should assume that those pupils (in the upper streams) who were good at other academic subjects might be good at the 'discipline' of music, whilst those pupils who had failed in other academic subjects (that is, those in the lower streams) would also 'fail' at music. This assumption clearly influenced the ways in which the different streams were taught. Whilst the top streams were taught the academic aspects of music, there was a general feeling amongst the music staff that there was little one could do with the lower streams in terms of teaching them music. It also affected which pupils were encouraged to take up playing musical instruments, since it was the Head of Music's view that a pupil in the lower stream, would have neither the ability nor the perseverance to play an instrument well and take full benefit from the peripatetic instrumental tuition provided.

Such observations, together with an examination of the literature on music education, tend to support the view that music educators with what I have called the 'traditional' paradigm of music teaching make the false assumption that only a limited number of people are 'musical'.                                    (Vulliamy 1976: 25–6)

In this passage he seemed to be suggesting, like Bourdieu (1976), that the style, as well as the content, of music education contributed to the false assumption on the part of teachers that many of their pupils lacked musical ability. Since it might further be argued that the features of music education to which Vulliamy pointed were more likely to 'make sense' or seem 'relevant' to the children of professional and managerial workers, rather than to those of the manual working class, there might well be grounds for suggesting that the selection of curricular knowledge, in this instance at least, was biased in the interests of the middle classes. On this view, the prevailing definitions of school music could be seen to encourage the failure of those who experienced a discontinuity between the culture of the school and life outside it and to legitimate the success of those with a prior familiarity with the culture embraced by the school. The argument that school music was culturally biased in this way was, of course, particularly strong in the case of schools with pupils from the various ethnic minorities.

If Vulliamy's argument about the nature of school music were generalizable to other aspects of the school curriculum, there would be some evidence that definitions of school knowledge could help to reproduce society in its existing form. Vulliamy himself did not necessarily wish to make such a broad claim. He suggested that school music was a 'particularly apt example of the potential of viewing school subjects from the perspective of the new sociology of education, because unlike the study of, for example, science subjects, it does not involve the epistemological problems associated with tendencies to extreme forms of relativity' (Vulliamy 1977). He implied that even if there might be absolutist justifications for prevailing definitions of certain subjects, there could be few tenable grounds for denying the relativity of aesthetic judgements. Certainly, some people did argue that knowledge in the natural sciences was less open to social relativization than in other fields. Jevons (1975) suggested that a 'dogmatic element in teaching physical science . . . [was] an epistemological necessity'. Students had to 'undergo a relatively dogmatic initiation, with temporary suspension of active participation in creating and criticizing theories'. Nevertheless, even a field like science education has seen different approaches to the subject competing for legitimacy, and Layton's work on the demise of the 'science of common things' in the nineteenth century concerned a view of science likely to have been far more meaningful to the majority of pupils than that which ultimately became established in the school curriculum (Layton 1973). It could be argued that it was the adoption of the latter that led to the widespread acceptance of a notion of science that defined the majority of the population as 'unscientific'. Young's work on science education attempted to explore these sorts of issues further (Young 1977a), and there certainly seemed to be at least some grounds for arguing that aspects of Vulliamy's case study of school music were paralleled in other aspects of the school curriculum.

Other studies (e.g. Whitty 1976) suggested that pupils were taught a particular view of the world in school and that, because there was no examination of the presuppositions upon which that view was based or of the social processes through which such a view developed, pupils were likely to accept as an immutable 'fact' what was but one ideological version of the world. A common criticism of courses in British political history was that, by concentrating on the activities of Crown, Lords and Commons, they served to 'naturalize' the existing British constitution and define the acceptable limits of political debate (Steed 1974). Hine's paper on school physics (Hine 1975) made a similar point about the nature of school physics. It suggested not only that prevailing approaches to the subject involved the selection and presentation of knowledge that legitimated the status quo and the omission of that which might challenge it, but also that the very organization of the curriculum into discrete units militated against the asking of the sorts of questions that might indicate that the world could be different.[1]

Whatever their relative plausibility, a clear implication of the various case studies of school subjects was that what was taught in schools acted as a means of social control and served to sustain the status quo. Nevertheless, there did seem to be an apparent contradiction between two aspects of the sort of work I have discussed here. In particular, there appeared to be some contradiction between arguments that stressed the curriculum's contribution to social reproduction by means of its cultural biases and those that suggested that what was actually taught made a much more direct contribution to social control. The first argument indicated that the majority of pupils failed because of the lack of relatedness of the school's criteria of success to their cultural experience outside school; the second implied that working-class pupils were kept in their place by learning a particular view of the way the world was. In one case the class structure was seen to be sustained because working-class pupils *failed* to learn what the school defined as significant, while in the other case the process depended on what they *did* learn in school – that is to accept (and if possible respect) the status quo.[2]

It might be suggested that this difference was trivial since the outcome, the efficient reproduction of the class structure of society, was the same in both cases. Certainly there was no reason to suppose that the process operated in a straightforward or non-contradictory manner or even that it operated in the same way for all aspects of the division of labour. Nevertheless, the issue could not be entirely evaded. One possible way of understanding the relationship between these two aspects of the process was hinted at in the following comments by Hand on the learning of literacy:

> On the one hand, then, high culture and children's literature develop an apparently universal content concealing form; on the other, the teaching of reading and writing as skills embodies a view of language as form without content. Actually, of course there is no paradox here. High culture is for, and shaped by, the middle class: instrumental language skills are for (but not shaped by) the working class. The middle-class child really learns to read at home. He learns through bedtime fairy tales, family story books, and so on – content and skill form one growing experience. Thus, from the first, reading comes naturally as a way of understanding and enlarging one's individual world. The working-class child learns to read if at all – at school. In toiling through the reading schemes he learns that reading is a mechanical task unrelated to anything he can understand. Thus he is prepared for a role in which reading is relevant only to the accomplishment of tasks ordained by others. For other purposes – apart from the reading of newspapers he abandons it as quickly as possible.
>
> (Hand 1976: 14)

This seemed to suggest that schools encouraged all pupils to acquire the sorts of skills and knowledge that ensured they could be dominated, but that only those with a prior familiarity with the prevailing cultural ethos of academic work were likely to show an interest in, and hence succeed at, those activities upon which educational success ultimately depended. Traditionally, of course, this process had been reinforced by institutional arrangements that provided separate schools, or at least separate courses, for those destined for different positions in the social hierarchy.

Most of the writers who were associated with the new sociology of education at this time implied, however, that by 'questioning of the "absoluteness" of many of the educator's assumptions about knowledge [and] illustrating the social origin of such assumptions, the way [was] open for the possibility of alternative definitions and assumptions' (Vulliamy 1976). Their work tended to lend support to Esland's view that sociological studies of the construction of school subjects would sensitize teachers to 'the open human possibilities of creating new knowledge structures and their modes of transmission' (Esland 1971) and to Gorbutt's optimism about the power of critical self-reflection to bring about change (Gorbutt 1972). Nevertheless, Keddie (1971) warned that, even in a comprehensive school context, 'hierarchical categories of ability and knowledge may well persist in unstreamed classrooms and lead to the differentiation of undifferentiated curricula' (Keddie 1971). Though she demonstrated in her own study of classroom knowledge how teachers themselves differentiated in selection of content and in pedagogy between pupils perceived as being of high and low ability, she also recognized (in a passage often ignored by her critics) that the origins of the categories involved lay outside the school in the wider distribution of power in society. Other writers rarely even mentioned this issue, let alone explored it, and thus most of the early empirical studies spawned by the new sociology of education over-estimated, at least by impli-cation, the ease with which change might take place.

Indeed, it was on this question of the relationship between curriculum change and the nature of the wider society that the early manifestations of the new sociology of education were at their weakest. A general optimism about the possibilities and consequences of change starting at school level was no substitute for a thorough analysis of the wider parameters of change (Sharp and Green 1975; Whitty 1974). A more rigorous exploration of the possibilities and problems of curriculum change therefore increasingly demanded a more rigorous analysis of the institutional and societal contexts of curriculum practice.

## The espousal of neo-Marxism

In a review of the state of the field, St John-Brooks (1980) argued that some of those associated with the new sociology of education in the early 1970s later took a mainly theoretical path, whilst others concentrated on the empirical study of classrooms. The theoretical path, which in practice turned out to be a largely neo-Marxist one, was taken by those whose major concern was with 'the ways in which the interests of dominant groups in society are translated into social values which inform schools, which in turn replicate the social structure'. The other direction was followed by those 'who were more interested in the question of what went on in schools' and led to the development of ethnographic techniques for studying classroom interaction. Although there seems no inherent reason why one of these sets of interests should necessarily lead to more theoretically inclined or empirically oriented work than the other, it did seem to be the case that those concerned with the broader issues devoted most of their attention to theoretical debate, while the other group concentrated upon the production of under-theorized classroom ethnographies. This created an unfortunate and, to date, enduring division between those concerned with so-called 'macro' issues and those engaged in 'micro' studies, a distinction symbolized in the contributions of Esland and Dale, on the one hand, and Woods and Hammersley, on the other hand, to a new Open University course, entitled *Schooling and Society*, that appeared in 1977.

In a way, the careers of Dale and Esland symbolized what was the dominant trend in the sociology of education in the mid-1970s. Initially proponents of a phenomenological approach, they became increasingly attracted to neo-Marxism, as represented in the work of Bowles and Gintis (1976). There was therefore a stark contrast between the theoretical orientations of their contributions to *School and Society* in the early 1970s and those to *Schooling and Society* in the middle of the decade. This both reflected and contributed to a major reorientation of sociology of education towards neo-Marxist perspectives that served to define the field, even for those opposed to this development, for the remainder of the decade. Once again, it was a combination of circumstances, fashion and political purpose that pushed many of those associated with the new sociology of education in the direction of Marxism as it became increasingly clear that their initial orientation was both theoretically and practically flawed.

The attraction of Marxism was, of course, linked to an increasing realization that social reality was not quite as fragile as students of the 1960s and the new sociologists of the 1970s had imagined. The over-emphasis on the notion that reality was socially constructed had led to the neglect of any consideration of how and why reality came to be constructed in particular ways and how and why particular constructions of reality seemed to have the power to resist subversion (Whitty 1974). While phenomenological and ethnomethodological studies endlessly illustrated how reality was sustained at a micro-level, they offered little purchase on the nature of the broader context in which this took place.

The changing mood was summed up by Apple in his review of Sharp and Green's book *Education and Social Control*:

> Phenomenological description and analysis of social processes, while important to be sure, incline us to forget that there *are* objective institutions and structures 'out there' that have power, that can control our lives and our very perceptions. By focusing on how everyday social interaction sustains people's identities and institutions, they can draw attention away from the fact that individual interaction and conception is constrained by material reality.
>
> One does not throw out social phenomenology here. . . . One combines it with a more critical social interpretation that looks at the negotiation of identities and meanings in specific institutions like schools as taking place within a context that often determines the parameters of what is negotiable and meaningful. This context does not reside merely at the level of consciousness: it is the nexus of economic and political institutions, a nexus which defines what schools should be about, that determines these parameters.
>
> (Apple 1977: 43)

The point was made even more strongly in Sharp and Green's own words:

> What seems to be crucial is whether in the last analysis one can control others and bring sanctions to bear against others, irrespective of their definition of reality. And the ability to do this derives not from language, the system of symbolic meanings itself . . . but from the distribution of power and authority in the macro-strucure.
>
> (Sharp and Green 1975: 34)

Initially, there was little evidence that this recognition would achieve more than a ritual restatement in the final paragraphs of studies which continued to focus on reality construction in the classroom. As Annette Kuhn put it:

> I noted for instance that many books and articles would conclude with injunctions to consider how power relations at work outside the school penetrate the structure of authority relations and inform the ways in which knowledge is organised and distributed within it. They would never specify how this was to be done. It was evident to me even then, that there was a block which could not be removed unless some notion of structure was to be mobilised: that is to say unless the phenomenological problematic were itself to be displaced.         (Kuhn 1978: 38)

The first response to such critiques of the earlier manifestations of the new sociology of education was to continue to place priority on meanings being constructed and negotiated in contexts of interaction –

but to displace those contexts outside the school. Thus the limits to negotiation in the classroom were set by the process of negotiation elsewhere. This could be seen in Young's paper, 'Curriculum change – limits and possibilities' (Young 1977b), in Vulliamy's later pieces (Vulliamy 1977) and, to some extent, in my own early work on school examinations (Whitty 1976). But, if Joan Simon was right to label the phenomenological work on classrooms as the 'blame the teacher school of sociology' (Simon 1974), the shift towards the study of constraints (and, in particular the focus upon the activities of those with apparent responsibility for influencing curricular decisions) merely seemed to identify new human culprits. It was in danger of merely blaming individuals or groups of examiners, academics, administrators, politicians or industrialists for the nature of education and the nature of society. Thus, ultimately, the need for a notion of an underlying structure was not only recognized rhetorically, but various notions of structure were actually invoked in seeking a more theoretically adequate answer to the question of why schools were as they were. It was implied that locating schools within the broader structures of advanced capitalist societies would help to identify both the possibilities of and limitations to change in and through education. Though initially such analyses were carried out with a view to identifying and informing more adequate strategies of change (Young and Whitty 1977), they too frequently came to look like retreats into mere theorizing (Demaine 1980).

Various types of macro-theory emerged during the mid and late 1970s as candidates in the quest to explain the relationship between education and the wider social structure. Most of them were, to a greater or lesser extent, influenced by Marxism, and they tended to identify the effects of 'the distribution of power and authority in the macro-structure' (Sharp and Green 1975) with the influence of capitalism on schooling. They could be roughly categorized as correspondence theories, reproduction theories and hegemonic theories, though many actual theorists straddled more than one of these categories.

Initially, the notion of structure was adopted in an extremely crude manner and little heed was taken of Apple's insistence that social phenomenology or the analysis of consciousness was not to be thrown out in the process (Apple 1977). Indeed Kuhn (1978) seems to have been nearer the mark in insisting on the necessity of a clear break with the phenomenological problematic before theoretical progress could be made. Thus, Kuhn points out, the first macro-theorists to be espoused with enthusiasm, particularly by Esland and Dale, were Bowles and Gintis and not, for instance, Bourdieu whose links with the new sociologists had already been established (Young 1971a) and whose developing concerns had somewhat more in common with the earlier tradition. Be that as it may, it was *Schooling in Capitalist America* (Bowles and Gintis 1976) that firmly established neo-Marxist theory at the heart of British sociology of education, even though it was a relatively crude piece of Marxist theory, based upon some highly questionable statistical data, and, perhaps strangest of all, one that mimimized the significance of the overt (as opposed to the hidden curriculum of schooling) in securing social reproduction and the legitimation of inequality.

What the work of Bowles and Gintis suggested was that the liberal or social democratic belief that education could bring personal fulfilment to all pupils and contribute to a reduction in social inequalities, at the same time as reproducing the sort of workforce required by capitalism, was essentially a myth – albeit an extremely powerful myth that had led even those least likely to benefit from schooling to accept its extension as unquestionably a 'good thing'. As they put it, 'the failure of educational reforms stems from the contradictory nature of expanded reproduction, equality of opportunity and self-development in a society whose economic life is governed by the institutions of corporate capitalism'. Behind the mask of what they called the 'liberal ideology of education', the educational system was seen by Bowles and Gintis and their British followers as getting on with its real job in society – that of producing a workforce that would fit into and accept as legitimate the patterns of inequality required by the capitalist system of production.

Bowles and Gintis argued that 'the social relations of educational institutions corresponded closely to the social relations of dominance, subordination and motivation in the economic sphere'. Their argument depended on identifying a series of parallels or correspondences between education and production in capitalist societies. The sorts of parallels that could be pointed to included the hierarchy between teachers and pupils that corresponded with the hierarchical authority in the workplace, the pupils' lack of control over the education that corresponded to workers' alienation in the factory, and the system of extrinsic motivation via grades that paralleled the system of wages for labour within capitalist production. In addition, the different levels of the educational system could be seen to feed workers into different levels in the occupational structure, and the internal organization of these different parts of the educational system to produce different habits and personality traits appropriate for different positions within the hier-archical division of labour. Thus there were different degrees of regimen-tation and autonomy for different groups of pupils, corresponding to differing degrees of responsibility within the adult workforce. The lower levels of the educational system, to which working-class and black pupils were usually confined, emphasized rule-following and behaviour con-trol as a preparation for the harsh labour discipline of the shop-floor. The middle levels of the system encouraged a greater degree of independent activity, thus preparing workers who would not require constant supervision. The highest levels of the education system, which were reached only by those who had internalized its dominant values, gave students even greater freedom and initiative since, in the workplace, such qualities were likely to be used in the interests of the enterprise rather than against it. Within the society as a whole, the social relations of the family, the school and the workplace were seen to reinforce each other to create and sustain a situation in which privileged students from good schools ended up in rewarding and highly paid jobs, whilst disadvantaged social groups were concentrated in poorly endowed schools that prepared them for the unrewarding slots in the workforce. The everyday experiences of being in school thus ensured that an appropriately skilled, fragmented and docile workforce for capitalism was reproduced in each generation.

The inequalities necessary to the capitalist system of wealth creation and distribution were seen in Bowles and Gintis's 'correspondence thesis' to be perpetuated and made acceptable by the workings of the school system. The fact that changes in schooling had generally *followed* changes in the system of production led Bowles and Gintis (1976) to argue that there was at least a prima facie case that the nature of schooling was determined by the nature of the economic system. At the very least, schooling could be seen to carry out a vital function on behalf of capitalism and one that was not compatible with some of the claims that were often made for the educational system by teachers. On this argument, the problem of working-class failure could not be seen as a mere aberration that could be overcome by further reform of the school system, but as an inevitable product of the structural relationship between schooling and the capitalist system of production. Though the emphasis in the book was on the fundamental importance of the *hidden* curriculum in this relationship, Bowles also argued that, 'if the children's everyday experiences with the structure of schooling were insufficient to inculcate the correct views and attitudes, the curriculum itself would be made to embody the bourgeois ideology' (Bowles 1976). The 'correspondence thesis' therefore began to have a considerable impact on studies of both the hidden and the overt curricula of schooling under capitalism (Apple 1979).

However, although Bowles and Gintis's work seemed to many to offer a plausible explanation for the failure of liberal educational reforms, many flaws were soon revealed in its account of the rise of mass schooling, in its picture of the capitalist system of production, and in its characterization of the correspondences between education and work (Hogan 1981). In addition, by concentrating our attention on the admittedly important relationship between education and capitalist production, it led to the neglect of other significant influences on the nature of schooling and those aspects of the education system that could be linked to the system of production only by a considerable stretch of the imagination (Collins 1977). Nevertheless, not only was the work itself somewhat crude in its analysis, British sociologists of education (including many who had earlier celebrated their release from the constraints of functionalist sociology) took it on board in a way that was often as functionalistic, deterministic and reductionistic as one could find anywhere in the literature. Even the subtleties that did exist in Bowles and Gintis's own analysis were often ignored in Britain, as were the cultural differences that made parts of the argument even less compelling in the British context than it was in the American one. The force of the argument that schools failed working-class pupils because they existed to do so seemed initially to blind many commentators to the complexities involved.

Other Marxist analyses were also taken up in a relatively crude way. Kuhn (1978) points out how the selective reading of one part of one of Althusser's papers led to a crude functionalist interpretation of his work. In this article, entitled 'Ideology and ideological state apparatuses' (Althusser 1971), he offered a theory of ideological state apparatuses (ISAs), some constitutionally within the state and others functionally related to it, all of which embodied ruling-class ideology and articulated together to reproduce the relations of production. Then, in trying to explore how it was that human subjects were formed in such a way as to fit into and accept the dominant system of production relations, he began to advance a theory of the formation of subjects, based on a concept of 'interpellation' in which individuals were transformed into particular kinds of subjects through being 'hailed' by ideology. In contemporary advanced capitalist societies, education was seen as the dominant ISA, making a massive contribution to the:

> reproduction of submission to the ruling ideology for workers, and a reproduction of the ability to manipulate the ruling ideology correctly for the agents of exploitation and repression, so that they, too, will be provided for the domination of the ruling class 'in words'.
> (Althusser 1971: 128)

The particular imaginary representations of the real world encountered as a material force within the educational system were thus seen to penetrate the individual (un)consciousness in such a way as to encourage acceptance of the existing order. Although the detail of his argument was extremely complex (and at times heavily qualified in footnotes), his characterization of the structures and processes involved has been the subject of considerable criticism, the most frequent charge levelled against him being one of functionalism (Erben and Gleeson 1977; Hirst 1979). Though Kuhn (1978) is probably right to suggest that this charge

was somewhat less applicable to Althusser than to his English popular-
izers, this work certainly presented too straightforward and unproblematic an account of the relationship between capitalist production relations,
ISAs and the formation of subjects. Indeed, it is somewhat ironic that,
in parts of this paper and despite the disclaimers, the sophisticated
conceptual repertoire of structuralist Marxism, designed to avoid the
mechanistic undertones of earlier approaches, appeared redundant.

Some of the central weaknesses of the Althusserian approach were
outlined by Johnson (1979b) in the following comments on the ISAs'
paper:

> The essay represents 'reproduction', which, in Marx, is a necessarily
> contradictory and antagonistic process, as the functional necessity of a
> system. . . . What is correctly understood as a condition or a contin-
> gency becomes, in the course of the argument, a continuously achieved
> outcome. Dominant ideology, organised especially through appar-
> atuses like schools, works with all the certainty usually ascribed to
> natural or biological processes. We are returned to a very familiar
> model of one-dimensional control in which all sense of struggle or
> contradiction is lost. . . . In general, the overriding concern with
> outcomes – reproduction – suppresses the fact that these conditions
> have continuously to be won or lost – in particular conflicts and
> struggles.                                            (Johnson 1979b: 229–30)

Nevertheless, the paper has been of central importance in provoking its
critics, including Johnson, into developing a more sophisticated and
useful form of Marxist analysis, as we shall see in the next chapter.

For a time, however, the introduction of neo-Marxism in its cruder
forms into the sociology of education was something of a mixed blessing
for the developing sociological analysis of the curriculum. In some ways
it meant that the project of *Knowledge and Control* was pushed to the
margins of the discipline. This was partly because the project seemed to
have been fulfilled in the sense that the 'interests and values involved' in
the construction of school curricula (Young 1971b) were now presented
as unproblematically capitalist ones, while in another sense the analysis
of surface phenomena such as curricula was seen as less important than
the proper task of Marxist science in laying bare underlying structures.
The political consequences of the shift in perspective were particularly
ironic. The theories, which, in part at least, had been looked to for the
basis of a more adequate strategy for radicals working within education
than the individualist stance adopted in the early 1970s, seemed to
suggest that little could be done until after the overthrow of capitalism.
They therefore helped to breed amongst sociologists of education a sort
of radical pessimism, reminiscent of the advice given by the dis-

illusioned staff-room communist to the idealistic young James Herndon in *The Way It Spozed to Be*:

> You've got to wait, Jim! You got to wait for the revolution! Socialism! This isn't a school! It's a place where those kids can find out once and for all what they're up against, where the ruling class says in no uncertain terms to them, Forget you! You ain't going nowhere. . . . But you, Jim, you got to live. You got your wife . . . that beautiful kid. You got to put those paragraphs on the board for them to copy as long as they'll still do it. . . . You're alone in there between the victims and the exploiters. . . .
> (Herndon 1970: 116)

In too many accounts, schools were seen merely as a part of the ideological apparatus of the state whose role was to secure the hegemonic control of the bourgeoisie and the perpetuation of the capitalist mode of production. Class domination was stressed at the expense of class conflict and, whether via a correspondence between schooling and the economy or via their relative autonomy, control and its legitimation appeared to be secured with little difficulty. Even those writings that paid more detailed attention to the ways in which the imperatives of capitalism could be seen to penetrate the overt as well as the hidden curriculum of schooling were only slightly more successful than Bowles and Gintis (1976) in escaping the charge of functionalism. The stress on the ubiquity of domination often obscured the existence of contradiction and conflict, so that even those readers who accepted what this sort of neo-Marxist told us about education were left with a problem in identifying possible sites of intervention for change. Thus, in correcting the naiveties of liberal analyses of education, neo-Marxism ended up in displaying naiveties of its own and seemed to justify what Demaine (1980) was later to characterize as ultra-left 'abstentionism'.

For a brief time, then, there may have been some validity in Lawton's charge that the neo-Marxist approach suggested that:

> control of the curriculum is simply a question of bourgeois hegemony . . . [and] the whole cultural super-structure, including education, is a reflection of the values of . . . the bourgeoisie or the capitalist ruling class. . . . Education is assumed to be a totally socialising influence.
> (Lawton 1980: 6)

However, as we shall see in the next chapter, this was no longer true even at the time that he wrote it. Not only were such crude versions of Marxism under attack from those outside the Marxist camp, they were also increasingly being called into question by those working within it. It is to these developments that we shall now turn.

# 2

---

# *The curriculum*
# *as ideological practice*

As we have seen in chapter 1, the sociology of the curriculum was opened up, but never fully developed, by the 'new sociology of education' of the early 1970s. Much of this work placed a major emphasis on the role of ideas and consciousness in the construction and maintenance of the existing social structure. In its more extreme versions, this new sociology of education envisaged that the questioning of teachers' taken-for-granted assumptions about prevailing curricular arrangements and peda-gogical practices, would not only transform education but also lead to wide-ranging changes in the wider society. By the mid-1970s, however, this 'naive possibilitarianism' (Whitty 1974) had largely been aban-doned. Some of those associated with the 'new' sociology of education began to replace their central concern with issues of curriculum and consciousness with a search for a broader social theory that could help them to understand the capacity of existing educational and social arrangements to resist subversion. In the initial stages of this quest, their early idealism was replaced with a rather crude version of Marxist materialism, which stressed the determining effects of capitalist produc-tion relations on the nature of schooling and consciousness in capitalist societies. In such formulations, the detail of the curriculum tended to be treated either as irrelevant or as a side issue, and the programme set out in *Knowledge and Control* (Young 1971a) for studying it was put on one side in the search for a more basic explanation of the nature of capitalist society and the place of schooling within it.

## Beyond correspondence theory

We have seen that it was the espousal of the Bowles and Gintis thesis that symbolized the beginning of a period in which neo-Marxist perspectives largely defined the terrain of the sociology of education in Britain. However, despite its initial appeal, this particular thesis not only generated dismissive scorn from non-Marxist sociologists of education such as Musgrove (1979), it was soon also found wanting even by those who shared the basic assumptions about society and education that underlay it. Such criticisms culminated in an interesting exercise in retrospective self-criticism by Gintis and Bowles (1981) themselves. The extent of the problems in the analysis offered by Bowles and Gintis can be gleaned from the fact that even a 'sympathetic' critique suggested that *Schooling in Capitalist America* (Bowles and Gintis 1976) was 'characterised by an ahistorical treatment of the functions of education, an economistic conception of the social structure, an inadequate theory of reproduction and contradiction and a seriously inaccurate account of educational politics' (Hogan 1981: 41).

Further criticisms were summarized particularly bluntly and succinctly by Giroux (1981c), who argued that inherent in Bowles and Gintis's correspondence theory there was a 'monolithic view of domination and an unduly passive view of human beings'. It had therefore outlived its usefulness and, in his view, had led teachers to overlook some of the important ways in which they could contribute to social transformation rather than social reproduction.

Even by the mid-1970s, Marxists in fields outside the sociology of education had rejected the search for a simple mono-causal explanation of the nature of capitalist societies and had become interested in the various versions of 'structuralist' Marxism. Rather than working with a simple notion of an economic base directly determining its political and ideological superstructure, writers in this tradition operated instead with a notion of the capitalist mode of production as a complex totality of economic, political and ideological practices. These practices were seen jointly to provide each other's conditions of existence and the economic was treated as determining only 'in the last instance'. The traditional superstructures were thus not merely dependent upon economic conditions but were themselves seen as having a specific and crucial role in the functioning of the whole. Any particular site within the social formation could be intersected by economic, political and ideological practices, all of which were relatively autonomous from each other. However, as we saw in chapter 1, Althusser's pioneering version of structuralist Marxism did not initially liberate British sociology of education from the excesses of Bowles and Gintis's political economy, and it was in fact often criticized in very similar terms for its stifling effects upon sociological analysis (Johnson 1979b) and upon radical initiatives in and around education (Erben and Gleeson 1977). For a time, the espousal of structure at the expense of human agency seemed complete.

Nevertheless, in other respects and in other fields, Althusser's work can be seen to have generated a release from over-economistic and deterministic accounts of the nature of capitalist societies and to have generated a resurgence of interest in the detailed exploration of ideological and political practice under capitalism. This resurgence was by no means always confined to work arising out of structuralist Marxism, but such work did help to put back on the agenda issues that had become unfashionable within British sociology of education. In particular, that form of practice that Johnson termed ideology/culture and which involves 'the production of forms of consciousness – ideas, feelings, desires, moral preferences [or] forms of subjectivity' (Johnson 1979b) excited renewed interest. Initially, this often involved a relegitimation of those forms of theory that emphasized the specific role of education and its apparent autonomy in cultural and social reproduction (Bernstein 1977a; Bourdieu and Passeron 1977), there being various attempts to integrate these neo-Durkheimian perspectives with Marxist analysis (Bernstein 1977c; M. Macdonald 1977). Gradually, the relatively autonomous dynamics of ideological/cultural practice came to take on more significance than merely that required for the efficient reproduction of capitalist relations of production. Eventually, sociologists of education began to shift from stressing the existence of a relationship between schooling and capitalism to a theorization of the complex and contradictory nature of that relationship and the degree of relative autonomy that at least some aspects of schooling enjoyed in their relations with economic production. This meant that, at the level of theory at least, a concern with ideological/cultural practice in and around the school curriculum received greater emphasis within the discipline. Interest therefore began to develop in the ways in which the curriculum worked to produce meanings and forms of consciousness and in the political struggles that developed around these processes.

Also significant for the sociological analysis of curriculum policy and practice was the attempt to develop a more sophisticated understanding of the contemporary state (Dale 1981, 1982; Jessop 1982; Offe 1984). Here, again, the initial move away from treating the state as a direct relay of the needs of capital involved conceptualizing its relative autonomy merely in terms of its role in reproducing the social relations of capitalism. Increasingly, however, the state came to be conceived as a site of struggle, the outcomes of which could not be taken for granted. In addition, the tendency to treat the state as a unitary or monolithic site was abandoned and replaced with a conception of the state as a constellation of sites whose determination by the economy was both general and varied rather than specific and identical (Saunders 1981). Crucial in linking these newer theories of ideology and the state was Gramsci's concept of 'hegemony' (Gramsci 1971). Ideologies were seen to become hegemonic when they made a contribution to the process by which 'commonsense is made to conform to the "necessities of production" ' and to the 'construction of "consent" and a political order' (Johnson 1979b). However, ideological practice in and around the state was not to be seen as economically determined in the sense that there was 'an external cause which totally predicts or prefigures, indeed totally controls'. Instead, there was, at most, a 'rather looser process of setting limits and exerting pressures' (Williams 1973). The relatively autonomous roles of ideological and political practice did not, then, mechanistically achieve the reproduction of the social relations of production. Indeed, far from this process being, as in Althusser's model, a continuously achieved outcome, it was a 'thoroughly contested and uneven process' (Johnson 1979b). Thus, both the possibilities for the construction of a potentially hegemonic discourse and its capacity to secure consent at the level of common sense were highly contingent upon the disposition of political and ideological forces within the state and civil society. It was within this context that both political struggles over the curriculum and classroom processes of meaning making came to be reconceptualized by the heirs of the new sociology of education (Reynolds 1984).

There is, however, a considerable tension within contemporary Marxist theory between the notions of relative autonomy on the one hand and economic determination on the other. As Hall (1977) pointed out, contemporary discussions of ideology present problems that are generalizable to all Marxist theory:

> it seems to be the case that the problem of ideology presents us with a paradigm instance of Marxist theory as such: what Althusser has called the necessity – and difficulty – of holding on to 'both ends of the chain' at once: the relative autonomy of a region (e.g. ideology) and its 'determination in the last instance' (i.e. the determinacy of ideology by other instances, and, in the last instance, by the economic). It is the necessity to hold fast to the latter protocol which has, from time to time, sanctioned a tendency to collapse the levels of a social formation – especially to collapse 'ideas' or ideology into 'the base' (narrowly defined as 'the economic'). On the other hand, it is the requirement to explore the difficult terrain of 'relative autonomy' (of ideology) which has given the field its awkward openness.          (Hall 1977: 29–30)

Although, as we shall see, this tension continues to run through many contemporary sociological analyses of the curriculum, some observers have seen it as making Marxism untenable. Thus, there are those who argue that Weberian perspectives have considerable advantages over

Marxist ones for the analysis of the sort of phenomena with which we are concerned in this book. A more general resurgence of interest in Weberian sociology has therefore had its parallel within the sociology of education (Collins 1977; King 1980). Thus Collins notes:

> Although the Weberian approach rejects the Marxian emphasis on the causal preponderance of the economic structure and its historical evolution, the Weberian approach is, to a degree, a sophisticated version of the Marxian tradition. That is, Weberians do see economic interests based on property divisions as key bases of group organization, or inter-group conflict, and of historical change. But, in contrast to Marx, Weber also pointed out that organizational resources, especially those of state and private bureaucracies, and cultural resources, above all religious traditions (but also secular ones such as education), can create and channel additional interest groups and conflicts. Three lines of societal division – economic, organizational-political, and cultural (or in Weber's terms, 'class', 'party' and 'status') – mesh so that economic classes or organizational politicians are stronger if they also possess the unity that comes from common cultural resources. But the three types of resources may be differentially distributed: strong ethnic, national, religious or other cultural divisions can shape struggles for economic or political domination into patterns very different from those emerging along class lines. There are many kinds of stratification system, and with the proper conceptual tools one may show the conditions for each. . . . [The Weberian approach sees] education as part of a multi-sided struggle among status communities for domination, for economic advantage, and for prestige. This approach allows the incorporation of a multiplicity of particular causes into an overall explanation, since it regards social structures as the result of the mobilisation of a variety of resources and interest groups within a common arena.                          (Collins 1977: 3)

Even if it can be argued that many varieties of Marxism can themselves accommodate this degree of complexity with ease, Collins's approach offers a starting point for analysis that does not grant privileged status to one particular form of explanation. Thus, it is sometimes seen to offer a more open opportunity to explore the articulation between, say, ideological cultural practice and economic practice rather than assuming a particular type of relationship. Equally, it is an approach that avoids the tendency to grant a 'residual' status to those aspects of stratification, or those elements of the educational system, that are not directly related to capitalist production relations.

A more profound challenge to neo-Marxist perspectives has, however, developed out of the tradition itself. Some post-Althusserian writers point not only to the theoretical limitations of theories of economic determination (and argue strongly that concepts like 'the last instance' and 'relative autonomy' do not ultimately avoid them) but also, and perhaps more significantly, to the way in which conventional Marxist approaches to ideological and political practice have served to mask possibilities for change. This group of theorists initially embraced Althusserianism as an escape from the economism and reductionism of classical Marxism but now regards Althusser's work as suffering, in the last instance, from similar defects. Although their work involves some very complex and controversial epistemological claims the main implications of their work for political practice in and around education are made clear in the following passage by Paul H. Hirst, one of the leading members of the group:

> In challenging the concept of totality which sustains Althusser's position we are also challenging its implications for the conception of politics. Our criticism challenges the basis for his characterisation of ISAs as state apparatuses and as forming a unity, a unity given in the ideology of the ruling class. The field of ISAs as the components of a unitary ideological instance serving to reproduce capitalist relations of production is thus decomposed. This decomposition has positive theoretical-political consequences. It follows from the criticism that all the institutions called ISAs (school, family, media, etc.) are not necessarily capitalist in character and effects. Nor are they 'state' apparatuses, dominated by ruling-class ideology. Whether constitutionally part of the state or not, they can be reformed and changed through state action, institutional initiatives and mass practice. The effect of such reforms and changes on wider social relations is not given and could be very radical indeed. Likewise particular institutions can possibly be transformed without radical change in other social relations as a concomitant or precondition. In the ISAs thesis legislative reform and state action to change institutions can only be within capitalist limits, apparatuses are merely differentiated parts of the state system subject to the necessities of reproduction. Reforms will merely be within the terms of and in order to serve that primary function. . . . Because its effect is to minimise the possible forms of change within capitalist and commodity relations Althusser's position reinforces traditional conceptions of revolutionary socialist struggle and is an obstacle to innovations in the political practice of the left. . . . The left needs to outflank its enemies, moving into areas and forms of struggle where the opposition is relatively unprepared and weak. The complex, inadequately denoted by the notion of 'ideological social relations', presents the primary example of such an opportunity.
>
> (Hirst 1979: 15–17)

Thus, in emphasising the real autonomy of ideological phenomena,

**Erratum** The publishers wish to point out that the passage above is by Paul Q. Hirst and not by Paul H. Hirst.

Hirst and other ex-Althusserians ironically find themselves in the position of denying the value of general explanatory theories in understanding specific historical conjunctures and the political possibilities inherent in them. As Golding and Murdock (1979) point out, their recent work has brought them strikingly close to the position of historian Edward Thompson, who has in the past been one of the fiercest critics of the over-theoreticist approach of Hirst and his colleagues (Thompson 1978). Such a perspective, when applied to the analysis of education, clearly implies a need to re-examine the possibilities inherent within schools as sites of ideological and political practice.

Hindess, one of Hirst's colleagues, has argued that 'either we effectively reduce ideological phenomena to class interests determined elsewhere (basically in the economy) . . . Or we face up to the real autonomy of ideological phenomena and their irreducibility to manifestations of interests determined by the structure of the economy' (Hindess 1977: 104). Power relations within particular arenas are the outcome of practices in those arenas rather than an automatic product of resources held elsewhere (Hindess 1983). Similar considerations to these inform yet another set of perspectives that is sometimes presented as an alternative to neo-Marxism. This tradition returns us to some of the concerns of the new sociology of education but claims to do so on the basis of more adequate notions of knowledge, power, structure and agency. Drawing upon a variety of post-structuralist forms of European social theory, and particularly upon the work of Foucault (1981), a potentially important new style of left theorizing relevant to our understanding of the curriculum has recently become discernible.[1] Initially appropriated by media studies in England, its value as a way of approaching the analysis and reconceptualization of the curriculum has now been recognized. The relationship of such a mode of theorizing to earlier approaches is complex, especially as some of those who have adopted it have been concerned to stress its differences from all other paradigms. Alvarado and Ferguson (1983) claim that:

> all other educational writers we know, do not raise the question of the way in which the world is *represented* to the pupil. (The 'new' sociologists of education began to raise some of these issues in the early seventies when they questioned the 'construction' and not 'representation') . . . of subject areas/academic disciplines . . . all offer representations of the world, discourses (usually educational) about the world and never (because it is impossible) the world itself. However, this is denied by the curriculum as it is currently conceived and constituted, for it is based on an essentially 'realist', i.e. empiricist, pragmatic and utilitarian, conception of both knowledge and the world. The 'new' sociologists recognised this fact but did not have the

theoretical tools at hand to solve the problem and hence they fell into a relative trap, of treating all knowledge as equally valid. . . . The main emphasis of the New Sociologists of education . . . was on the crucial importance of human agency in the move towards radical social change.                                   (Alvarado and Ferguson 1983: 25–8)

In contrast, they claim that their emphasis, following Foucault, is to combine a theory of institutions with a theory of symbolic systems and specific signifying systems. What teachers teach is 'not knowledge . . . [but] preferred discourses', which are inscribed within institutions and everyday practices. The task of the radical teacher, whether of sociology of education, curriculum studies or of school subjects, should therefore be 'to *de*naturalise various discourses rather than to endlessly validate them by a complicity with the unspoken norms of a powerful state apparatus'. Recognizing the importance of the 'power–knowledge relationship' (Foucault 1979), Alvarado and Ferguson (1983) suggest that an important contribution to social transformation can be undertaken in school by developing approaches to teaching which shatter the naturalization of school knowledge via a deconstruction of the dominant 'realist' discourse and the identification of other discourses.

In practice, some of the suggestions that arise from this approach do not seem radically different from those that emerged out of the new sociology of education (Whitty 1974). It also seems that, despite its origins within a French intellectual tradition distinct not only from phenomenology but also from Marxism, this perspective's sectarianism has not been entirely rigorously carried through to the British scene.[2] Thus, certainly within the sociology of education, theories and methodologies that, in their original form, were used to critique Marxism have been used to refine neo-Marxist approaches rather than to discredit them. In their very different ways, for instance, both Donald (1979) and Sarup (1982, 1983) have tried to use the perspectives and methods of writers such as Barthes and Foucault to develop an analysis of ideological and political practice around education under capitalism within a broadly neo-Marxist paradigm.

Indeed, it does seem that the theoretical strand of the British sociology of education may now be emerging from a period of purely theoretical development in which a succession of different approaches were seen as exclusive and incompatible. Many of the oppositions that have characterized the different phases of the sociology of education over the past decade now seem less rigidly drawn. Within broader fields of social theory, the dichotomy between structure and agency is being increasingly rejected and attempts are being made to synthesize elements of the humanist and structuralist strands of contemporary Marxism (Giddens 1979; Johnson 1979b). There has also been an increasing rejection of the tendency to veer 'from the view that representation is an unmediated reflection of material conditions of existence to the view that representation is necessarily totally autonomous of those conditions' (Barrett *et al.* 1979). If these developments become established within the sociology of education, the obsession with theoretical purity may give way to the development of theoretically informed empirical research. If, for instance, it is clear that the relationship between economic, political and ideological practice is not, except perhaps in the very broadest terms, to be understood at a purely theoretical level, it becomes necessary to study the relations between such practices in specific historical conjunctures (and even sites) within a particular mode of production. Thus, it is to be hoped that the theoretical strand of the sociology of education will follow its parent discipline in recognizing that the immediate future of studies of ideological practice lies in 'the analysis of . . . meaning production in historically specific conditions of existence' (Barrett *et al.* 1979). If so, there is an assured future for detailed studies of ideological and political practice in and around the school curriculum.

None of this should, however, be taken to suggest, that after a decade of increasingly obscure theoretical debate, we are right back to where the new sociology of education started in the early 1970s. The perspectives now developing recognize more clearly the articulations between hegemonic ideological practice and its economic and political conditions of existence and hence the necessity of effective challenges to that practice being more than individual acts of defiance. On the other hand, such work also does question the validity of the overreaction of many sociologists of education to the 'possibilitarianism' of the 'new sociology of education' in so far as this led to the adoption of a rather crude version of Marxism, in which it was difficult to see any possibility of change in or through the school curriculum in the absence of a prior transformation of the social relations of production.

The recent perspectives point to the relative autonomy and specific effectivity of ideological practice rather than treating it as epiphenomenal. They therefore suggest that just as hegemonic ideological practice has a particular and crucial role in social reproduction, so can oppositional ideological practice, if appropriately organized, play a significant role in social transformation. In the current conjuncture the school curriculum has itself become an important site of ideological struggle, even though it almost certainly lacks the overwhelming significance that the 'new sociology of education' sometimes seemed to attribute to it.

## Empirical applications

At the same time as the more theoretical strand that developed from the new sociology of education has reached a position where empirical research on the curriculum may once again become a central part of its project, the empirical strand has also showed signs of broadening the scope of its concerns. For a number of years this latter group has held an annual conference at St Hilda's College, Oxford, which, in its initial phase, was highly exclusive in both its composition and its concerns. Though a few of the contributions addressed broader issues and attempted to make links with the work of those outside the narrow tradition of English classroom ethnography (e.g. A. Hargreaves 1980), most were concerned with classroom and staff-room ethnographies and their references (other than disparaging ones) to work outside this tradition and its informing theorists were as sparse as those to this tradition within the work of the neo-Marxists (Woods 1980a, 1980b). The conference in 1981, however, was concerned with what it termed the 'sociology of curriculum practice' and was self-consciously designed to recall some of the questions raised a decade earlier in *Knowledge and Control* (Young 1971a) and assess what progress had been made in answering them in the ensuing period. Though the outcome of the conference hardly lived up to this aim (Hammersley and Hargreaves 1983), it did signal an end to the more myopic tendencies within the ethnographic tradition. Hammersley and Hargreaves (1983) expressed the hope in their introduction to the conference papers that:

> this kind of sociologically informed empirical work on curriculum at the level of the classroom, the subject department or the examining body will enable us to test and develop the rather more speculative explanations of curriculum practice that sociologists have advanced to date which are epitomised in concepts like ideology, hegemony and cultural capital. At the same time, it might give curriculum theorists and curriculum planners a fuller and more realistic sense of the problems they are likely to encounter when they seek to implement their ambitiously prescriptive models of curriculum change.
>
> (Hammersley and Hargreaves 1983: 12)

The return to the concern of the new sociology of education with an analysis of curricular knowledge was sustained at the following year's conference, which was devoted to histories and ethnographies of school subjects. This conference was particularly reminiscent of some of those in the early 1970s and the themes of the conference papers had much in common with the sorts of dissertations produced by students in the sociology of education department at the Institute of Education in that earlier period. What was newer was the wealth of empirical detail in the studies and a greater concern with methodological rigour, which perhaps reflected many of their authors' association with the ethno-graphic rather than the theoretical tradition in the later 1970s. Unfor-tunately, however, this same feature produced a relative ignorance of theoretical developments in that same period, or perhaps a conscious dismissal of their relevance., The references in most of these studies (e.g. Cooper 1983; Goodson 1983) are mostly drawn either from theoretical writings of the early 1970s or from empirical work in the ethnographic tradition. Again, however, there is now some indication that those involved in this sort of work in Britain recognize a potential value in the interrogation of their empirical work with neo-Marxist theory and vice versa (Goodson 1985). Nevertheless, the divisions between theoretical and empirical traditions continue to run deep and the real fruits of a possible rapprochement between them have yet to be seen in Britain.

It is partly for this reason that the real fruitfulness of the coming together of theoretical developments and substantive research on the sociology of the curriculum has hitherto been glimpsed more clearly in work originating from outside the British context. In particular, the work of the so-called 'critical' curriculum writers in the USA, such as Apple, Anyon, Giroux, Taxel and Wexler,[3] demonstrates the advantages of a more dynamic relationship between theoretical and empirical developments, though it also demonstrates some of the difficulties of relying upon theories whose origins lie in a different empirical context. Nevertheless, the work shows some of the potential that lies in a sociological approach to the study of the school curriculum that involves a process of mutual interrogation between theoretical and empirical work. I shall therefore outline in some detail the development of this American work in three areas of substantive interest – their analyses of the overt curriculum, the hidden curriculum and the curriculum-in-use.

Initial interest in the content of the overt curriculum, via the analysis of school textbooks and instructional materials, stemmed from a political concern about their overt censorship during the Cold War era and the more covert methods of exclusion typical of the mid-1960s. Studies focused upon the patterns of discrimination within school texts, the incidence of stereotyping and the distortion of reality or the 'absence of realism'. Most of this work was largely descriptive and often decontextualized, and it was left to the critical curriculum writers to develop a more theoretically informed analysis, partly inspired by perspectives imported from the new sociology of education in Britain and Bourdieu's work in France. These writers set out to explore why educational texts took the form they did and why some messages were transmitted rather than others. The 'selective tradition' in school knowledge was initially studied in science and social science textbooks, where Apple (1971) and Popkewitz (1977) identified a static view of society and a predominently functionalist perspective that stressed social harmony and stability and gave a negative view of the nature and value of conflict. Such tacit assumptions were seen to have considerable potency for legitimating the existing social order. However, as Anyon's study of elementary social studies textbooks (Anyon 1978) argued, the origins of such 'naive and unrealistic' images of society were not to be sought in the mindlessness of educators or the inattention of textbook producers to critical thought, but in the 'powerful nexus of social forces in which schools operate'. The omissions, distortions and misrepresentations in texts were thus seen to reflect the social structure as well as contributing to its legitimation.

In the more recent development of such work, one can observe more clearly the productive interplay between the insights of European social theory and the detailed textual research being carried out by the American writers. Thus, in a discussion of high school history textbooks, Anyon (1979) analyses the ideological import of their content and absences and tries to relate both the textual messages and their mode of production to the interests of capital. Anyon's paper is somewhat like the style of content-analysis that Sumner (1979) has termed 'speculative criticism' though it is arguably less speculative and more grounded in textual evidence than the sorts of work on the mass media for which Sumner coined the phrase. Nevertheless, like those studies, it is concerned to register a political protest about the features that it identifies in the texts as much as to offer an explanation of them. The study focuses on the broad patterns of inclusion and exclusion of content within seventeen widely used secondary school history textbooks. Particularly important, and an advance on much other work in this vein, is her emphasis on what is excluded, an emphasis that echoes, at the level of content, the claim by Macherey, a French literary theorist, that 'a work is tied to ideology not so much by what it says as by what it does not say. It is in the significant *silences* of a text, in its gaps and absences, that the presence of ideology can be most positively felt' (Eagleton 1976: 34–5). Anyon's central claim seems to be that patterns of inclusion and exclusion, as well as certain recurrent stereotypical representations, serve to portray the nature and history of both dominant and oppositional groups in American society in a remarkably consistent and, to her, misleading way.

The texts, then, serve to emphasize and legitimate the existence and activities of some groups at the expense of others. In particular, Anyon argues, militant trade unionists and socialists are denied the place in history that other sources suggest they ought to occupy. Although her main emphasis is on the broad patterns of inclusion and exclusion, she also points from time to time to the ways in which the use of particular terms structures our reading of the texts and thus helps to construct the particular sense of history that they produce. This, for Anyon, is a version of history that serves to 'naturalize' the status quo by providing support for the interests of the dominant groups in American society and hiding from view the sorts of political action that might effectively challenge them. Perhaps most significantly of all, she argues that the texts actually make it difficult to call to mind a working class as a meaningful entity in American society at all. This, and other elements of her analysis, have something in common with the claim by Poulantzas (1973) that one of the effects of the dominant ideology in class societies is the fragmentation of classes into 'individual persons', who are then reconstituted into various imaginary and non-antagonistic unities such as the 'nation' and the 'community', thus masking and displacing class relations and economic contradictions.

However, there are problems with an analysis such as Anyon's when we come to consider the origins and effects of the phenomena that she describes. It seems clear that she is committed to analysing texts in a way that does not eschew questions of their material origins and their actual effects, but the paper also illustrates some of the difficulties in dealing with these questions. Thus, while she appears to have established the existence of a close relationship between contemporary capitalism and the symbolic representation of capital–labour relations in history books, it is not altogether clear how she would wish to characterize the nature of that relationship. At the beginning of the article she seems to be stressing the way in which the content of textbooks is dependent upon the activities of multinational companies and the demands of the capitalist market, that is the very institutions whose position in American society would seem to be legitimated by that content. By the end of the paper, Anyon is arguing that, if the school curriculum helps to form attitudes and thus provides a subjective basis for social control in American society, it might also be used to change those attitudes and thereby foster social change and the creation of a more equal social structure. She therefore celebrates the possibilities for changing textbook content and thus helping to effect changes in the broader social structure, possiilities whose existence signficantly detracts from the determining power assigned to the dominant economic and political interests earlier in the article.

It may be that Anyon conceives of a rather tight and unproblematic relationship between these different elements, in which interventions for change are not only possible at any one point but also have clear implications for other parts of the system. If so, her argument would be open to the same charge of over-simplifying the nature of the broader structure of power relations in capitalist societies, which was often levelled at the 'new sociology of education' of the early 1970s (Ahier 1977). Alternatively, Anyon may be adopting (though it is more implicit than explicit) a rather more sophisticated position that stresses not only the location of textbook production within capitalist economic relations, but also the relative autonomy and specific effectivity of ideological representations within texts. In this case, however, the possibilities for and the significance of interventions to transform the nature of school texts would be highly contingent upon their conjunctural articulation with broader political struggles.

One way of exploring the complex articulations that remain relatively unexplored or unproblematic in Anyon's study would be a programme of research around the contexts of textbook production and consumption (Apple 1984). An understanding of the extent to which the content of textbooks is currently determined in the way that Anyon suggests would require both a political economy and an ethnography of textbook production. Questions about the significance and effects of textbook discourse would also require studies of their consumption, both at the point of adoption and, more importantly, at the point of use. The implication of most studies of textbook content that we have to date is that they actually serve to form attitudes and values of the sort suggested by Anyon. But, of course, readers are interpellated by a whole range of intra- and extra-textual discourses that prevent even the most closed of texts from absolutely determining its reading by readers who bring to it different knowledges, prejudices and resistances (Willeman 1978). Studies of texts thus also need to be related to the broader discursive contexts in which they circulate. Although a detached reading of textbooks as text may suggest that they foster a particular type of subjectivity, it is likely that, in the concrete contexts of their use, they would have a differential effectivity in relation to different groups of readers. As we shall see later in this chapter, Anyon's own work elsewhere on class differentials in curriculum provision (Anyon 1980) and in conceptions of knowledge (Anyon 1981a) itself points to the importance of such questions and of research along these lines. Ethnographies of textbook use would also be crucially concerned with the pedagogical contexts in which they are employed, since we need to know far more about the ways in which styles of pedagogy mediate teaching materials for pupils. Although, in some cases, there may be a relationship of correspondence between the ideology of textbooks and the ideology of teaching style, in other cases the relationship may be a contradictory one. Particularly interesting would be the significance of radical pedagogies and especially those approaches that involve the critical reading of texts and the decoding of their messages (Alvarado and Ferguson 1983; Giroux 1983). I have no doubt that, were all these various lines of enquiry to be pursued, they would produce a picture of the relationship between textbook producers, textbook content and the attitudes of their readers that was considerably more complex and contradictory than that which emerges from Anyon's paper, but this is no way to detract from the importance of her pioneering work.

It is, however, important to note one particular limitation of Anyon's study, albeit one that I have already hinted at in my earlier discussion. This is its almost total concentration on the ideological work of the content of school textbooks, in terms of their inclusions and exclusions, rather than on that which emanates from their form. As Taxel (1980) says, her study is 'conspicuously silent on the question of the possible legitimating function which the form of these materials might play', though it is fair to add that there are some aspects of her analysis where she discusses features of textbooks very close to what Taxel terms 'form'. Nevertheless, there is, as Taxel states, considerably more scope for studying the narrative form or structure of textbooks along the sort of lines suggested by Eagleton (1976) for the study of works of literature, particularly when many contemporary theorists regard form as a more significant producer of ideological effects than content. Taxel (1980, 1981, 1983) himself has made a start on this sort of analysis in his own study of ideology in children's fiction about the American Revolution. This work is particularly important in its attempt to explore the interaction and interpenetration of form and content in constructing a particular version of history and a particular notion of abstract individualism that

> may serve to 'symbolically buttress' sets of social relationships which are not, in and of themselves, natural but are, instead, specific to an existing 'balance of forces' . . . [which] is not ideologically neutral but serves instead to legitimate the interests of those who occupy positions of power and wealth in society.          (Taxel 1980: 303)

Taxel points out that the form of the novel, with its focus on individual perception, is particularly ironic in this context given that the revolution was a collective movement. Here again there are some parallels with the ideas of Poulantzas on the effects of the dominant ideological practices in class societies (Poulantzas 1973).

In discussing another approach to the analysis of artistic form, as employed by W. Wright (1975) in his study of the deep structure of westerns, Taxel suggests that

> a by-product of the transition from a market to a corporate economy is the need for an alternate set of rules to govern social relationships and interactions [and that] such changes . . . make their way into, and are reflected in, imaginative works such as children's Revolutionary War fiction and Western films.          (Taxel 1980: 300)

Like Bourdieu (1971a, b), he argues that culture 'reproduces in trans-figured, and therefore unrecognizable form, the structure of socioeconomic relationships', thus making the cultural part of the dialectic of reproduction. But he also points out that, in some respects, Wright's analysis provides rather too neat an illustration of the correspondences between textual structure and socio-economic context, and it is signifi-cant that his own study only partially lent support to Wright's claim. He suggests that Wright's analysis has similar dangers to Bowles and

Gintis's work on the form of schooling in that it suggests a rather too mechanistic conception of the relationship between text and context. His own study argues for the importance of the 'notion of partial, or relative, autonomy' and he suggests that the analysis of this particular set of novels lends credence 'to the notion that social and material conditions exert pressures which influence and shape . . . cultural practice and creation' but not the notion that they 'mechanistically determine' them (Taxel 1980: 307). He also emphasizes that cultural practice involves not just the process of reproduction or legitimation, but also the processes of production and creating meanings. The independent work of authors, publishers and editors points to the necessity, in his eyes, of developing an analysis of the 'production of texts' that can integrate with a theory of the reproduction of meanings and values.

Nevertheless, most of these studies still operate with a basically 'reflectionist' model of explanation where school materials are structured by the underlying 'reality' of society. This sets limits or boundaries on the form or content of the materials in the texts while it is itself affected, in the long run, by the boundaries laid upon individual's social perceptions of reality as constructed by such educational materials themselves. Thus the powerlessness of the working class is not only reflected in the texts, it is also reinforced and added to. However, the complexities thrown up by these empirical studies have helped, at least as much as purely theoretical developments, to identify the limitations of such an approach to the study of texts and to the weaknesses of reproduction theories more generally.

As a result of this, there are now several authors who wish to argue that we must go beyond reproduction models of culture and develop the sort of theory that stresses the work of the school in the 'production of meanings', though this does not mean that they thereby abandon a recognition of the social and political location and function of schooling. Thus, for example, Wexler (1982a) demonstrates the limitations of the reproduction model of schooling and the reflectionist approach to the study of texts. He suggests that a sociology of school knowledge trapped within such traditions of analysis cannot cope with the 'tenuousness, disjunction, interruption and possibility' that is inherent in educational contexts, materials and processes. He argues that 'a critique of ideology requires a mode of analysis which makes the tenuousness of the object apparent, not by contextualising it, but by *deconstructing* it' (Wexler 1982a: 279, my emphasis).

Rejecting the 'mirror' analogy, Wexler argues that knowledge production is constituted by transformative activities that are the series of editings and recodings during which the raw materials are continuously transformed. 'Social montage' is therefore more apt a metaphor for the sociology of school knowledge, which should concern itself with the labour involved in constructing the montage, the social historical processes by which knowledge is produced and converted into school texts, and the processes of selection and recoding – all of which are involved in the 'social organization of meaning production'. For the analysis of content, Wexler recommends a critical semiotics of school texts that avoids idealism by relating internal structures and content to external conditions:

> A semiotics of school text, descriptions of the operation of structure to produce textual effects, counters the reification of knowledge as a solid, though socially reflective, object. In this sense it supports opposition against the pervasive commodifying processes . . . that incorporate even such critical analyses as those of cultural reproduction. It makes it possible to understand knowledge production as a chain or series of transformative activities which range from the social organisation of text industries, to the activities of text producers, through the symbolic transformations of the text itself, and to the transformative interaction between text and reader, or school knowledge and student.
>
> (Wexler 1982a: 286)

Whether or not a 'semiotics of school text' is the best description for this enterprise, such work demonstrates the analytical, political and pedagogical importance of not collapsing the different levels of meaning production that have been obscured too often in the cruder and over-generalized version of reproduction theory. It thus provides some justification for the pedagogical strategies of deconstruction and de-naturalization suggested by Alvarado and Ferguson (1983).

The second area of focus for this American work is the hidden curriculum, and it is particularly American in its origins. In its original definitions it was influenced by the functional theory of socialization and described the process of transmission of implicit norms, values and beliefs through the underlying structure of the curriculum and, more particularly, the social relations of school and classroom. Subsequently, as we have seen, the approach of Bowles and Gintis (1976) pointed to a correspondence between the social relations of the school and the social relations of capitalist production, and the nature of this relationship was further explored in the work of a number of the critical curriculum writers (Apple and King 1977; Giroux and Penna 1979). Increasingly they came to recognize that the political economy of schooling as presented by Bowles and Gintis had severe limitations. It failed to describe and explain classroom life, the conflicts and contradictions *within* the school and the distance and conflict *between* the school and the economy. Further, it could not account for the variety of responses of teachers and pupils to the structures of the school – some of which were liable to threaten the successful socialization of the new generation.

The neo-Marxist analysis of the hidden curriculum did, indeed, seem at one stage to have adopted a strangely monolithic view of the school as a conservative force, oddly reminiscent of the functionalist tradition that it had sought to counter. However, as crude correspondence theories had themselves been called into question in Britain by, for instance, Willis's *Learning to Labour* (Willis 1977), American writers such as Apple (1980) and Giroux (1981a) were amongst the first to make use of this work in the development of a more adequate conception of the hidden curriculum. They recognized the effects of class culture on the ways pupils made sense of and responded to the ideologies and culture of the school. They further argued that the hidden curriculum of schooling was not merely the terrain of social control but also the ground on which ideological and political struggles were fought and hence a potential site of interventions for change.

Such arguments initially pointed towards what we might call a 'complex correspondence' theory of the hidden curriculum that emphasized the reproduction of conflict rather than merely the maintenance of domination. This redefinition of the hidden curriculum was explored in a more empirical way by Anyon (1980), in an article entitled 'Social class and the hidden curriculum of work'. Here she presented some preliminary results of research into the curriculum, pedagogy and pupil evaluation practices in five East Coast elementary schools, located in contrasting social class communities. Using data on the social composition of their intakes, she characterized the schools as (in two cases) working-class schools, a middle-class school, an affluent professional school and an executive élite school. She employed classroom observation and informal and formal interviews, together with an analysis of curriculum materials, to explore the nature and effects of the differentiated hidden curricula to which the different groups were exposed. What makes her study different from earlier empirical tests of the hidden curriculum thesis is that she examined not so much the creation of specific dispositions and personality attributes but the fostering of particular *relationships* to production.

From her observations and analyses, Anyon argued that working-class children's school work was an appropriate preparation for mechanical and routine work. In the middle-class school, the work tasks and relationship encouraged a *bureaucratic* relation to capital, appropriate for white-collar technical jobs. Children from the affluent professional school acquired *symbolic capital* – linguistic, artistic and scientific skills suitable for the professional middle classes. The executive élite school, on the other hand, gave children 'grammatical, mathematical and other vocabularies and rules', which are another form of cultural/symbolic capital. This type is more suited to the *control* of production rather than that appropriate for the conceptualization and creation of new knowledge, which was transmitted in the affluent professional school.

Anyon also identified, in the hidden curriculum of working-class schools in particular, the reproduction of the forms of resistance and struggle that characterize working-class resistance and struggle in production. She argues that: 'The working class children are developing a potential *conflict* relationship with capital. . . . [They] are not learning to be docile and obedient in the face of present or future degrading conditions or financial exploitation. They are developing abilities and skills of resistance' (Anyon 1980: 88).

However, this paper by Anyon perhaps represents the limits of the concept of the hidden curriculum as it has generally been utilized. Giroux (1981c) now argues that we need to go beyond not only the earlier approaches to the study of the hidden curriculum but also some elements of these more complex versions. He implies that, even where forms of resistance have been acknowledged, their significance has not been recognized because of inadequate conceptions of consciousness and culture. Thus, seemingly radical theorists have pointed to few possi-bilities for oppositional teaching in schools because their perspectives have remained too 'undialectical' to contribute significantly either to a comprehensive understanding of the relationship between schooling and capitalism or to the development of a more critical mode of pedagogy. He therefore proposes that a 'one-sided concern with cultural reproduction' should be compensated for by a 'primary concern with cultural intervention and social action' (Giroux 1981c). Drawing on Giddens's (1979) discussion of structure and human agency, Giroux argues that the concept of the hidden curriculum should refer to its potential for *both* reproduction and transformation.

Many of the issues raised in the work I have discussed on school texts and the hidden curriculum point towards the importance of studying the 'curriculum-in-use'. This is increasingly the direction in which much of the American work has been moving. Something of the nature of this shift and the issues it raises can be seen in a paper by Apple. This paper, entitled 'Curricular form and the logic of technical control' (Apple 1982b) can be seen as a transitional stage in the development of Apple's work. In it, he claims that there is a clear, though mediated, relationship between the movement towards packaged curricula in schools and the changing modes of control within capitalist production relations. He argues that the form these teaching materials take makes a particularly significant contribution to the formation of the type of 'possessive individual' appropriate to the current stage of development of capitalism. He suggests that these curricular packages constrain teachers in ways that make it difficult for them to organize the social relations of the classroom in a manner that would contest the messages implicit in the materials. Nevertheless, although he has a pessimistic view about the possibilities for more than token resistances to the logic of capitalist control in the present conjuncture, Apple accepts the theoretical possibility that resistances and contradictions within schools can be a significant site of political education and intervention. There remains, however, a certain tension within the paper between the early part, which seems to illustrate an almost *a priori* claim about the necessary outcome of the dynamics of capitalist development, and the later part, which quite explicitly recognizes that 'the creation of the kind of hegemony "caused" by the increasing introduction of technical control is not "naturally" pre-ordained . . . [but] something that is won or lost in particular conflicts and struggles' (Apple 1982b: 264).

What this work certainly does recognize is that the precise relationship between the political economy of schooling, the form and content of the curriculum and the social relations of the classroom cannot be resolved at a purely theoretical level. Thus the theoretical exploration of the broader dynamics of capitalist societies and the historical and situational analysis of curricular practice need to be brought together. What some of the curriculum writers in America are trying to do is to identify the different levels of cultural production and potential transformation in a more empirical manner than has so far taken place in Britain. Though I would not wish to claim that their progress has been substantial, I would argue that only work that moves in this direction is likely to be helpful in the development of strategies of pedagogic and political intervention.

An example of work that has this potential is to be found in another paper by Anyon (1981a) where she develops and presents new material from her research project in five elementary schools, to which I referred earlier. This work tries to demonstrate the importance and the possibilities of analysing the curriculum at several different levels and of identifying the contradictions within and between them as possible sites of transformative interventions. Particularly interesting is her attempt to explore which aspects of school knowledge in the different school contexts may be seen as reproductive in their effects and which as 'non-reproductive' and potentially transformative. In the working-class schools she found that knowledge was presented as a series of fragmented facts, isolated from their conceptual context and divorced from the 'lived experience' of the pupils. Copying was a major classroom activity and much of the learning emphasized by teachers was practical, rule-governed behaviour, leaving little room for pupil choice or decision-making. Nevertheless, while there was certainly no attempt to teach working-class pupils their own history, the emphasis was more on physical containment rather than on winning their hearts and minds to the dominant ideology. Anyon suggests that the pupils were, to some extent, able to 'see through' or *penetrate* the system and that this produced considerable passive and a certain amount of active resistance to the school knowledge with which they were confronted. They never-theless lacked the conceptual tools to develop any real alternatives.

In the middle-class school, knowledge was more conceptual but took the form of reified and mystifying understandings derived from socially approved sources. The knowledge had little immediate relevance to pupils and they felt little in the way of an active relationship to its pro-duction. However, the pupils did regard it as an important commodity that could be exchanged for a good job. The emphasis was thus, on the part of both teachers and pupils, on the *possibilities* the possession of this knowledge opened up for them in the labour market. In the affluent professional school, knowledge was seen as having both this exchange value and a more direct *use value*. The emphasis was upon learning as a creative process involving meaning-making rather than on the con-sumption of inert pre-defined knowledge. Yet, Anyon (1981a) suggests, it also produced a very individualistic and narcissistic orientation towards knowledge and experience. Whilst the curriculum encouraged a certain amount of care and compassion towards the less fortunate, history was seen in individualistic rather than collective terms. The curriculum of the executive élite school was academic in orientation and stressed tradition, rigour and rationality. Pupils were encouraged to understand systemic rules and practice problem-solving on the basis of the understandings so developed. Most pupils seemed to have internal-ized a sense of necessity to pursue 'excellence' at all costs, though there was already emerging in the fifth grade a distinct 'radical' subculture that self-consciously adopted 'street values'. Thus Anyon suggests that the clarity of the understandings engendered by this curriculum was a double-edged sword in that it might produce a *rejection* of ascribed roles rather than a commitment to them.

While some of Anyon's (1981a) data may be seen as confirming crucial elements of reproduction theory, she also begins to demonstrate that schools cannot be seen unproblematically as sites of social and cultural reproduction. She argues, for instance, that the lack of successful ideological incorporation of working-class pupils and their spontaneous perspicacity is a possible source of vulnerability in the reproduction cycle. An emphasis in the middle-class school on the possibility of individual success is likely to be contradicted by the realities of a contracting job market and restraints on social mobility. The emphasis on creativity and meaning-making in the affluent professional school is seen as coming into potential conflict with demands increasingly being made on the newer professional classes by the bureaucratic rationality of the corporate state. Even the understandings generated by the executive élite curriculum could, she suggests, be turned to very different political purposes than the maintenance of class advantage.

Elsewhere, Anyon (1981b) has made some more explicit suggestions about how she, as a teacher, might make use of contradictory and non-reproductive elements in developing a radical pedagogy or what she calls a 'transformative pedagogics'. Her strategies involve using (rather than merely 'celebrating') penetrative consciousness, politicizing cultural resistance and developing counter-ideologies. These strategies can be seen as closely related to the categories generated in her empirical research. There is thus a clearer relationship between the discourse of sociological analysis and the discourse of radical practice within her work than has typically been the case in Britain where, apart from a brief period in the early 1970s, the two modes of discourse have tended to remain distinct. Indeed, some of Anyon's concrete suggestions about pedagogy are still somewhat reminiscent of the possibilitarian phase of the new sociology of education, as is her rather optimistic claim that non-reproductive knowledge can facilitate 'fundamental transformation of ideologies and practices on the basis of which objects, services and ideas (and other cultural products) are produced, owned, distributed and publicly evaluated' (Anyon 1981a). Nevertheless, what is crucially important in this work is its recognition that whether contradictions and penetrations prove reproductive or transformative in practice depends partly on how they are worked upon via specific pedagogical strategies. Her work thus moves decisively beyond any tendency to romanticize and applaud working-class resistance *per se*, a tendency that has often been a feature of other work in this field.

Despite the promise of this sort of work, however, it is open to considerable criticism and has indeed been subjected to a savage critique by A. Hargreaves (1982). My own reservations about the work are not, by any means, as fundamental, as will become clear when I return to Hargreaves's arguments in chapter 4. However, I shall briefly note here some of the issues on which the work of these writers can be faulted. First, their criticisms of mainstream curricular research in the USA initially generated a rather uncritical openness to European radical social theory, even though they subsequently went on to modify and refine it. Second, although the eclecticism of these writers certainly produced some original and productive insights, it also obscured some very real incompatibilities between the different forms of theory that they have imported. Third, it must be said that, while these writers have recognized the importance of doing empirical research to a much greater extent than most British neo-Marxist theorists, they have been much less explicit about the problems of research methodology than those writers working within the ethnographic tradition in Britain. Fourth, there is the underdeveloped political dimension of these analyses. In many of them, there is a certain ambiguity in their political goals and an assumption that there is a general agreement about what sorts of educational and social changes are desirable in American society. Indeed, McNeil (1981a) has pointed to an unwarranted tendency in some of the writings to assume that there is a pre-constituted audience of vaguely socialist teachers who share the authors' political orientations which therefore do not need spelling out in more detail. In addition, the political focus of many of the studies is strangely narrow. Despite its apparent commitment to a broader transformation of society, much of the work has, until recently, limited its concerns to the professional arena and seems to assume that innovations in curricula and pedagogy in schools will necessarily have radical effects independently of their articulations with broader political struggles. This is a criticism I shall discuss in more detail in chapter 4.

Finally, some of this American work has, like the British influences upon it, focused upon social class differences in curriculum provision, enactment and response and has neglected the significance of other factors and the articulation between them. Thus, Ramsay (1983) suggests, for instance, that Anyon's concentration on class may have led her to neglect the significance of ethnicity. On the other hand, Taxel (1979) was amongst the first writers in this tradition to address the issues of racism and sexism in instructional materials. Recent work by Anyon (1983) and Kelly and Nihlen (1982) has anyway begun to remedy the weakness in respect of gender issues and that by Weis (1983) in respect of race, while the work of McNeil (1981b) and Popkewitz (1981) is also, in some respects, a corrective to any over-emphasis on class.

## Class, race and gender

I suggested earlier that the dominant concern of British sociologists of education, including those associated with the so-called 'new directions' of the 1970s, has been with the relationship between education and social class. Yet Spender (1982) points out that, while *Knowledge and Control* (Young 1971a) actually makes few references to women, its approach could well be adapted to the study of gender inequalities in and through education. In practice, however, only a very few studies in the tradition of the new sociology of education or its immediate successors concerned themselves with this issue.[4] The study by Wynn (1977) of home economics teaching was something of an exception. Similarly, as I pointed out when discussing Vulliamy's work on music education (Vulliamy 1972, 1976, 1977), some of the issues he raised were particularly relevant to the exclusion of the music of ethnic minorities from the school curriculum in Britain. Yet, here again, the new sociology of education paid little attention to the question of racial oppression, while initially, nor did the various neo-Marxist perspectives that succeeded it. As I have indicated above, some of the American work that used these perspectives to inform its empirical research also suffered from this same limitation.

However, in Britain, one of the influences on the sorts of developments in theory discussed earlier in this chapter was a growing recognition that the cruder forms of neo-Marxist theory, even of the structuralist variety, were unable to deal adequately with the theorization of gender and race. Feminist writers (Deem 1978; Nava 1980; M. MacDonald 1981) and black sociologists (CCCS 1982; Mullard 1981) drew attention to the limitations of white male Marxist sociologists' neglect of such issues or their attempts to subsume them under patriarchical and ethnocentric conceptions of class. At the same time, at the level of official policy and, to a lesser extent, curriculum practice in schools, multi-cultural education programmes and equal opportunities initiatives demanded forms of analysis that moved beyond seeing the state and education merely in terms of the reproduction of class relations. The development of a coherent response from the left also required a means of exploring the ways in which anti-racist and anti-sexist initiatives related to conventional left politics (Culley and Demaine 1983).

A great deal of the work that has arisen from these concerns demonstrates the importance of developing analyses in the sociology of education that explore the relationship between economic, political and ideological cultural practices in perpetuating and legitimating inequalities in school and society. Arnot (1981) shows, for instance, how the cultural perspective, which focuses on sex role socialization as the basis of gender inequalities, and the political economy perspective, which focuses on the requirements of the labour market, are both inadequate in their existing forms. Work in a culturalist perspective varies in the extent to which it is compatible with the developments in the new sociology of education discussed in this chapter, with that by McRobbie (1978), for example, exhibiting a number of features in common with them. Other studies, such as those contained in Kelly (1981), stem from rather different research traditions, which focus on the significance of attitudes, values and institutional practices in fostering unfavourable attitudes to the physical sciences on the part of girls. This sort of work points to the possibilities of reducing gender inequalities by providing common curricula for boys and girls, rewriting instructional materials to eliminate sexist vocabulary and images, reforming careers guidance and improving the representation of women in the higher levels of school hierarchies. Some of it also seems to suggest a strategy of teaching science in single sex groups.

Arnot (1981) implies that many of those who adopt the culturalist perspective tend to be over-optimistic about 'the extent of change brought about by [such] reforms' and need to beware of the 'danger of overstressing the possibilities and impact of internal reforms without recognition of external structures and attempts to change them'. This broader perspective is supplied by the political economy approach, though this, at least when adopting a traditional Marxist orientation 'tends to under-theorise and under-represent the impact of specifically patriarchal forms of domination and control'. Much current feminist theory and research is devoted to exploring the relationship between class and gender or capitalism and patriarchy. This work should help to clarify the extent to which strategies that specifically address gender inequalities in the curriculum are likely to be effective and the extent to which they need to be linked to broader attacks on prevailing patterns of capitalist and/or male domination in contemporary societies.[5]

Similar, though by no means identical, considerations underlie much of the work being done on race and schooling. Again, there are writers who place their major emphasis on attitudes (Milner 1975) and others whose analysis focuses on the influence of the capitalist economy (Sivanandan 1982). Some of the best work explores the relations between ideology and structure and the significance of cultural resistance for broader strategies of change (CCCS 1982). Clearly, though, an emphasis on culture is increasingly seen to be inadequate on its own and, indeed, in so far as it is officially sponsored through multi-cultural education policies, there is some agreement amongst writers in the field that it has the political function of diverting attention away from broader structural issues (Carby 1980; Sivanandan 1982). There is also a growing recognition that the sponsoring of progressive multi-racial, multi-ethnic or multi-cultural policies in schools is not, by itself, going to alter the power relations that sustain racial inequalities (Milner 1983). However, although Stone (1980) has argued strongly that such policies should therefore be eschewed in favour of a highly traditional curriculum for black pupils, her argument is based partly upon a misapprehension of the possibilities inherent in such programmes and the limited, but arguably significant, role that anti-racist approaches might play in broader strategies of change (Green 1982). Hatcher and Shallice (1983) suggest that multi-culturalism is a classic case of a curriculum innovation sponsored by the state but whose inherent contradictions make it susceptible to oppositional interventions.

In this field, as in the studies of gender, there is considerable concern to establish the relationship between the specificities of a particular form of oppression and those of others, such as class and gender. Most contemporary sociologists of education seem to share the view of Edwards (1979) that 'the histories of racism and sexism, intimately linked though they are to that of capitalism, are not sub-sets of the latter' and hence their dynamics require separate types of analysis.[6] They differ considerably, however, about the nature of that intimate link and the types of separate analyses required. There remains a tendency amongst many writers in the field to regard class relations as somehow more basic than gender and race relations, but this view is hotly contested by others. For the moment, it is only possible to say that the rising concern with those issues has helped to make the cruder forms of neo-Marxist theory inadequate to an understanding of contemporary social relations. At the same time, it does seem that the work that offers some of the most plausible conceptualizations of the relations between the dynamics of different forms of oppression draws heavily upon some of the more sophisticated developments in and around Marxist theory discussed in this chapter.[7]

# 3

# Curriculum studies and the sociology of school knowledge

It might be expected that work within the sociology of education that concerned itself particularly with aspects of the curriculum would make a major impact on curriculum studies, a field of enquiry concerned with relating curriculum theory and practice. This is happening to a growing extent in North America and much of the American work discussed in chapter 2, which owes part of its inspiration to the British new sociology of education, is being carried out in departments of curriculum and instruction. In Britain, however, there has so far been little constructive interchange between scholars working on the sociology of school knowledge and those involved in the field of curriculum studies. Although *Knowledge and Control* (Young 1971a) made some initial impact, the criticisms of it by writers such as Lawton (1973, 1975a) and Pring (1972) seem to have satisfied most curriculum studies specialists that there is little to be gained by keeping abreast of developments within the sociology of education. In this chapter, I attempt to explore some of the limitations of curriculum studies as presently constituted in Britain and suggest ways in which both curriculum studies and the sociology of school knowledge might benefit from the development of closer links between them.

Curriculum studies, as a distinctive field of educational theory and practice, is a relatively new arrival on the British scene. Nevertheless, two approaches to curriculum studies can be thought of as distinctively British in inspiration – the work of Denis Lawton and his colleagues in the Curriculum Studies Department at the Institute of Education in

London[1] and the activities of the group that formed around the late Lawrence Stenhouse at the University of East Anglia.[2] Both these groups have self-consciously distanced themselves from the banalities of the sort of technicist approaches to curriculum planning, development and evaluation they saw as dominating the American scene and which looked in danger of determining the nature of the field in Britain in the 1960s and early 1970s. They have both also had a powerful influence on the character of curriculum studies way beyond the confines of their own institutions, particularly through their involvement in Open University curriculum courses (OU 1976, 1983). They have thus helped (even today when many American curriculum writers are themselves beginning to reject the earlier approaches and British officialdom has started to flirt with something not unlike them) to give curriculum studies in Britain a more liberal and humanistic flavour than its transatlantic counterpart. Their work may well appeal therefore to all those who are increasingly coming to question and reject the traditional paradigm in curriculum studies and, in particular, to those who see their own work in education as contributing to a quest for greater democracy and social justice in society.

However, even though these approaches have distinct advantages over the more conventional ones which they criticize, they themselves need to be subjected to critical appraisal. Although this chapter will focus mainly on the work of Denis Lawton, it will also argue that, despite important differences of emphasis between the different writers in-volved, they all share a similar ambiguity about the purposes of the enterprise in which they are engaged and a collective refusal to address certain crucial structural issues raised, for instance, in contemporary work in the sociology of education. This detracts not only from their understanding of many of the phenomena they discuss, but also from the viability and significance of their proposed or implied strategies of change.

First, I want to make some general comments about the nature and importance of the curriculum studies field in Britain today. As we have seen, for much of the post-war period the curriculum was sadly neglected as an area of concern by educational theorists and educational policy-makers alike, its nature having either been taken for granted or treated as a matter for teachers' professional judgement. Educational studies and social democratic education policy were both organized along lines that made it difficult to discuss curriculum issues in a meaningful way, and this was to have serious implications for their capacity to influence the reality of schooling. It is therefore very much to the credit of those writers whose work is considered in this chapter that they have helped to bring curriculum issues into sharper focus even if, as I will argue, they have allowed our vision of the broader context of those issues to become blurred in the process. Yet it must also be said that the reluctance, until recently, of theorists and politicians to involve themselves in the curriculum field has contributed to its relative underdevelopment and thus to the disproportionate influence of the work discussed here.

In one of his public pronouncements about the state of the field he helped to found in Britain, Denis Lawton claims that 'curriculum studies is not a field of educational enquiry to specialize in for those who want a quiet life in an ivory tower'. He suggests that it is a 'rather aggressive world' in which 'even jokes about the curriculum tend to have a cruel edge' (Lawton 1979). But, to other people, the curriculum studies field gives little impression of being intellectually alive, let alone 'aggressive' or 'cruel'. In many ways it has been largely parasitic upon the work of philosophers and sociologists of education who have themselves often been at pains to eschew the curriculum studies field, and indeed sometimes any direct concern with pedagogical and policy issues at all. This has meant that curriculum theorists have often drawn upon outdated and simplistic versions of their work, with the unfortunate consequence that it has often been only via the emasculated versions of such work, as utilized in curriculum studies departments, that philosophical and sociological perspectives have entered the consciousness of serving teachers and the ideological discourse of policy-making contexts. It also means that, in a period when the curriculum has suddenly emerged as a live issue in the British political arena for the first time since the war, the curriculum studies 'specialists' are those most likely to be called upon to contribute to the debate. Although, as I implied earlier, the DES initially responded to political demands for accountability with some rather crude and outmoded models of curriculum planning and control, there are also signs (Lawton 1980, 1983; Sockett 1980) that the advocates of the more liberal approaches are seeking to influence the direction of policy. The nature of curriculum studies is thus potentially of more than purely academic or even professional significance.

## The work of Denis Lawton

I now want to explore the work of Denis Lawton in some depth since not only is he one of the most prolific writers in this field, he is also, as director of London University's Institute of Education, the one nearest to the major arenas of educational debate and policy formation. One of the strengths of Lawton's approach is that he certainly does not regard curriculum planning as purely, or even largely, a technical exercise and he recognizes that curriculum decision-making involves crucial cultural and political choices. Indeed, he was one of the first occupants of the middle ground of British politics to face up to this and to try to explore the implications of the work of those theorists to his right and left (Bantock 1968; Williams 1965; Young 1971b) who had been arguing that case for some time. More than most writers in the curriculum field, at least until very recently, he has attempted to address theoretical issues about the nature of culture and to link his discussion of the curriculum to broader political concepts like social justice. He has made some specific proposals for the reform of the curriculum and has also proposed a new model of curriculum decision-making around which a consensus about the curriculum might be achieved. I want, however, to suggest that both the style and the content of his argument often serve to obscure rather than clarify the nature of the issues he seeks to address and that by emphasizing the construction of consensus he fails to consider in sufficient depth how such consensual curricular arguments would, even if they were to be achieved, articulate with broader structural features of society. Indeed, I would argue that his proposals derive from a misrecognition of the social formation in which they have arisen and that they may effectively contribute to the construction of the sort of new hegemonic discourse about education that could help bolster a society antithetical in nature to one in which his concept of social justice could have any real substance.

Let me therefore illustrate the way in which Lawton's basic approach seems almost to be designed to avoid confronting such issues and to mask them in the construction of a spurious consensual position to which it is assumed all rational persons will assent. Lawton adopts a tone of informed common sense and in his writing for teachers and adminis-trators, as much as in his writing for school pupils, his tendency is always to establish 'what most sociologists would accept' (Lawton 1975a) rather than to engage seriously with the very basic issues around which they differ. Yet, significantly, he only seems able to justify his own position by a distortion of some of the more interesting arguments he hopes thereby to defuse, and the institutional separation of curriculum studies from other areas of educational theory ensures that only a minority of his readership will have had direct access to the arguments he claims to have disposed of. It is interesting to notice how, like Entwistle (Entwistle 1978, 1979), whose work has a certain affinity to his own, Lawton always chooses to discuss, and hence dismiss, the extreme version of any argument that differs from his own – and often merely a caricature of such an argument. Thus, for instance, his target is 'Naive Progessivism' (Lawton 1977) rather than those forms of progressivism that are actually influential, while elsewhere (Lawton 1975b) he attacks a *'naive and simplistic* interpretation of the Marxian assumptions about the *direct* relationship of the economic substructure and the cultural superstruc-ture'. In the same book he opposes the view that *'everything* that the school offers is middle-class culture and, therefore, of *no* value' and the suggestion that '*all* science, history, art, philosophy, and morals' can be labelled as 'bourgeois' (my emphases).

Even where his strictures have a more genuine target, as in parts of his critique of the work of Michael Young and his associates (Young 1971a), one scans his work in vain for any mention of the way in which these writers have themselves taken criticism on board and attempted to refine their arguments. In this way, Lawton can appear to dispose of positions that might call his own into question without ever seriously addressing them in their more sophisticated forms, which actually stress the complex and contradictory nature of schooling, and seek to explore the nature of the relationship between economy and culture rather than assuming it to be a 'direct' one (Willis 1977; Young and Whitty 1977). Even if we accept that, because of the institutional divisions between sociology of education and curriculum studies, Lawton might not always have been aware of these developments, it is clear that by 1980 he was aware of some of the vocabulary used in this work even though he again employed it in typically caricatured fashion. This can be seen in the following passage, parts of which were quoted in chapter 1:

> Some recent sociologists specialising in the sociology of the curriculum would have us believe that control of the curriculum is *simply* a question of bourgeois hegemony. They assume that in a capitalist society the *whole* of the cultural superstructure, including education, is a *reflection* of the values of the dominant group – i.e. the bourgeoisie or the capitalist ruling class. For this group of writers education is assumed to be a *totally* socialising influence. But I am suggesting that the question of the control of education is much more complicated than that.                                       (Lawton 1980: 6–7, my emphases)

Even if such a crude view of the curriculum was ever propagated, and I suggested earlier that only in the mid-1970s did it take anything resembling that form, it is to the exploration of the very complexity to which Lawton points that sociologists have been committed over the past few years.

I have spent some time showing how Lawton's method of argumentation involves exaggeration and caricature because I believe it helps to explain the apparent plausibility of his position and also serves to make us wary of being seduced by his prescriptions. In fact, because he chooses to mount his argument via a series of supposed refutations of the work of other theorists, Lawton is able to avoid mounting a carefully constructed positive argument. Thus, in the context of caricatured alternatives, but possibly not in the context of some of the more real alternatives, an ill-defined pluralism can easily appear the most plausible social theory on offer and a consensual approach to curriculum decision-making the strategy most likely to contribute towards social justice. His claims to have uncovered flaws in other theories and strategies create the space into which his own conception of a common culture curriculum or a democratic model of curriculum planning can be slotted, with predictable regularity, at the end of virtually every volume he produces. While some of the flaws he identifies in other theories do undoubtedly exist, and while some of his policy prescriptions may have much to commend them, we would be better able to judge them in the light of a firm foundation of positive argument and a more genuine exploration of other views of the society and educational system in which they are intended to operate. It is, I am suggesting, as much his style of writing as the substantive content of Lawton's position that makes it appear highly plausible and something to which all but a 'few extremists' (Lawton 1977) could easily agree.

Let us turn, then, to his substantive proposals for a common culture curriculum and co-operative model of curriculum decision-making and control. These proposals have been developed over the past ten years or so in a series of complementary and overlapping publications, the most significant of which have been *Social Change, Educational Theory and Curriculum Planning* (1973), *Class, Culture and the Curriculum* (1975b), *Education and Social Justice* (1977) and *The Politics of the School Curriculum* (1980). The earlier volumes outlined his conception of the curriculum as a 'selection from culture' and suggested that, in the interests of social justice, all pupils should be exposed to a selection from our 'common culture'. This produced his prescription of a curriculum centred around five core areas of knowledge – mathematics, the physical and biological sciences, the humanities and social studies, the expressive arts and moral education. He recognizes however, that the selection of these and, to an even greater extent, other elements of the curriculum is never likely to be an entirely uncontentious matter and, in the light of recent disputes between politicians and professionals over curriculum issues, the later volumes focus upon the idea of a new model of curriculum decision-making.

Lawton proposes a multi-level scheme of co-operative control in which all the relevant parties can reach broad agreement on the nature of the curriculum, with its detailed implementation and assessment being assigned to different groups at the different levels of decision-making from the context of national policy through to the individual teacher planning his/her lesson. He suggests that such a scheme should be implemented in the near future 'if we are to avoid further confusion and unnecessary conflict' (Lawton 1980). While there might appear at first sight to be a certain tension between his own conviction that the curriculum should take a particular form and his proposals for a co-operative mechanism through which decisions about the curriculum should be made, it is clear that he regards the two proposals as essentially complementary and both as suggestions on which it ought to be possible to reach agreement with all rational and fair-minded people.

What is disturbing is that Lawton almost seduces us into believing that his prescriptions are manifestly 'a good thing' on the basis of very little careful sociological analysis of the context in which they are intended to operate, and without even giving us a very clear idea of what precisely his common culture curriculum and his co-operative decision-making model are for – other, of course, than a basis for agreement. It is only when we pause to reflect upon such questions that we recognize the dangers of accepting his stunningly simple solutions to our current educational problems. The immediate appeal of a *common culture* curriculum or a *co-operative* approach to curriculum planning is perhaps hardly surprising in the context of a prevailing educational ideology that has tended to mask fundamental conflicts and inequalities in contemporary society. Yet in the context of the underlying power relations of that society, which he does not analyse in any depth, such proposals may well have effects very different from those which Lawton himself envisages. It is even quite conceivable that his rhetoric will merely be used to provide a legitimating gloss for the implementation of the sort of core curriculum that will actually contribute little to the realization of social justice. In other words, the achievement of social justice in the context with which we are actually faced may necessitate not so much the avoidance of 'unnecessary conflict' as the bringing into sharper focus of some *necessary* conflicts over, amongst other things, the nature of the school curriculum.

The instant appeal of Lawton's demand for a consensus around his proposals is not necessarily a useful measure of their efficacy as instruments for the extension of democratic rights and the pursuance of social justice. There may, in fact, be a certain irony in a statement in *Education and Social Justice* where Lawton points to the way in which dangerous psychological half-truths about 'three types of children' entered the public consciousness and helped to legitimate that earlier supposed instrument of social justice, the tripartite system of secondary education. Of that episode, he said:

> In this, as in many other respects, it was not the scientific evidence or the opinions of experts which really mattered, but the oversimplified view which had been created in the minds of the population as a whole, and of teachers and educational administrators in particular.
>
> (Lawton 1977: 46)

This should serve to remind us that the patent 'reasonableness' of a view is not enough to ensure its accuracy; nor, indeed, is an appearance of egalitarianism sufficient to ensure that a policy is egalitarian in its effects. Thus the role of Lawton's own work in the reconstruction of hegemony out of the current crisis in education, and in the legitimation of the forms of élitism and injustice he claims to attack, must itself be subject to careful scrutiny, and any temptation to accept uncritically his notion of a common culture curriculum should be resisted by those committed to an extension of social justice. This is not, however, to suggest that his work should be dismissed by such people, but rather that it should be subjected to a serious critical analysis.

Interestingly, in the light of my foregoing comments, Lawton's work has, as yet, come in for very little critical appraisal in this country. In what follows, I shall therefore be drawing quite heavily upon a critique of his work produced by Uldis Ozolins of the University of Melbourne in Australia, where the work of the sociology research group in cultural and educational studies seems to span the gulf between sociology of education and curriculum studies that has bedevilled the British scene. This paper (Ozolins 1979) is particularly concerned with Lawton's *Class, Culture and the Curriculum* and concentrates upon his supposed refutation of the idea of a 'working-class curriculum' and claim that his own 'common culture curriculum' would be to the benefit of the working class.

Before looking at Ozolins's criticisms, I want to suggest that the nature of Lawton's work is partially to be understood in terms of its relationship to conventional social democratic education policy in Britain, a relationship that becomes clearer in his later book *Education and Social Justice*. Certainly there can be little doubt that Lawton's work represents something of an advance on the conventional social democratic notion that educational and social justice are to be attained by improving access to an education whose content remains largely unproblematic. His sympathetic critique of Labour Party education policy (Lawton 1977: ch. 7) follows similar lines to other recent commentaries on this point. However, his recognition of the significance of curricular arrangements for the perpetuation and legitimation of social inequality, and his subsequent argument that social justice would best be served by the introduction of his common culture curriculum, should not necessarily be seen to stand or fall together. The suggestion that a differentiated curriculum is as divisive as a differentiated school system does not necessarily lead one to the conclusion that the addition of a common curriculum to a formal policy of comprehensive schooling will be any more successful than the latter alone in achieving social justice. But, given Lawton's somewhat reified conception of the curriculum as something to be transmitted, his argument often does appear to be merely an extension of the formal equality of access position that has dominated Labour Party policy.

Yet it was surely not just because the knowledge dimension of educational provision was neglected in traditional social democratic thinking, nor even because professional administrators with a vested interest in the preservation of the status quo outsmarted the politicians, that Labour Party education policies failed to realize their promise. Rather it was because (as some of the architects of those policies have now recognized) the nature of society, the state and education and the articulations between them were far more complex than such policies assumed. Again it is noticeable that Lawton almost entirely neglects, even in his most recent work, to discuss any of the literature that attempts, however unsuccessfully, to come to grips with such issues.

It seems to me that it is also this continuity with traditional social democratic approaches to education that helps to explain why 'Lawton tells us surprisingly little about what he expects the consequences of [his common culture] curriculum to be' (Ozolins 1979). While, in places, Lawton seems to recognize some of the tensions involved in what Finn, Grant and Johnson (1977) term the 'dual repertoire' of Labour Party policy, his own position retains many of the ambiguities this entails. Thus, Ozolins is able to quote from *Class, Culture and the Curriculum* to suggest that Lawton's main purpose is to 'produce a few more good sixth formers' and thus he is able to locate him in the Fabian 'capacity-catching' tradition. In *Education and Social Justice*, however, Lawton shows a more 'egalitarian' concern with education as a 'right' and his common curriculum can thus be seen as recognizing the right of all children to 'real education'. Elsewhere in both these books he stresses the importance of transmitting a common culture as a way of reducing social division and antagonism. There is then not only something of an ambiguity about what his proposals are designed for, but also the usual reluctance to explore rather than gloss over the relationship between arguments about social justice *in* education and those about social justice *through* education, or even to tell us what precisely social justice might mean in either context. The difficulty of knowing what the consequences of Lawton's curricular proposals are expected to be is, then, a feature of the continuity between his work and prevailing social democratic traditions, even though he himself rightly suggests that the Labour Party needs 'to clarify fundamental principles . . . about society and education' as a prelude to doing 'their homework more carefully on important questions of detail in education' (Lawton 1977). It is, however, the very congruity between his lack of clarity and a more general one within the labour movement as a whole that contributes to the ease with which we can be lulled into accepting his policy prescriptions as self-evidently a good thing, without really analysing their purposes or implications or their relationship to other aspects of social policy.

None of these issues can really be adequately dealt with in the absence of an analysis of the social formation and the role of education within it. This is not to say that Lawton entirely fails to recognize that schools are located in society or even that he is unaware of the dangers of seeming to suggest that schools can remedy all of society's ills. Indeed, he explicitly tells us at one point that 'the question of social justice in education cannot be separated from social justice in society at large, particularly the question of access to certain kinds of occupation' and that it 'is difficult to promote social justice in education without going some way towards eliminating social injustice in the wider community' (Lawton 1977). Equally, he admits that 'schools cannot compensate for society, and schools should not be blamed for all the imperfections of society as a whole', although education can, he tells us, 'equip people to understand . . . society better and improve it' (Lawton 1977). But, for the most part, such issues are bracketed and it is significant that all these quotations are, once again, comments made during critiques of other writers rather than part of an explicit theory of society upon which Lawton's position is based. Even when he is discussing the essential bases of a prescriptive educational theory, he does not include amongst its components a theory of the nature of society, even though the last of his comments quoted above implies that practical interventions in the social world are most likely to be effective if they are based on a proper understanding of society. The problem may arise because he draws heavily here (Lawton 1977) on the work of Moore (1974), a philosopher of education.

Yet, although sometimes (Lawton 1973, 1975b, 1983) somewhat greater prominence is given to the role of sociological questions in curriculum planning, it is surely *only* in the context of an explicit theory of society, and a clearer conception of how struggles for social justice in education relate to similar struggles elsewhere, that we can judge whether Lawton's prescriptions for a common culture curriculum and a consensus model of curriculum planning are likely to be efficacious in achieving even the somewhat ambiguous social objectives to which he adheres. In some cases, as part of a clearer broader strategy designed to further the interests of those currently disadvantaged in society, they might well have some merit. But, on their own, they might equally well contribute towards the construction of a new hegemonic settlement that effectively sustains the status quo. Only a more adequate analysis of the structural and conjunctural features of contemporary society could put us in a position to make an informed judgement about their merits.

If *Education and Social Justice* thus helps us to locate the ambiguities of Lawton's work within the ambiguities of a broader political tradition, it does little to remedy the essential weaknesses Ozolins identifies in *Class, Culture and the Curriculum*, and it is to a fuller consideration of those weaknesses that we now turn. In a careful analysis of the case set out in that book, an analysis Lawton himself has subsequently characterized as 'interesting' (Lawton 1983), Ozolins demonstrates quite convincingly that Lawton avoids some of those crucial questions about the nature of contemporary society to which I have pointed above. He concludes that Lawton is:

> politically ingenuous: he presents his idea of a common curriculum with very much the feeling that it is a philosophy whose time has come, but it is only arrived at by systematically ignoring class and culture conflict on a massive scale.                          (Ozolins 1979: 62)

The paper shows Lawton's conceptions of class and culture to be crude in the extreme and indicates that he is highly ambivalent, if not somewhat inconsistent, about the admittedly highly complex relationship between culture and the social and economic environment. His case about the existence and nature of a common culture is seen to be developed via the mode of argumentation I outlined earlier and 'without any substantial analysis of the working class in the contemporary class structure'. Yet, ultimately, Ozolins suggests, Lawton's curricular proposals emerge not so much from his somewhat confused discussion of class and culture but rather from a strategic retreat into the Hirstian 'forms of knowledge' (Hirst and Peters 1970). The core areas of his curriculum are therefore derived from a 'structure and organisation of knowledge [which] is universal rather than culturally based'. But, even if such 'universal' forms can be distinguished analytically, the real problem facing those committed to social justice is not thereby removed. While Lawton does make brief mention of the problems of changing teachers' and pupils' attitudes, he seems to assume that the essential work has been done once the abstract analysis has been carried out, and certainly does not face up to the complexities of translating it into a curriculum that can be taught meaningfully to all pupils in the real world. These complexities can, of course, only be grasped adequately via an understanding of the broader context in which the cultural transactions of schooling take place. It is not therefore simply a matter of distinguishing basic knowledge forms which should be made available to all pupils from 'middle-class manners, etiquette and lower-level middle-class values' (Lawton 1975b), even if that were indeed a simple matter in itself.

The most telling part of Ozolins's critique is where he pursues this point and considers the likely effects of Lawton's 'common culture curriculum' as a curriculum-in-use rather than as a reified abstraction. He points out the way in which Lawton conveniently ignores the work of Bourdieu (Bourdieu 1971a, b, 1976) which would raise major questions about the likely articulation between Lawton's curriculum-in-use and aspects of the broader social structure. It is therefore worth quoting Ozolins at some length on this point:

> Bourdieu . . . is concerned to show how it is that the academic curriculum itself serves as an instrument of differentiation and

exclusion: it is not that pupils are taught vastly different sorts of curriculum, nor that teachers have prejudicial outlooks on their pupils; rather it is that a common curriculum, 'effectively' taught, will itself be a biased form of education. In *Knowledge and Control* (Young 1971a), Bourdieu discusses the education of elites, and the way in which education of certain forms encourages homogeneity among elites by emphasis on an academic curriculum. This curriculum serves to distinguish the elite and (because they fail to master it) severely restricts and rationalizes the life-chances of the working class pupils. Elsewhere (Dale *et al.* 1976), Bourdieu has amplified these views in two directions: first that the school works in a biased manner by demanding of *every* child what only some children can give – a certain orientation to the culture of the school and the academic curriculum, a certain 'cultural capital' that reflects the cultural level of the home and provides the children of *some* families with the essential skills and attitudes ('cultural ethos') that lead to success in school. It is these children who are rewarded in school when their social gifts are interpreted as natural ability and interest. Secondly, the curriculum of the school cannot be treated as a neutral object: some elements, particularly the letters, humanities and social sciences, are peculiarly dependent on the child's cultural capital. They are taught by a pedagogy which makes continual *implicit* demands on a child's own social and cultural skills of subtlety, nuance, taste and manner which some children acquire 'naturally' from their own cultural milieu *and which are not capable of an explicit pedagogy.*

Bourdieu's critique seriously questions the 'fairness' of a common curriculum. Bourdieu's work, by pointing to the profoundly inegalitarian consequences of a common curriculum, negates Lawton's . . . main thesis; argumentation on this point is not forthcoming from Lawton.                                              (Ozolins 1979: 46)

It is true that Lawton does recognize that we cannot assume that a curriculum that is common in conception will necessarily be enacted and received in an undifferentiated way, nor indeed would he consider it desirable that all pupils should have a *uniform* curriculum (Lawton 1973, 1975b). Yet, as Ozolins points out, these seem to be essentially side-issues for Lawton and he clearly believes that, if we can persuade teachers to reflect upon and change inappropriate attitudes, it will be quite feasible to provide all children with the basic core understandings he has identified. But Bourdieu suggests the problem is an altogether deeper one and one much less capable of simple solution, certainly within the school. It is not that Lawton's proposals for a common culture curriculum are without their strengths, but there are also strong grounds for taking seriously Bourdieu's argument that the elevation of the cultural arbitraries of particular social groups to the status of universals can contribute to a self-legitimating system of cultural and social reproduction. He tells us that there is *no* pedagogic action 'which does not inculcate some meanings not deducible from a universal principle' and that the work of schooling can always be carried out 'without either those who exercise it or those who undergo it ever ceasing to misrecognise its dependence on the power relations making up the social formation in which it is carried on' (Bourdieu and Passeron 1977). While this argument clearly creates problems of its own, those who see current proposals for a common curriculum as a major route towards social justice ignore it at their peril. It is therefore little short of astonishing that Lawton, whose familiarity with at least one of the volumes in which Bourdieu's work appears is established via his other citations of it, should choose to do so.

While Bourdieu shows the issues surrounding a common curriculum to be much more complex than Lawton admits, Ozolins himself does not take refuge in these complexities to preach a counsel of despair. He is not to be counted amongst those who argue there is no form of curriculum strategy that can usefully be employed in schools by those seeking social justice in society, and he demonstrates that Lawton tries to justify his own consensus curriculum via a refutation of a caricature of other supposedly 'left' approaches. Lawton is shown to base his critique of left theorists on the attribution to them of the notion that a curriculum in the interests of the working class means a curriculum rooted in and *restricted* to a *celebration* of working-class life as it is – a view Ozolins suggests it may be appropriate to attribute to Bantock on the right, but is hardly attributable to any serious theorist on the left.

Ozolins admits that 'we are only at the beginning of being able to define and elaborate a viable working class curriculum', but says that 'it is neither philosophically nor educationally an incoherent concept of curricular development' and argues that attempted 'refutations' such as Lawton's should not be a serious deterrent to those who wish to pursue the idea of a curriculum that would really be in the interests of the working class. Thus, in place of Lawton's concern to establish a consensus around the concept of 'worthwhile' knowledge, Ozolins himself makes some tentative proposals for a curriculum that discriminates positively in favour of knowledge that would be really useful to working-class pupils. This might well overlap with much of the content of Lawton's own curriculum as he has subsequently claimed (Lawton 1983), but the criteria of selection are clearly different. Ozolins's idea resonates with the educational programmes of the nineteenth-century radicals described by Johnson (1979a), who saw '*really* useful knowledge' as including knowledge 'concerning our conditions in life . . . [and] how to get out of our present troubles'. While fully democratic access to all forms of knowledge was seen as a future ideal, the immediate priority was a sort of 'spearhead knowledge' committed to the emancipation of the working class and the creation of a form of society in which all would have the right of access to knowledge and justice. Though the modern equivalent of such a curriculum would clearly relate to the realities of working-class life, and presumably seek to develop a critique of prevailing society via the sorts of cultural penetrations already present within working-class culture, it would hardly be a mere celebration of it. As Ozolins says:

> rather than just a study of working class culture and working class life [such a curriculum] must be a study of the relations of the working class to the rest of society: the forces by which this relationship can be investigated, questioned and eventually transformed.
>
> (Ozolins 1979: 50)

In such a curriculum, 'situation-centred learning' is neither inherently limiting nor, as in Lawton's work, merely a way of catching pupils' interest in the disciplines.

While Ozolins's own brief curricular proposals are clearly only in an embryonic stage of development, and indeed are not entirely free from the sorts of weaknesses he attributes to Lawton's, they do at least make clear that Lawton's is not the only approach to curriculum planning to be considered by those pursuing social justice. It also seems likely that such an approach would be less susceptible to hegemonic incorporation in that it has a much clearer and consistent view of its purpose than is evident in Lawton's work and, in a section of the paper on the institutional form of schooling, Ozolins (1979) also demonstrates an awareness of the realities and difficulties of pursuing that purpose within such an institutional form. The paper is rather less clear about how its curriculum strategy articulates with other strategies of social change, but its author is quite clear that its purpose is to contribute to the struggle against the hegemonic forces in contemporary society rather than to risk the sort of accommodation with them that might legitimate rather than challenge the status quo. Yet he is clearly not the sort of caricatured 'extremist' with whom Lawton likes to take issue and he takes Lawton's own position seriously enough to want to engage in dialogue about it and its effects. To Lawton's credit, he has been prepared to take Ozolins's contribution to that dialogue more seriously than he has taken British contributions (Lawton 1983).

However, even in Britain, not all Marxists are 'naive and simplistic' and Ozolins is merely one of many serious socialist educators in various countries who are struggling to understand the complex nature of education under capitalism, to recognize its specificities in particular national and cultural contexts and to devise appropriate strategies of educational and social change. Their work might, if taken seriously, assist Lawton to explore the conditions under which it could make sense to claim, as he does in an optimistic conclusion to a recent article, that in 'increased struggles between the periphery and the centre on curriculum issues . . . the professionals – in the end – might win' (Lawton 1984). Much of it would suggest that whatever the capacity of the teaching profession to frustrate change, the current disposition of political and ideological forces in and around the state makes it highly unlikely that progressive curriculum change could any longer be won by the teaching profession alone. This makes it especially important that, if Lawton and others working along similar lines are genuinely committed to the realization of social justice, they begin to engage in serious dialogue with writers on the left, including sociologists of education, rather than reducing their arguments to caricature.

## The contribution of CARE

I now want to make some rather briefer comments about the work of those writers associated with the Centre for Applied Research in Education at the University of East Anglia. One of the major criticisms which can be made of Lawton's work is that it remains largely at the level of formal curriculum analysis and is therefore able to avoid confronting the complexity of the real contexts in which educational transactions take place. Culture and curriculum become reified and detached from the contexts of lived experience and hence also from the broader structural relations that interpenetrate that experience. The strength of most of the writers associated with CARE lies in their commitment to the integrity of lived experience and their abiding interest in the subjective interpretations of curricular reality made by teachers and pupils. This results partly from the different focus of their interests, for while Lawton puts most of his emphasis on curriculum planning, the East Anglian group have been more interested in the study of curriculum implementation, evaluation and diffusion. However, while their emphasis on the subjective dimension of curriculum change is a useful complement to Lawton's work, and certainly a necessary corrective to the crude centre-periphery models of curriculum development imported from the USA, it has often attained such a centrality within the work of these school-centred writers that it has served to divert attention away from the broader sociological and political realities of schooling.

An understanding of the ways in which curricular meanings are inter-subjectively negotiated and the institutional factors that facilitate or hinder change in schools (Walker and MacDonald 1976) is absolutely vital to any effective strategy of change, but so is an understanding of the ways in which they articulate with the broader power relations of society. The role of teachers' 'habitual and unconscious behaviour patterns' in sustaining traditional modes of pedagogy, and the development of self-monitoring techniques amongst teachers as a way of producing and sustaining change (Elliott and Adelman 1976), are also important areas of work, but their real significance can only really be grasped in the context of a fuller exploration of the reasons why teacher behaviour is apparently so generalizable 'across classrooms, subject areas and schools'. In other words, while this work correctly recognizes that any realistic strategy of change must address itself to the problems of ideologies *in* education as well as ideologies *about* education (Finn, Grant and Johnson 1977), it has tended to sidestep the issue of the economic and political conditions of existence of both. It has therefore tended to over-emphasize the possibilities for teachers to effect change in schools, and for researchers to develop democratic modes of evaluation by bracketing out those wider considerations. Significantly these writers have, like Lawton, chosen either to ignore the considerable litera-ture generated in the sociology of education on these very issues (Bartholomew 1974; Whitty 1974) or to misrepresent it (Elliott 1983).

This avoidance of broader sociological issues, together with a related distrust of political 'movements' (Stenhouse 1975), means that such perspectives on the curriculum are, despite their frequent association with liberal and progressive modes of pedagogy, singularly ill-fitted to respond to the current wave of reactionary initiatives in the curriculum field. Barton and Lawn (1980) have put this case in even stronger terms:

The CARE unit lays little emphasis on explicating its underlying political assumptions. Where it is evident or implied, one can deduce that there is a strongly optimistic view that revealing information about processes and people will result in increased awareness, participation and change by ordinary people. It is radical in that it takes the views of ordinary people seriously, but it can also be seen as conservative in that it does not introduce new questions or challenge the perceptions of the practitioners. Indeed, it may expose in an efficient way its practitioners to the policy-makers and powerful public institutions. It also does not enter into a public debate or theoretical argument which would directly challenge the technological determinism or radical political alternatives evident today.

Perhaps CARE will take note of the warning made by George Orwell in his essay 'Inside the Whale' when he saw in the future a new quietist, passive writing arising which would not fight the world but would be content to 'simply accept, endure it, record it'. Or will they be influenced, like Mass Observation, which tried to move from a 'naturalistic' to a 'political' perspective because of the political context of the thirties and its crises. Will a siege economy and political conflict in Britain in the 1980s change CARE?        (Barton and Lawn 1980: 14)

While this passage glosses over some important differences between the various writers at CARE, to which the authors point elsewhere in the paper, it does demonstrate how, although the CARE unit's work differs in significant ways from that of Lawton, it shares his work's ambiguities about the purpose of the enterprise and is even less concerned to place the study of the curriculum and the process of curriculum development within its broader social context. There is, however, now some indication (Elliott 1980; B. MacDonald 1979) that at least some of the writers associated with CARE are moving into areas of work which make it increasingly difficult to avoid such issues.

Nevertheless, although there are those, such as Elliott, who are beginning to make considerable use of a version of neo-Marxist critical theory in their work, they have drawn largely on the work of Habermas and often adopted a particularly idealist interpretation of his work. Though this work certainly leads them to consider questions of educational change and human emancipation in a broader context than hitherto, they retain an emphasis on professional process at the expense of political action. Alongside the recognition of broader constraints, whose prominence is hard to ignore in the current political climate, there remains, to an even greater extent than in Lawton's work, a naive optimism in the countervailing power of a born-again profession that is somewhat reminiscent of the new sociology of education of the early 1970s. Thus, after defending CARE from my charge about its lack of attention to constraints upon teacher autonomy, Elliott (1983) goes on to say:

> The action-research movement is grounded in the assumption that teachers can exercise a measure of control and influence over what educational changes are brought about, through practical discourse about the validity of the practical theories and norms which underpin their established practices. By enabling teachers to reconstruct their educational norms, action-research strengthens their capacity to resist political manipulation and to hold the state to account for its policies.
> (Elliott 1983: 23)

This seems as naive as the over-deterministic sociological models of the education–society relation that Elliott is attacking. Though the understandings of the state offered by neo-Marxist theory may initially have been rather crude, the more recent work in this field (Apple 1982b; Dale 1982) explores both the possibilities and the limitations inherent within the state form. In the current conjuncture in Britain, the capacity of the teaching profession as a whole, let alone the minute fraction of it enlightened by action research, to resist political manipulation and hold the state to account seems to beg a great many questions. Even if the case studies in Part Two of this book indicate the power of professional inertia to frustrate certain aspects of official policy, they also suggest that the more progressive elements of professional practice are likely to be realized only if linked to other political forces operating in and around the state arena. Stenhouse's fear of 'movements' seems to be reflected in his colleague's uneasiness about a politics that goes beyond that of the profession, and there remains a stubborn refusal within Elliott's work to recognize that the sort of change to which he aspires requires the deconstruction of institutionalized relations far beyond those over which the profession alone has control. None of this is to deny that the sort of work in which he is engaged might become an important part of a broader strategy of change, as appears to be happening in the rather different political climate which, as we shall see, currently prevails in parts of Australia (Kemmis *et al.* 1983).

## *Overcoming institutional separation*

I have pointed in various places to the problem of the institutional separation between curriculum studies as an enterprise and the more established academic disciplines of education. I have also suggested that many of the issues neglected by curriculum writers, and which are of absolutely central importance to the very areas of concern into which curriculum theorists are now beginning to move, have been the subject of considerable debate within the sociology of education over the past decade. Yet there is still little sign that those working within the curriculum field in Britain either recognize the significance of those debates for their own work or, where they do, that they are attempting to come to grips with their implications. Thus they have tended to ignore or caricature such work and have thereby avoided entering into critical dialogue about the nature of education and society and the educational and social policies necessary to change them. Nevertheless, I would argue that, for instance, the whole debate within the sociology of education about the relationship of macro-theories of society and studies of classroom interaction (A. Hargreaves 1980) is directly relevant to the very issues I have suggested have been consistently neglected or underdeveloped within curriculum studies.

Further, I would argue that it would be most fruitful to interrogate recent work in curriculum studies with real, as opposed to imagined, forms of contemporary neo-Marxist theory. Thus, for instance, Lawton's model of curriculum decision-making could be explored in terms of those forms of Marxist theory which do recognize the specificities and relative autonomies of the different levels with which he is concerned, rather than seeing the education system as a monolithic expression of the interests and values of the capitalist ruling class. Recent theoretical work on education and the state within the sociology of education, especially that by Dale (1982, 1983b), could be usefully integrated with empirical observations made by Lawton about the segmentation of the DES into 'politicos, bureaucrats and professionals' (Lawton 1984). Similarly, work in cultural studies (e.g. Clarke *et al.* 1979) has made a much greater impact in the sociology of education than it has in curriculum studies. Yet it addresses questions about the nature of 'lived experience' and the ways in which cultures are formed and transformed, issues which relate directly to some of the central interests of the East Anglian Group.

In calling for more of a dialogue between sociologists and curriculum theorists, I am not, however, suggesting that curriculum studies would be better incorporated within the sociology of education as we know it. One of the great strengths of curriculum studies from the point of view of those committed to social and educational change is that it claims to speak to the worlds of policy and practice and is concerned with developing educational theory as a 'guide [to] action in a desirable direction' (Lawton 1977). The sociology of education in Britain has sometimes been even more lacking in a sense of purpose than curriculum studies, and observers of theoretical debates in the field could well have been excused for wondering what the whole exercise was for.

This relative lack of interest in exploring the implications of sociological work for educational policy and practice has ironically been at least as true of those who have followed the micro-sociological path into classroom ethnography as it has of those who have taken the more macro-sociological and theoretical direction. At least until very recently, ethnographers working within the sociology of education have favoured a research model based upon a supposedly disinterested style of anthropological fieldwork. Although St John-Brooks (1980) represents Hammersley as unusual in adopting this stance, his position does not seem to me at all unrepresentative of the orientation of most classroom ethnographers within the sociology of education in Britain. Indeed, Delamont (1978) has explicitly tried to distance sociological ethnography from classroom studies in the 'illuminative evaluation' tradition associated with CARE and has suggested that this latter style of work, which is very clearly committed to the improvement of classroom practice, is liable to get ethnography a bad name. There is little evidence amongst classroom-oriented sociologists of education of writers like those who, in the early 1970s, saw sociological studies of classrooms as a radical possibilitarian endeavour. Those who have identified with the more theoretically inclined direction have had a somewhat more ambiguous view of the relationship between the sociology of education and issues of policy and practice. However, even their interest in such issues has generally been restricted to the sociological critique of prevailing policies and practices and substantive proposals for alternatives have been much rarer.

Nevertheless, the issues at the centre of sociological debates have often had considerable potential relevance to issues of curriculum policy and practice, whether or not writers in either field have chosen to recognize it. It is therefore to be hoped that all those genuinely concerned to explore the relationship between educational practice and social justice in society will seek to overcome some of the suspicion and institutional separation between curriculum studies and the sociology of education. As we saw in chapter 2, the sociology of school knowledge has had more influence on curriculum studies in North America, though ironically mainstream sociology of education there remains relatively untouched by it. Attempts to forge connections between sociology, curriculum studies and educational policy and practice have perhaps been most successful in Australia. There, even the traditional discipline of educational administration has been influenced by the new sociology of education and subsequent developments (Bates 1980, 1981) in a way that has not so far happened elsewhere. Indeed, as we shall see, there are aspects of the current conjuncture in Australia that make it perhaps the most likely context within which a synthesis between sociology of education and applied educational studies could have a real impact on policy and practice in and around education. It is to the possibilities and problems of such developments that we turn in the next chapter.

# 4

---

# *From academic critique
to radical intervention*

If curriculum studies is committed to using theory to 'guide action in a desirable direction' (Lawton 1977), it might be that the reluctance to enter into serious dialogue with sociologists stems from a fear on the part of curriculum specialists that a serious confrontation with the issues raised would lead those of them committed to the pursuance of social justice or human emancipation to advocate a new and more politically radical set of actions. These might involve, if the analyses offered by sociologists have taught us anything, a shift away from narrow education-centred professional strategies towards ones linked much more directly to other modes of political action. This is clearly a threatening development for those who have generally spent their working lives within professional rather than political contexts in the wider sense. I suggested in the last chapter, however, that sociologists of education have themselves often been reluctant to take that step, since many of them do not regard their work as informing either pedagogical practice or political action. In this chapter, I want to say something more about what I regard as the unfortunate gulf between British sociology of education and issues of policy and practice and then reflect upon the value of attempts by various sociologists of education to bridge that gulf.

The terms 'policy' and 'practice' are merely very approximate shorthand terms for the sorts of issues with which I am concerned. 'Policy' is thus intended to signal an area of political and ideological practice around the curriculum, while 'practice' in its more restricted sense is intended to refer to curricular and pedagogic practice within schools.

Both terms clearly entail 'practice' in its broader sense and my concern is thus with the relationship between the sociology of education and political and ideological practice in and around the curriculum. I am particularly concerned to consider the extent to which the ways in which sociologists of education have conceived their relationship to curriculum policy and practice have restricted the possibilities for their work to become radical in its effects. In fact, my central emphasis will be on the relevance of sociology of education to the curricular policy and practice of the radical left. This focus reflects not only my own long-standing tendency to select areas of work within the field on the basis of their potential relevance to left pedagogical and political practice, but also the central concerns of many of the writers whose work has been discussed in this book – and, indeed, those of many of its critics. However, I do not wish to claim that the sociology of education is relevant only to the development of curriculum policy and practice by the political left, or that work in the field must necessarily be guided by such interests.

We have already seen that there is a sense in which issues of policy and practice were progressively marginalized in British sociology of education during the 1970s. The radical 'possibilitarianism' of the new sociology of the early 1970s gave way to a much less optimistic and interventionist stance. The recognition by many writers associated with this work that the transformation of lived reality was a more complex undertaking than they had initially envisaged provides part of the explanation for the subsequent attraction of, on the one hand, more sophisticated work on the nature of advanced capitalist societies and, on the other hand, more detailed investigations of the nature of life in classrooms. What is less clear is why so few writers have returned to questions about what would constitute significant interventions for change in ways that are consistent with the insights of new theory or with the findings of empirical research. Thus, in the mid and late 1970s, few sociologists of education showed much interest at all in influencing policy and practice in and around education. Rather, they tended to retreat into a spurious academicist and abstentionist stance that eschewed both the possibilitarian excesses of the 'new sociology of education' and the policy orientation of earlier traditions.

We noted in chapter 3 that this lack of a practical orientation may have been more true of those sociologists who concentrated on classroom ethnography than it was of those engaged in theoretical debate. Nevertheless, while the initial interest in neo-Marxist theories may have sprung from the relative neglect in the early 'new sociology' of the broader contexts of educational practice, and was often part of a search for more adequate strategies of educational and social change than those implied in that work, questions of policy and practice have subsequently tended to be confronted only as issues within Marxist *theory*. Thus, the principal orientation of both empirical and theoretical work in the sociology of education in the latter half of the 1970s was essentially an analytic rather than a practical one.

There are, of course, those on the left who see this as being an appropriate defensive tactic in the current political and ideological climate. Personally, I am not convinced that it is even that. Sociology has come under attack in recent years not only because of its 'subversive' image (Gould 1977) but also for its lack of utility of any sort. Digby Anderson, a right-wing critic of 'radical' sociology, has scathingly written of its 'adolescent' approach to sociology, which treats the subject as more of a debunking exercise rather than a practical enterprise (D. Anderson 1980). Left academics often try to sidestep such charges of uselessness with the rhetorical question 'useless for whom?'. I do not, however, believe that this is a sufficient response any more than is the argument that sociology is itself a form of 'practice' when it is used to avoid questions about its relationship to *other* forms of practice. For it is not only those on the right who question the utility of much that passes for left academic work in sociology, such charges also frequently come from the political left. The lack of any significant practical or policy orientation in much sociology of education, including that which claims to be radical, is paralleled by a lack of any organic relationship between such work and those groups for whom one might have expected left theoretical work to have some political value. Such a separation has certainly had unfortunate political and educational effects and, for this reason, it is important not to dismiss the comments of writers such as Demaine (1980), who make this point, however much they may exaggerate and misrepresent the nature of the problem.

While some have argued that what is needed is a return to value freedom in sociology of education (A. Hargreaves 1982), it can also be argued that the present conjuncture is one in which it may be feasible to begin to rework in a more sophisticated manner the links between theory, research, policy and practice that were naively glimpsed by the 'new sociology of education' in the early 1970s, but subsequently obscured from sight in the fragmentation described earlier. Indeed, as I indicated in chapter 2, the possibilities for doing this certainly seem brighter now than they have done for some years. As we saw, the reasons for this are various but it is somewhat ironic that neo-Marxist theoreticism seems to have run its course for the time being, leading some of its former advocates both to re-assert the importance of empirical research and to re-emphasize the need to locate their work within a specific political project. Thus, theory itself has begun to direct us back to the analysis of specific conjunctures rather than merely general systemic relationships, and has encouraged us to conceive of wider possibilities for intervention than those prescribed by the more restrictive modes of neo-Marxist theory, which reached their zenith of popularity in the mid-1970s.

One does not have to go all the way with Hindess and Hirst and their colleagues (Cutler *et al.* 1977/8), since many other contemporary writers, including many discussed in this book, continue to believe that the basic tenets of contemporary Marxism can be recast in terms that do *not* result in theoretical incoherence and political inaction. Indeed, the increasingly complex theoretical armoury of relative autonomies, conditions of existence, specificities and specific effectivities they have begun to develop is not of purely theoretical interest. For some writers, at least, it has resensitized them to the possibilities for and significance of left political and ideological practice within those institutions Althusser characterized rather too simply as Ideological State Apparatuses.

Thus, even if Demaine (1980) was right to claim that one effect of the importation of over-simplified versions of neo-Marxist theory into the sociology of education in the mid-1970s was to minimize the possibilities for left policy and practice in and around state education, this should no longer be the case today. Interestingly, writers in other fields have been somewhat quicker to grasp the significance of recent developments in Marxist theory. Media studies, a field which arguably has suffered even more from theoretical excesses and theoretical dogmatism than the sociology of education, has begun to overcome the separation between theory, empirical work and the development of left practices within and around the media. Similarly, a new journal called *Critical Social Policy* has been successfully launched, a venture which only a few years ago might have been considered by some to be a contradiction in terms. Again, in the sociology of race relations, writers such as Ben-Tovim and Gabriel (1979) have also argued that recent theoretical developments can be used to justify a reconsideration of the sorts of policy issues Marxist analysis in the mid-1970s tended to regard as 'outside its scope', if not positively 'diversionary'. Indeed, many of Ben-Tovim and Gabriel's comments about the sociology of race relations would be almost equally appropriate as a commentary on the history of the sociology of education.

Very recently it has even been possible to discern some stirrings of a greater concern with issues of policy and practice within sociology of education itself. This is the case even within some of the approaches which, as I noted in chapter 3, have hitherto tended to eschew such considerations. Certainly, at a theoretical level, recent Open University courses in the sociology of education have paid far more attention than did *Schooling and Society* (OU 1977) to the specificities of political and ideological practice in and around education, even if they have still to consider their implications for future strategies. Further, even a number of interactionist sociologists have retreated somewhat from their earlier 'disinterested' stance, partly as a result of their political as well as academic interest in issues of gender inequality (Delamont 1983), and partly in response to pressures on them to demonstrate their 'usefulness' to society in a period of contraction in higher education (Pollard 1984).

Nevertheless, such initiatives are certainly not yet typical of the field in Britain, although my own view is clearly that they should be welcomed and encouraged. If the sociology of education is to make a significant contribution to left policy and practice, it will have to explore the implications of recent theoretical work for our understanding of political and pedagogic practice in and around education. Therefore, I now want to discuss the lessons of some of the work that does attempt to link theoretical and empirical work in the sociology of the curriculum with policy and practice on the part of the left. First, I shall reflect on the work in which I myself was involved with Michael Young in the mid-1970s, second, I shall discuss further the American contributions outlined in chapter 2, and third I shall consider recent work being done by sociologists in Australia.

## *Young, Whitty* et al. circa *1976*

The work which I was engaged with Michael Young and other collaborators in the mid-1970s (Whitty and Young 1976; Young and Whitty 1977) was dubbed by Bates (1980) as 'new developments in the new sociology of education'. Such work was a conscious attempt to transcend the prevailing separation between theoretical and empirical work in the sociology of education and to relate both to questions of left pedagogical and political practice. The intended nature of our intervention was recognized by some of its earlier reviewers, with Mardle (1977) describing *Explorations* (Whitty and Young 1976) as 'an important part of the radical left's attempt to respond to the Great Debate' and Williams (1977) claiming that *Society, State and Schooling* (Young and Whitty 1977) was the 'most *hopeful*, serious and vigorous book on English education [he had] read for many years' (my emphasis). Yet both these assessments contrasted sharply with other claims that this sort of work was pessimistic, nihilistic and utterly irrelevant to contemporary educational concerns. Not only did mainstream educationists such as Taylor (1978) dismiss this work as of limited or even negative value to teachers and policy-makers, but other writers on the left – themselves apparently concerned with the relationship between sociology of education and socialist educational and political practice – also suggested that it was irrelevant or even damaging to their concerns. Thus our political stance was represented as typical of an 'ultra-leftist ideology [which] invites abstentionism from political work and substitutes revolutionary slogans and despises all "reforms" ' (Demaine 1980), whilst our observations on educational practice were characterized as, at best, vacuous and, at worst, contributing to the educational deprivation of working-class pupils (Demaine 1980; Entwistle 1979; Reynolds and Sullivan 1980).

Given the nature of our original objectives in producing the volumes, it is obviously quite alarming that the work was open to such interpretations. Thus, while it is also important to notice that the relevance of this same work was far more positively evaluated elsewhere (Bates 1981), such criticisms need to be taken seriously. This is particularly the case given that the present book has expressed similar disquiet that the sociology of education should apparently have so little to say of relevance to left policy and practice in contemporary Britain.

Clearly, my work with Young was ambiguous in so far as it was open to the variety of interpretations described above. Never the less, it is not easy to see how either of the two volumes could have been read as typical of the sort of neo-Marxism that dismissed the viability of socialist struggles – within the Labour Party or within state education – by theoretical fiat and political dogma. Although, as Williams (1977) pointed out, this type of work 'is still labelled and caricatured by orthodox politicians and the press', one might have expected colleagues on the left to share his own view that it was typical of a more 'open, enquiring, but still deeply committed' form of Marxism. The work was, as some of the critics grudgingly admit, self-consciously exploratory and hence probably inevitably flawed with the sort of inconsistencies and confusions the critics claimed to have identified within it. Though some of these were more the product of our critics' proclivity for lifting sentences out of context than genuine internal inconsistencies, others were an understandable consequence of the attempt to explore what was, as we explicitly argued, largely uncharted territory. Nevertheless we were concerned to explore that territory and to suggest that the terrain, and the intervention strategies appropriate to it, had a far more complex and contradictory character than most available theories – whether liberal, social democratic or Marxist – seemed to attribute to it. Given the exploratory, tentative and, on occasions, contradictory nature of our writings, the charge of theoretical and political dogmatism is surely hard to sustain, whilst that of inconsistency is, in part at least, the result of our attempt to confront the complexity of an empirical world whose reality Demaine implied we ignored. A more appropriate target of criticism would perhaps have been the failure of most of those involved in this venture – and, one must add, most of its critics – to undertake the sort of work necessary to refine and clarify some of the ambiguities and inconsistencies within these embryonic sketches of the nature of the terrain and possible ways of traversing it.

However, it is worth exploring a little further some of the criticisms made of this work, in the hope that this will help us to clarify the nature of the contribution work in the sociology of education might or might not make to left policy and practice in the future. One frequent criticism was that our work was merely sloganistic and essentially vacuous in its prescriptions for practice. Another was that the sociologists of education of the 1970s lacked the close links with policy-makers that were typical of their predecessors of the 1950s and 1960s. Both these points had an element of truth in them, but both of them failed to grasp that the relative lack of *detailed* policy prescriptions in the work was consistent with the critique of prevailing policy-making procedures which had been a central feature of the new sociology of education in all its various guises (CCCS 1981). Since part of the critique of provided schooling for the masses had been concerned with the political and professional processes that traditionally defined its form and content, it was hardly surprising that – as both Williamson (1974) and Demaine (1980) pointed out – the sociologists of the 1970s did not share the same sort of relationship to leading Labour Party politicians as that enjoyed by Halsey and Floud. The practical implications of our work for socialist political and educational practice were as much concerned with the ways in which policy is made as with specific substantive policies.

To this extent, it might even be argued that Bates (1980) was correct to defend Michael Young from those of us he saw as wanting to impose upon Young a more detailed prescriptive programme. However, over-generalized injunctions *can* easily merge into vacuous rhetoric, and work that claims to speak to a specifically socialist political constituency certainly needs to define its ultimate aims in rather more explicit terms than a catch-all phrase like 'human betterment'. Sharp (1980) was therefore right to demand a clearer political programme than had hitherto been offered, but that programme would almost certainly have needed to involve a search for new procedures for clarifying the nature of appropriate 'new forms of knowledge and pedagogy'. Bates's own suggestions about how tangible policies were to be arrived at were almost entirely ones of intra-professional process and, in this respect, the suggestions of Johnson (1981) were more consistent with the sort of analysis Young and I were offering in *Society, State and Schooling*.

In his article, Johnson argued that the Labour Party should break with its traditional approach to producing policy for education and approach its development in a manner more in keeping with its democratic and egalitarian socialist ideals. Policy, he suggested, should be developed from the grass-roots, growing out of popular experience, not merely handed down by professional politicians and the professional educationists who randomly emerged as advisers to its NEC subcommittee. Further, he argued that the party itself should become a more important context of education, just as radicals in the past often established their own agencies of self-education. But that was not by any means the same thing as arguing that those committed to socialist conceptions of democracy and equality should leave capitalist schooling to its own devices and advocate a policy of de-schooling, a position both Demaine (1980) and Reynolds and Sullivan (1980) suggested Young and I adhered to – or at least, 'flirted outrageously' with! Rather, it was to suggest that socialists would be better placed to intervene in struggles over the form, content and control of state education and remedy some of the crucial absences of traditional Labour Party policy on such issues (Bleiman and Burt 1981) if they were also constantly struggling to develop new skills and forms of democratic practice within the labour movement itself. A strategy of linked struggles was precisely what was being advocated in *Explorations* and *Society, State and Schooling.*

Although one might therefore have expected the 'new sociologists' to be active in the grass-roots of the labour movement rather than merely 'well-connected' (Williamson 1974), a recognition of the long-term importance of grass-roots struggles did not imply that the more conventional contexts of educational policy discourse should be spurned, since into these are inserted initiatives that demand an immediate response. Nor did the argument that it was politically essential for socialist educators to be involved in and build alliances with other elements of the labour movement constitute a retreat in 'worker-ism' (Donald 1979). Nor was the left somehow faced, as Demaine seemed to imply, with a straight choice between the new sociology of education and the Islington Labour Party as the authentic voice of socialist education. Rather, our suggestion was that a basis for constructive dialogue between different sections of the left urgently needed to be constructed. One would not have expected sociologists either to carry off-the-peg policies into the labour movement or to celebrate uncritically the conventional wisdom of that movement. Nevertheless, one might have expected that those sociologists of education who were committed to that movement would have something valuable to contribute towards the clarification of its aims in the realm of education, and to their translation into political and pedagogical strategies appropriate to the current conjuncture. Certainly the over-theoretical orientation of much neo-Marxist sociology of education proved a barrier to this, but this is exactly what Young and I were suggesting in our writings. Far from being written off by theoretical fiat, as Demaine and Reynolds and Sullivan argue, the Labour Party and its policies for state education were seen by us as a vital context of intervention.

Interestingly, at the same time as suggesting that our work had nothing of significance to say to educational practitioners, the same writers suggested that the work could have some very dangerous consequences for practice. Specifically, Entwistle (1979) and Reynolds and Sullivan (1980) argued that those few practical suggestions that did exist in our work were mischievous and anti-socialist. They suggested that we sought to trap working-class pupils in a curriculum rooted in and restricted to a celebration of working-class life as it is. This, I suggest, was a wilfully misleading – indeed mischievous – reading of our work. Thus, as I pointed out when discussing Ozolins's work in chapter 3, radical curriculum practice would clearly have to *relate* to the realities of working-class life, but it could hardly be uncritical of it. Although, in order to be meaningful to working-class children, it would almost certainly make use of the sorts of penetrations already present within working-class culture, it would not celebrate that culture *per se*. Given the racist and sexist nature of that culture, as described by such writers as Willis (1977, 1979), and the role it clearly plays in the process of social reproduction, there would be little mileage for socialists in mere celebration and reinforcement.

What Denis Gleeson and I were explicitly arguing for in our work on the social studies curriculum was a meaningful *and* critical education (Gleeson and Whitty 1976), a contribution to debates about the nature of a genuinely progressive curriculum that is conveniently ignored by most critics. Even so, we recognized that the nature of a genuinely progressive curriculum was highly dependent upon its articulation with other cultural phenomena; it was therefore by no means fixed for all time in a particular mould, as the defenders of the traditional curriculum as the only hope for a socialist future seemed to believe.

The thrust of our work was, then, precisely against dogmatic solutions to both theoretical and practical questions. Certainly, neither the curriculum of state education nor the Labour Party as a context of educational policy-making was defined *a priori* as an inappropriate context of socialist intervention. Indeed, it was just because (as Demaine argued, apparently believing that we claimed the opposite!) their character is not theoretically given, but rather historically constructed and struggled over, that the position of Entwistle, Reynolds and Sullivan over what constitutes a definitive socialist strategy for education was the dogmatic and unhelpful one.

I do not therefore find the argument that our own position was wrong – though well it may have been – *because* it was different from either Lenin's or Gramsci's an especially convincing or compelling one. Indeed, I would find it odd if, for example, what was a progressive policy for working-class education in Italy in the 1920s was appropriate for the context of Britain in the 1970s or 1980s. Thus, when Entwistle said that our attack on traditional left policies for education in Britain for ignoring the issue of ideology would put Gramsci in error as well, it would not – even if it were true – be quite the damning criticism that Entwistle took it to be. In fact, it could only result from his taking a position totally at odds with Gramsci's own highly developed sense of history and conjunctural politics. Hegemony takes different forms in different contexts and hence counter-hegemonic struggles must, if they are to contribute to the struggle for socialism, take forms appropriate to the specific historical context in which they take place. A sociology of education that can contribute to left policy and practice therefore needs, as Sharp (1980) has argued, to offer us a clearer understanding of the nature of that context, a project that requires the sort of articulation between a theoretical, empirical and political programme which has been largely absent from the British scene. Our own work certainly did not provide it, but neither was it as irrelevant to that project as its critics have suggested.

## American contributions

Shepherd and Vulliamy have argued that

> although a sociology of school knowledge has been on the forefront of the agenda for over a decade and despite a few British analyses in this field (Whitty and Young 1976; Whitty 1977), we owe the recent resurgence in this area to the work of American sociologists, many of whom have a background in both curriculum studies and sociology of education.                                        (Shepherd and Vulliamy 1983: 4)

I have already examined some examples of this American work in chapter 2 of this book.[1] In discussing the importance of this critical sociological work on the curriculum, Arnot and I have suggested that it had three characteristics that distinguished it from most British sociology of education in the late 1970s and early 1980s (Arnot and Whitty 1982).

The work we had in mind, which included that of Anyon, Apple, Giroux, Taxel and Wexler, varied considerably in other respects, but had these three characteristics in common. The first distinguishing characteristic lay in its greater openness to a variety of theoretical perspectives at any one time. Thus, some of these writers often drew simultaneously from approaches to theory that were treated as mutually exclusive in the sectarian atmosphere of British sociology at that time. Apple's edited collection of papers (Apple 1982a) was centrally concerned to demonstrate the potential complementarity of often disparate traditions of economic and cultural theorizing. In Giroux's work, it was evident that the phenomenological 'new sociology of education', neo-Marxist political economy, and social and cultural reproduction theories – together with the work of the Frankfurt School and Paulo Freire's conception of a critical pedagogy – all had a significant influence on the development of his own approach to curriculum theory and practice. In Britain, such perspectives tended to be treated as alternatives, but Giroux did not see any of them alone as adequate either to an account of the complexities of classroom life or to the furtherance of his political project of social transformation.

The second characteristic of this American work that made it distinctive lay in its attempt to relate theoretical and substantive concerns, and its professed belief in the importance of interrogating theory with empirical research and vice versa. This was, in part, a legacy of the tradition of empiricism that has characterized mainstream social science and educational research in the USA, a research paradigm that had both negative and positive implications for the critical curriculum writers. On the one hand, it meant that much of the theoretical inspiration for their work had to be imported from British or European social and educational theory, but it also meant that the use of this theory to criticize mainstream empiricism did not also produce a tendency to eschew empirical research altogether. Thus, while Apple acknowledged the importance of English theoretical work in keeping Marxist scholarship alive, he was also quite explicit that the real test of the fruitfulness of the conceptual repertoire of contemporary Marxism lay in its 'applicability to the interrogation of concrete situations' (Apple 1982a: 5). Though this was not always evident in Apple's own work, or that of Giroux, studies by Taxel (1980, 1981) and by Anyon (1979, 1980, 1981a, 1981b) demonstrated that this commitment to a programme of theoretically informed empirical research was not purely rhetorical.

The third distinctive feature of this work was that it attempted to move beyond a sociological critique of existing school practice and sought to explore the implications of that critique for radical practice in and around education. In practice, the work often lent support to the view that educational interventions could make an important contribution to social change and it contrasted starkly with the pessimism and abstentionism that Demaine (1980) and others argued was a prime characteristic of neo-Marxist sociology of education in Britain, including ironically my own work with Young. Thus the American papers in this field frequently included sections with such titles as 'Beyond resistance and domination' (Giroux 1981b), 'Transformative pedagogics' (Anyon 1981b) or 'Towards political and educational action' (Apple 1981) in which one found at least the seeds of prescriptive methodologies and programmes of action for teachers.

Our belief that the American work exhibited these characteristics led us to make a positive evaluation of the direction in which it was moving, a direction clearly compatible with that which I have been advocating in this book. However, in response to our argument, A. Hargreaves (1982) seriously called into question the usefulness of most of this work and contested our evaluation of it. Since A. Hargreaves (1980) has appeared in the past to be one who shared my own reservations about the fragmentation of the sociology of education in Britain, his arguments have to be taken seriously as a challenge to the sort of work being favoured here. He argued that, although Arnot and I correctly identified the three areas in which the American work was distinctive, we were wrong about the nature of its distinctiveness on two of the counts and, though we were right on the third count, we overlooked the fact that it was this very feature of the work that seriously undermined the whole enterprise.

Thus, Hargreaves suggested that our claim that the American work was theoretically pluralist was unsound, and that, on the contrary, the distinctive nature of this work was that it was theoretically closed, since it refused to engage seriously with work in non-Marxist traditions such as English ethnography. Second, he claimed that far from being committed to the interrogation of theory with empirical research and vice versa, the American work was lacking in empirical rigour and consistently ignored empirical evidence that might serve to disconfirm its preconstituted theoretical position. The reason for these shortcomings lay he argued, in the third feature of the work, a blind commitment to social transformation and using schools to foster radical social change. Their optimistic view about the possibilities for using schools for such a purpose had led these writers to interpret everything that they saw in schools as a contribution to this end. Thus a specious optimism had replaced the specious pessimism of earlier correspondence theories of schooling and now all pupil responses, from passivity to rebellion, were to be seen as resistances to the reproductive functions of schooling. Resistance spotting, he implied, had replaced the correspondence spotting that was typical of an earlier phase of this work (e.g. Apple and King 1977).

The tendency to interpret all responses to schooling in a particular light, and to ignore any embarrassing disconfirming instances, was seen to be a particularly stark feature of the ethnographic studies by Anyon discussed in chapter 2 (Anyon 1980, 1981a, 1981b), but it also applied to the very selective use that all these writers made of other people's ethnographic work. The only way to develop a genuinely open and rigorous set of procedures, suggested Hargreaves, was by bracketing an interest in the possibilities of social transformation and returning to a concept of a value-free social science.

Clearly Hargreaves chose, for the purposes of his argument, to exaggerate our own claims about the nature of the American work and to present our enthusiasm for the direction that the work was taking as a statement about is solid achievements up to that point. Thus he translated our argument that the work was more open to a variety of theoretical perspectives than equivalent British work into a much more easily refutable claim that the work had shown itself to be open to all conceivable theoretical traditions. More seriously, he glossed our claim that the American writers were more committed than British neo-Marxists to interrogating theory with empirical research and vice versa into a statement that their work had been empirically rigorous, a claim that was impossible to substantiate or refute without considerably more evidence of the procedures adopted by these writers than we had available. This was why we had noted (and were, in fact, in agreement with Hargreaves) that the American studies were relatively inexplicit about their methodological procedures and that this deficiency needed to be remedied in future work in this tradition. We were also in agreement with Hargreaves that the term 'resistance' had tended to become a catch-all concept whose initial usefulness had probably been exhausted. What was needed was some limitation upon its applicability or some differentiation of types of resistance within the overall concept, either of which would make it a more sensitive tool for the interpretation of empirical situations (see Aggleton and Whitty, 1985). What was not clear to us, however, was that the third characteristic of the American work made it improbable that empirical research could be carried out in a rigorous manner. In other words, we could not accept Hargreaves's suggestion that the political interest in radical social change on the part of these writers was almost bound to produce a lack of empirical rigour in their work. Indeed, it might equally be claimed that a concern to interrogate situations with a view to informing policy and practice would create more of an incentive to be empirically rigorous than producing knowledge supposedly for its own sake, or for the sake of one's career. In reality, though, all research traditions can be more or less rigorous and the tenets of all of them are open to abuse.

Hargreaves's central criticism of the American writers was, then, that their apparent optimism about the fact that educational practice could make a contribution to transformative politics was 'specious' and a *result* of their political commitment to social transformation. Yet presumably their overall political viewpoint was not markedly different during the period when studies in the sociology of education were characterized by the 'radical pessimism' of correspondence theory. To this extent it is easier to locate the problem in inadequate theory or methodology than it is in political commitment. However, whatever the theoretical flaws of the earlier work, our point about the current optimism about the role of education in social transformation was that it was not a dogmatic or blind one. Indeed, as I argued earlier, Anyon's work suggested that whether aspects of education were ultimately reproductive or transformative in their effects was not given but rather a result of how they were actively worked upon pedagogically. What was crucially important in such work was its recognition that whether or not contradictions and penetrations proved reproductive or transformative in practice depended upon this active pedagogic work. This was clearly an advance on the sort of work that romanticized and applauded working-class resistance just because it was there, even when it took a form that was ultimately reproductive.

Indeed, far from taking Hargreaves's view that it suffers from too much political commitment, I am tempted to argue that there is a sense in which the American work would benefit from a clearer political commitment that would sharpen its broader political analysis and its conception of an adequate strategy of change. Certainly, the political dimension of this work does require considerable clarification. To this extent at least, McNeil's (1981a) criticism about the ambiguity about the authors' political goals and the nature of the audience they are addressing, which we noted in chapter 2, has some validity. If these writers see their work as contributing to a transformation of society, they clearly need to address the question of the relationship between education and oppositional politics, as it is upon this relationship that any transformative effects of supposedly radical interventions in education ultimately depend – except, of course, when they are purely fortuitous. This is why it was unfortunate that some of the earlier work by these American writers was overly school and teacher-centred in its approach to the sociology of the curriculum. Possibly because of their links with a longer tradition of curriculum reform as a basis for social reconstruction, some of these writers tended to assume that pedagogic interventions would necessarily have radical effects independently of their articulation with broader political struggles.

Anyon has paid little attention to the disposition of political forces in and around the educational arena and this perhaps explains the similarity, mentioned earlier, between some of her prescriptions and those of the phenomenological phase of the new sociology of education in Britain. Giroux's earlier work on radical pedagogic strategies (Giroux and Penna 1979) sometimes seemed to have similar implications. Nevertheless, Giroux has more recently argued that in the current context interventions within schooling can play a small but significant part in broader oppositional strategies and has linked the work of radical educators to Aronowitz's proposals for the building of an alternative public sphere by the American left (Aronowitz 1983; Giroux 1983). Apple's exploration of the possibilities for the development of 'more democratic institutions . . . and socialist pedagogical and curricular models' (Apple 1981) has also been increasingly located in an analysis of how such interventions might articulate with the broader disposition of political and ideological forces within American society (Apple 1982c; 1983).

Hargreaves's central criticism of the work of these writers would only be a damning one if they were not prepared to entertain the possibility that the role of schools in social transformation might be a negligible one. Yet some of the literature under discussion has been increasingly concerned with a consideration of this very issue and in establishing the precise circumstances in which schools may or may not have a significant role in social transformation. Certainly Apple has been quite adamant in his discussion of whether the left should give support to liberal educational reforms, that there are 'no easy answers' (Apple 1982c). The question is 'decidedly dependent on the balance of forces within a specific arena' and it is 'only by analyzing the specificity of each individual location [that one can] make a decision on appropriate strategies'. Whether schools, or particular instances of resistance in or around them, contribute to reproduction or transformation is not then a question that can be settled on a once and for all basis, and thus neither a blanket optimism nor a blanket pessimism can be a viable position to uphold. Ironically, Hargreaves's own prescription that we should seek to study schools as either determined or determining, but not both at the same time, seems to be just the sort of research programme that would encourage a constant alternation between specious pessimism and specious optimism on the part of the left.

What the American work increasingly recognizes is that whether or not particular aspects of education are ultimately reproductive or transformative in their effects is essentially a political question concerning how they are worked upon pedagogically *and* politically, and how they become articulated with other struggles in and beyond the school. Therefore, I continue to believe that the sort of work in which these American writers are now engaged can usefully inform the development of pedagogical and political strategies, and that the fact that it is often conducted with a *view* to informing such strategies in no sense automatically devalues it. Whatever criticisms can be made of the work carried out to date, the charge that it is fundamentally flawed cannot be sustained. I remain convinced that this work has pointed us in a valuable direction, and that there are important lessons to be learnt from it if we are to overcome the characteristic separation between theoretical and practical concerns in British educational studies in general, and the separation between a sterile theoreticism and a blind empiricism within the sociology of education in particular.

As far as actually building an organic and potentially radical connection with the broader political movements of the left in the current conjuncture is concerned, there are, of course, still substantial difficulties facing these American writers. The relative lack of an appropriate broader political tradition with which to connect limits the capacity of much of the American work to become radical in its effects.[2] Though Giroux, for instance, has recently made it quite clear that he himself is committed to 'a radical transformation of the existing society in all its manifestations' (Giroux 1983), and now fully recognizes the absurdity of any notion that this could be achieved by teachers alone, he is still far from explicit about who the potential allies of radical educators might be. References to working more closely with 'community people' or to the need for 'various groups' to come together, and even the notion of an alternative public sphere, can sometimes obscure this issue.

Many of the groups occupying such an alternative public sphere espouse, as the term implies, 'alternative' rather than 'oppositional' views of culture and politics in Williams's (1973) terms. In other words, they are merely seeking spaces for peaceful coexistence alongside mainstream society rather than mounting a challenge to the prevailing system of social relations. Yet it is only on the basis of a clearer conception of oppositional politics that one can make tactical judgements about appropriate pedagogic strategies or about forming alliances around liberal reforms. So, although this work seems committed to replacing the prevailing system of social relations with a more demo-cratic, egalitarian and equitable society, its contribution to the fostering of social emancipation for the subordinate and systematically disadvan-taged groups in society is still not sufficiently located within any broader programme of oppositional political activity. While clearly intended to go beyond approaches concerned only to provide pupils and future citizens with a somewhat better deal within existing social arrange-ments, this often seems a somewhat rhetorical aspiration in the American context. An effectively radical approach to education needs to move beyond statements of intent to an active exploration of the pedagogical and political implications of its work among the political constituencies in whose interests it is supposedly being carried out. In this respect, recent work coming out of Australia perhaps provides a more useful example of a developing relationship between sociology of the curriculum and left policy and practice than do the American writings discussed here.

## Australian contributions

Sociologists of education in Australia, whether of Australian or British origin, seem to have been particularly active in developing a sociological approach to the curriculum.[3] It is also a feature of the Australian scene that philosophers of education have been quicker to recognize the significance of sociological questions to our understanding of the nature of educational knowledge than have their colleagues in Britain (Harris 1979; Walker 1983). Amongst sociologists working in Australia, Musgrave (1973) produced one of the earliest books concerned to 'under-stand the sociological forces at work on the creation and change of the curriculum'. Though working from within a mainstream sociological tradition, and himself doubting the value of Marxist perspectives for exploring detailed political and cultural struggles over the content and control of the curriculum (Musgrave 1979), some of his empirical work on conflicts over the curriculum in Australian society concerns itself with just the sorts of nuances that neo-Marxist work needs to address if it is to be of relevance to policy and practice.

Sharp (1980, 1982a) has argued, however, that it was just this sort of obsession with surface phenomena within the new sociology of education of the 1970s, and its consequent neglect of the significance of underlying structures, that limited its value to the left. Her book (Sharp 1980) is one of the most trenchant critiques of the work of Bernstein, Bourdieu and Young from a Marxist perspective, but its mode of theorizing and style of critique seemed somewhat dated even by the time it was published (Wexler 1982b).

In her more recent work, Sharp (1984) has engaged in theoretically informed empirical enquiries, even if, as I suggest in chapter 5, the particular theory she employs is limited in its capacity to account for the complexities with which sociologists of the curriculum need to be concerned, if they are to make a fruitful contribution to the development of curricular practices that may further the political programme of the left. Nevertheless, Sharp herself has always urged that such links with left policy and practice need to be developed and, in reply to Wexler's criticisms of her work, has stated:

> If we have failed, it is by not following up our analyses either with practical and concrete suggestions which could guide teachers in the mass schooling system or with the production of well worked-out curriculum materials which could substitute for the profoundly liberal, and hence ideological, materials presently available . . . [But] it is not only the content of the curriculum that matters; equally important is the form of its elaboration and transmission, which will determine its reception. A pedagogical practice of counter-hegemony needs to go beyond an affirmation of good intentions to develop a theory that can inform the realization of the intentions. (Sharp 1982b: 75)

There is, in fact, within various traditions of work in Australia, evidence of a commitment both to take account of the sort of neo-Marxist scholarship that has developed since the mid-1970s, and to move beyond it by addressing more directly the relationship between theoretical, empirical and policy issues. Certainly, as I intimated in the last chapter, there is less evidence of institutional separation between those concerned with these various issues than there is in Britain. Thus, for instance, Smith and Knight (1978) made considerable use of the theoretical work of Bernstein and Young in an empirical analysis of a political controversy over whether use of progressive curriculum projects such as Bruner's *Man: A Course of Study* (MACOS) or the federal Curriculum Development Centre's *Social Education Materials Project* (SEMP) should be permitted in Queensland schools. Convinced by studies such as this of the importance of combining cultural analysis with political economy, they have also been concerned to explore the extent to which recent developments in neo-Marxist analysis have produced common ground with liberal opinion about the sort of educational initiatives that deserve support (Smith and Knight 1982). Faced in Queensland with a government of the New Right long before those of us in Britain or even America contemplated such a possibility, Smith and Knight were clearly aware from a very early stage of the dangers of merely theorizing the curriculum terrain rather than contesting it. On the other hand, to an even greater degree than Giroux in the USA, they seem to minimize some very real differences between alternative and oppositional political aspirations.

Other Australian writers, more clearly committed to oppositional political goals, have also seemed to move more easily between sociological analysis of the curriculum and the exploration of its practical implications than most left sociologists of education in Britain. Amongst these, Gilbert is an interesting case of an Australian academic who, as a doctoral student in the Curriculum Studies department at the London Institute of Education, made far more use of contemporary sociological approaches to the analysis of the curriculum than (as we saw in the last chapter) has been typical of that department. Drawing upon the insights of British and American sociologies of school knowledge, he recognized the importance of 'addressing the ideological aspects of the reproductive role of schooling, in such a way as to avoid romanticism, idealism and naive empiricism, and yet to provide a theory on which progress in curricular practice might be based' (Gilbert 1983). After a theoretically informed empirical study of the extent to which hegemonic ideology is penetrated by students within the English school system, and after giving serious consideration to Hargreaves's critique of the American work discussed above (A. Hargreaves 1982), he concluded that:

> [informal] oppositional practices in schools are, by virtue of their informality, susceptibility to appropriation and lack of conscious analysis, unable to confront dominant ideologies. And yet it is also clear that these dominant ideologies are, in any particular context, not immune to critical practice which questions their contradictions, gaps and evasions. The moral is that an anti-hegemonic formal practice is a necessary condition of ideological penetration if it is to produce policies and political action.                        (Gilbert 1983: 20)

As we saw in chapter 3, Ozolins (1979) has also followed his sociological critique of the work of Lawton with an embryonic attempt to sketch out what a 'working-class curriculum', utilizing the penetrations and confronting the limitations of the Australian equivalents of Willis's 'lads' (Willis 1977), might look like.

One of the reasons why there has not been quite the same divorce between theoretical analyses of the curriculum and a concern with policy and practice may be that in some Australian states, both sorts of work have been carried out within teachers' unions. This has been particularly the case in Victoria, where some of the writings published by the second-ary teachers' union under the editorship of Bill Hannan display a much greater sociological awareness than is typical of the stance taken in the journals of Britain's National Union of Teachers (VSTA 1976). In addition, although Ashenden (1979) pointed to a crisis in the relationship between academic Marxist writers on education and left teachers which was reminiscent of the situation in Britain at the time, Australian Marxists seem to have been quicker than British ones to develop links with the realms of both professional and political practice. Thus, for example, Freeland, whose earlier work (Freeland 1979) I shall suggest in chapter 5, was amongst the less helpful modes of neo-Marxist analysis for informing policy and practice, has shifted the focus of his work towards just such a concern (Freeland 1981). That his earlier work was carried out when he was a trade union official and his later work when an academic perhaps merely underlines the relative fluidity of the boundaries between these contexts when compared with Britain! In his recent work, Freeland has become increasingly interested in the 'refrac-tions' through which state policy passes in the process of implemen-tation, and has begun to analyse the pedagogical and political potential of the specific contradictory sites and practices generated by the dynamics of contemporary capitalist societies. In doing this, he has also made the potentially radical link between such analyses and left policy and practice, by working with trade union and left groups to exploit the space offered for critical work within the developing policies for unemployed youth in New South Wales (Freeland 1982).

Perhaps the most influential example of a radical synthesis between sociological theory and research and left policy and practice can be seen in the work of Connell and his colleagues (Connell *et al.* 1982). Their book, *Making the Difference*, is based upon some of the data generated from a major study of home and school relations in a dozen 'ruling class' and 'working-class schools' in Sydney and Adelaide. The ruling-class schools were exclusive independent schools and the working-class schools were urban comprehensives. In broad terms, cohesiveness was seen to characterize the relationship between ruling-class families and their schools, while disjunction was more typical of home–school relations in working-class schools, even in the case of families well-disposed towards education as a personal and social 'good'. Working-class schools were seen to deny influence to parents through a system of relations that was essentially bureaucratic in nature, while the fee-paying ruling-class parents entered into a market relationship with their schools, as well as having close informal relationships with the teachers (and especially the principals) in a shared cultural milieu. There was, then, an organic link between ruling-class schools and ruling-class culture, whereas no such link existed in the case of the working class. Indeed, its culture of co-operation and collectivism was seen to contrast with many of the values espoused in the schools which working-class children attended.

When summarized in these stark terms, this may appear little different from other work in the sociology of education in Britain and America. Yet what this study contained was rich ethnographic material with which the authors tried to be sensitive to diversity and contradiction, at the same time as making defensible generalizations from a comparison of the various families and schools involved. As a result, class relations took on 'life' in a way that was absent from many other studies and, indeed, one of the intentions of the book was to demonstrate that 'Classes are not abstract categories, but real-life groupings, which like heavily-travelled roads are constantly under construction; getting organised, divided, broken down, re-made.' The authors claimed to show how class and its relationship to schooling worked as a living dynamic, a set of relations constantly being reconstituted and changed through human interactions, rather than as an imposed set of inhuman structures. The case-study method allowed the authors to stress the unique dynamics of these relations in particular cases, and to remedy some of the failings of reproduction theories. Only the most partisan of critics could argue that the ethnographic material in this study was violently twisted to fit a pre-existing theory, though the authors' attempts to integrate discussion of class and patriarchy may be susceptible to the charge that their concern with the latter is something of an afterthought.

The analysis is not, of course, without its problems (Toomey, 1983; White, 1982), but a particularly refreshing aspect of the book is the way in which it attempts to express complex ideas in a manner comprehensible to an audience well beyond the sociology of education. Equally important is the fact that the authors make it clear that they wish their work to be judged in terms of its political effectivity. It is as much a political intervention as it is a contribution to academic scholarship, though it is also one of those books that makes it hard to sustain the dubious notion that these are clearly separable enterprises.

The final chapter, entitled 'Inequality and what to do about it' begins with an attempt to draw together the theoretical threads of the study, but the authors' priorities become clear when they suddenly stop and declare, 'Enough of theory'. Though the discussion 'may have been useful in clearing the air, it is time to try spelling out what some of the potentials and constraints in the present situation are'. The subsequent section, headed 'A democratic strategy for schooling' is an example of the sort of work that is, as I argued earlier, all too rarely regarded by British sociologists of education as an important part of their brief.

The concluding pages of the book attempt to move beyond traditional social democratic notions of education policy and begin to conceive of an education for the working class in different terms from either of the received models, based upon the academic disciplines on the one hand or immediate 'relevance' on the other. The general course of action the authors suggest is 'one of making working-class schools organic to their class' by utilizing a 'third notion' of the curriculum, actively linking academic knowledge to working-class concerns. Of course, much more work needs to be done to develop such a notion if it is really going to win support from those groups who have traditionally supported the social democratic strategy of seeking to provide 'elite education for all', even when, in practice, it has not served their interests. Since writing the book, the authors have themselves continued to consider critically the viability of their proposals and recognize that their proposal for 'organic working-class schools' might in certain circumstances 'amplify the enclosure of the working class and the exclusion of working class people from society and culture as a whole' (Connell *et al.* 1983). There is therefore now some debate between the authors about whether they should instead argue for the reconstruction of the common curriculum for all classes in such a way as to ensure a greater representation of working-class interests. What should be clear from my earlier argument is that debates about the extent to which any solution is in working-class interests cannot usefully be conducted in the absence of an analysis of the broader disposition of political and ideological forces in society at large.

What is encouraging about the Australian scene, when compared with Britain, is that sociologists are more actively engaged in a lively debate about what might actually constitute a left approach to curriculum policy and practice in the current conjuncture (Ashenden *et al.* 1984; Radical Education Dossier 1984). This debate is beginning to move well beyond the confines of the academy to a much greater extent than is apparent in the USA. The authors of *Making the Difference* are themselves keen to see 'the people who are normally just the objects of research . . . develop their capacity to research their own situations and evolve their own solutions'. As part of this process, they are using their work, and videotapes arising from it, to stimulate consideration of the issues it raises with teachers' workshops and community groups. At the same time, they are trying to develop links with broader political movements, though hopefully the emergence of one of the authors as a major policy adviser to the Minister of Education in the new Labor federal administration is only one part of such a strategy.

Perhaps more important than the work of Connell *et al.* themselves, or the particular conclusions they draw from it, is the context in which it circulates. Reactions to the book, and other work relating to it, illustrate the extent to which many Australian writers are concerned to explore in some detail the implications of sociological work for left policy and practice. The authors' debate with White in a left journal (Connell *et al.* 1983; White 1982) demonstrates not only a lack of consensus on the Australian left about the nature of the relationship between academic scholarship and left policy and practice, but also a determination to continue to grapple with this issue. Connell *et al.* agree with White that, as yet, their work constitutes 'theory about practice' rather more than it demonstrates theory that is 'organic in practice', but suggest that their ways of working do begin to point towards new forms of relationship amongst education workers. They acknowledge problems about the book's focus and agree that more might usefully have been said about the relationship of their work to broader political struggles. However, they counter White's disparaging reference to the 'micro' orientation of their work with the suggestion that they might actually have said rather more about the implications of their work for the day-to-day practice of radical teachers in schools. While recognizing the limitations of recommendations made 'in the absence of an account and analysis of [the] objective conditions for the consolidation of working class opposition and assertion', they suggest that daily practice is 'consistently ignored, denied, or under-valued in left argumentation'.

The question of the relationship between different modes of left policy and practice is addressed by another set of writers working in Victoria (Dwyer *et al.* 1984). Their work demonstrates a clear political commitment to social transformation, based upon a recognition of 'both the destructiveness inherent in the present social structure and the possibilities inherent in the human spirit'. The focus of their book is the plight of Australian youth in a period of high unemployment and the actual and potential role of education in sustaining and challenging the existing situation. The empirical content of the book derives from the experience of a community project concerned with the transition between school and work, and the analysis offered tries to take account of the complexities of class, ethnicity and gender in exploring both the possibilities and problems of such a project contributing to a broader process of social change. The authors argue that 'education must be considered as part of a social action programme' and they conclude the book with an important, albeit brief, assessment of the sorts of political movements with which radical educational practices might become articulated. The particular possibilities that the authors explore include a revitalized and radicalized Australian Labor Party, working-class members of the labour movement and the advocates of an 'alternative culture'. The authors conclude:

None of these approaches seems to us to be adequate in itself, and yet each contributes elements that must be present in order for social change of a desirable nature to occur. There must be a political vehicle that is a party structure, which must at some point assume political power. The working class should be an important element in that political party, and play a leading role in shaping its development. The working class, through its industrial movement, should also assume an increasing share of economic power. Culture, and cultural formation are important, and feminists, ecologists and others have an important role to play in providing examples and models of lives lived in ways different from those more directly shaped by Australian capitalism.                                                   (Dwyer *et al.* 1984: 160)

Whatever the strengths and weaknesses of this particular conclusion in the current conjuncture in Australia, the authors have at least shown themselves to be prepared to consider the relevance of a variety of modes of political theorizing and practice to their educational programme. They have also tried to identify more precisely than their American counterparts the sorts of alliances that would further their political aspirations at the present time. To this extent, it seems clear that the work of left sociologists of education in Australia indicates something of the change of emphasis that will be required in Britain, and indeed North America, if the sociology of the curriculum is to make a useful contribution to the development of a coherent educational and political programme on the part of the left. I hope that, to some degree at least, my own explorations in the sociology and politics of the curriculum in contemporary Britain, which are contained in the second part of this book, will demonstrate that this change has begun to take place.

# Part Two

## Current curriculum conflicts in a sociological perspective

# 5

## *The Great Debate and its aftermath*

One of the major criticisms that sociologists of education have made of social democratic education policy is its tendency to neglect the significance of the content of education and concentrate on increasing access to élite styles of education. Indeed, this was one of the themes of the introduction to a collection of papers edited by Michael Young and myself in the mid–1970s (Young and Whitty 1977). By the time the book was ready for publication, however, we felt it necessary to add a postscript to discuss the significance of a break with this tradition on the part of the Labour government in the aftermath of a speech by Prime Minister James Callaghan at Ruskin College, Oxford, on 18 October 1976. It was this speech that launched what we now know as the Great Debate on education.

In that postcript, we pointed out that it was

> ironical (though probably predictable) that when leading Labour politicians do attempt to intervene directly in what have convention-ally been regarded as 'professional matters', their views seem barely distinguishable from those of the Conservative Right. Two themes seem to underlie their pronouncements . . . First, the emphasis is on greater control over content and methods – expressed through the possibility of a 'common' national curriculum, regular monitoring of standards, and giving increased powers to the Inspectorate. The second and related theme (for this is what gives control its purpose) is the importance of responding to the 'needs of industry'. This is

expressed variously in an emphasis on 'vocational preparation', an increase in the funding of courses sponsored via the Training Services Agency, a greater technological emphasis in school science, and the priority placed upon instilling in pupils the importance of industry to our 'national survival'.                    (Young and Whitty 1977: 269–70)

## The Great Debate

Virtually a year to the day before Callaghan's Ruskin College speech, an article had appeared in *The Times Educational Supplement* on 17 October 1975 claiming that during the previous fifteen years there had been a 'breakdown of the "understood" curriculum' in schools and that 'compulsory education is a farce unless all schools follow the same basic syllabus as preparation for society' (Boyson 1975). Its author, Rhodes Boyson, was in the process of emerging from the backwoods of the *Black Papers* (Cox and Dyson 1969; Cox and Boyson 1975), whose impact amongst the Conservative rank-and-file had been largely ignored by the national party leaders, to become one of the major party commentators on educational affairs. During the following year, such was the mounting popular disillusion with the social democratic education settlement (CCCS 1981) that the Labour leadership did indeed come to accept not only the agenda set by Boyson and his associates but even some of their solutions. As we shall see, however, this also involved accepting some of the contradictions that were implicit in their arguments and which Young and I failed to make explicit when we were commenting on these developments at the time.

The agenda of Labour's Great Debate reflected, then, an acceptance by the party leadership in parliament of the claim that the sort of progressive education that had developed in a period of relative professional autonomy[1] in the 1950s and 1960s had produced at least a decline in the rate of increase of educational standards and was ill-suited to the needs of British industry. Some aspects of education were represented as having neglected the needs of the wider society for an appropriately skilled and disciplined workforce and citizenry. Among the solutions might be the development of a common core curriculum and a closer relationship between school experience and working life. Such themes have, as we shall see in succeeding chapters, informed many of the policy initiatives not only of Callaghan's government but also of the Conservative administrations that have followed it.

Underlying many of these initiatives and their concern to increase central control over a system in which a partnership between central government, local government and the teaching profession (Kogan 1971) had involved the devolution of curriculum matters to the profession, was a growing view that the professional mandate of teachers had been abused in the preceding period. An influential article by Weinstock, a leading industrialist and head of GEC, that appeared only a few months before the launching of the Great Debate had been entitled 'I blame the teachers' and argued:

> Teachers fulfil an essential function in the community but, having themselves chosen not to go into industry, they often deliberately or more usually unconsciously instil in their pupils a similar bias . . . And this is quite apart from the strong though unquantifiable impression an outsider receives that the teaching profession has more than its fair share of people actively politically committed to the overthrow of liberal institutions, democratic will or no democratic will.
>
> The most insidious and 'respectable' version of this anti-industry bias has impeccable antecedents. At least since Plato, there has been a deep-seated preference in Western culture (reinforced in Britain by our class structure) for the life of the mind over the practical life. But why should children be taught that the products of the brain will be valued more highly than the products of the hands?
>
> (Weinstock 1976: 2)

The suggestion that there were teachers consciously committed to the overthrow of liberal democracy and who had tried to utilize their professional autonomy to decide on the curriculum to further this end was given added credence by the publicity surrounding the William Tyndale affair. It has been suggested (Dale 1979) that this incident, which eventually culminated in the sacking of the head teacher and most of the staff at William Tyndale Junior School in Islington, provided Callaghan with the necessary legitimation for launching an assault on the profession's autonomy.

However, it is clear from the quotation from Weinstock's article that disquiet with the activities of the teaching profession was by no means directed only at those members of it who espoused radical, or even progressive, approaches. Rather, it was also fuelled by the predominant cultural ethos of the upper reaches of the educational system, where traditional academic approaches and standards still held sway. Certainly there was a concern with the lack of skill and motivation amongst those who had failed within the educational system, though arguably the attitude of Willis's 'Lads' towards mental labour (Willis 1977) should have won Weinstock's approval! However, there was at least an equal concern with the attitudes of those who had clearly succeeded in educational terms. This theme was taken up by Callaghan who was not only dismayed 'to find complaints from industry that new recruits from the schools sometimes do not have the basic tools to do the job', he was also:

concerned to find that many of our best trained students who have completed the higher levels of education at university or polytechnic have no desire to join industry. Their preferences are to stay in academic life or to find their way into the Civil Service. There seems to be a need for a more technological bias in science teaching that will lead towards practical applications in industry rather than towards academic studies.                                          (Callaghan 1976: 333)

Such concerns with the prevailing cultural ethos of the British educational system and its contribution to Britain's economic decline, were not, of course, new (Reeder 1979; Roderick and Stephens 1981, 1982) and can be traced back, as Weinstock implied, to the peculiar history of class formation in nineteenth-century Britain (Wiener 1981). However, they were expressed with an unprecedented level of official sponsorship during the Great Debate.

During that debate there were frequent suggestions that the prevailing modes of educational practice had become, if not directly antagonistic to the survival of capitalism, certainly inappropriate to its needs in a period of economic crisis. The Great Debate culminated, at least formally, with the publication of the government's Green Paper *Education in Schools: A Consultative Document* in July 1977. This paper stated that:

It is vital to Britain's economic recovery and standards of living that the performance of manufacturing industry is improved and that the whole range of government policies, including education, contribute as much as possible to improving industrial performance and thereby increasing the national wealth.                          (DES 1977: 6)

At the level of curriculum content, this meant (again in the words of the Green Paper) that pupils should be taught to 'appreciate how the nation earns and maintains its standard of living and properly to esteem the essential role of industry and commerce in this process'.

The Great Debate was clearly more of an opinion forming exercise than a direct government intervention in the day-to-day management of the schools. Nevertheless, it was accompanied and followed by a whole spate of official and semi-official documents intended to influence the climate of public and professional opinion about education. Virtually all of them displayed the assumption that it was desirable to introduce a greater degree of standardization into the form and content of the English educational system and to make teachers more accountable to those outside of the profession. Amongst the documents emanating from Elizabeth House in the years following the Great Debate were ministerial documents entitled *A Framework for the School Curriculum* (DES 1979) and *The School Curriculum* (DES 1980), and Inspectorate documents such as *Curriculum 11–16* (HMI 1977), *A Survey of Primary Education* (HMI 1978),

*Aspects of Secondary Education* (HMI 1979) and *A View of the Curriculum* (HMI 1980).

The Inspectorate documents revealed considerably more sophistication than the ministerial ones and a greater awareness of the sensitivities of the teaching profession, even if, in some ways, their implications were more far reaching. Certainly, the documents were by no means identical in their understandings of the nature of the curriculum and of the difficulties and significance of changing it. However, although one could not claim that there was anything like a monolithic set of views emerging even from this one department of state, one could say that all these documents were based upon an implicit (and sometimes explicit) assumption that a clearer and more consistent definition of the school curriculum was desirable, that it should have more relevance to the demands of adult and working life, and that central government had a role in bringing this about.

Clearly such developments created considerable concern amongst the teaching profession and the local authorities, since they implied a change in the division of responsibilities between the parties to the post-war consensus. The response of the local authorities was often to mount their own curriculum reviews, and indeed the Inspectorate surveys required this, so that this whole exercise resulted not only in national guidelines on the curriculum but often local ones as well. The Schools Council response to the debate in the form of the working paper *The Practical Curriculum* (Schools Council 1981) emphasized the role of the Council as a forum for 'central government, local authorities, teachers' organizations, further education and higher education, employers, trade unions, parents, churches and examining bodies' to meet and discuss the content and process of education in schools. To this extent, even the curriculum body dominated by official representatives of the profession had become more fully involved in fostering a climate conducive to standardization than had traditionally been the case (Young 1972).

Meanwhile, further centralizing tendencies could be discerned in the work of the Assessment of Performance Unit (APU) at the DES. Although officially this concerned itself with the monitoring of standards and eschewed any role in curriculum control, it was nevertheless felt by many to be likely to have a significant backwash effect on what was actually taught in schools (Hextall 1984; Lawton 1980). Some of the developments within school examinations, which will be the subject of more detailed discussion in the next chapter, have also been interpreted as increasing central control. Similarly, the abolition of the Schools Council has led to its replacement with curriculum and examinations committees whose memberships are more directly under the control of the Secretary of State. Perhaps even more significantly, especially in terms of the resources available to it, has been the growing influence of the

Manpower Services Commission (MSC), another agency of central government but outside the control of the DES. Though initially concerned, amongst other duties, with the curriculum of youth training outside the schools, the MSC has, since 1983, begun to exercise a direct influence on the school curriculum through its Technical and Vocational Education Initiative (TVEI). In this situation, it does seem, on the surface, that Eggleston's claim (1975), that the constraints that keep conceptions of the school curriculum in line with the needs of the existing social system come from teachers' own consciousness rather than external agencies, is no longer true – if, indeed, it ever has been.

## Sociological interpretations

These developments present certain difficulties for sociologists of the curriculum, in so far as much of their work (Bourdieu and Passeron 1977; Young 1971b) has seemed to suggest that the apparently autonomous academic curriculum is ideally suited to the needs of advanced capitalism. Yet, as we have seen, it was not only the perceived failings of progressive and radical teachers that were the focus of the Great Debate. Rather, it was also the conventional academic curriculum that was being characterized as out of tune with the needs of the time and thus as a contributory factor in the mounting 'crisis' of British capitalism and, indeed, of other national capitalisms. Even if there was within the Great Debate some emphasis on a return to traditional academic standards, the dominant refrain in its initial stages was the call to make the curriculum respond more directly to the needs of industry.

Many observers have regarded all these developments as part of the same generalized tendency to functionalize education for a new phase of capitalism. In this connection, it is worth observing that similar developments have been discerned in the educational policies of other advanced capitalist societies, such as Australia and the USA. To this extent, the notion that the basis of such policies is to be found in the needs of capitalism has a considerable degree of plausibility. In the Australian case, Freeland (1979) saw, during 1978, 'a sharpening of the ideological class struggle' and a 'unity of purpose among the fractions of capital and their political and ideological representatives' in the face of 'the necessity to secure the essential conditions for a restructuring of Australian capitalism in its international context'. Drawing upon a fairly crude version of Althusserian analysis, he argued that:

> Those essential conditions are to secure widespread commitment to, or at least acquiescence in, the reduction in the real level of return for labour and redirection of State expenditure from welfare, teachers and health to the various fractions of capital. . . . Repeated attacks are being

made on the liberal progressive reforms in schooling structures and processes of the past decade; 'declining standards of literacy and numeracy' are blamed for youth unemployment; the pool of unemployed teachers is being used to secure a politically and ideologically more docile teaching service; social science education has suffered severe reversals; pressures are rising for the return to externally imposed examinations; and the relative autonomy of the Schools Commission and the various State Departments and educational boards is being reduced.                    (Freeland 1979: 29–30)

Such analyses, appealing as they are in their simplicity, are problematic for a number of reasons. In particular, they often imply a homogeneity in disparate developments for which empirical warrant is hard to find, while in so far as they imply that capitalist imperatives can be relatively easily identified and implemented, they can be both empirically and politically misleading.

Even more sophisticated neo-Marxist accounts can suffer from similar difficulties if they do not rigorously explore the relationship between theoretical tendencies and the empirical processes through which history is made. The work of Holloway and Picciotto (1977) is illustrative of both the strengths and weaknesses of the sort of neo-Marxist work that has sought to explain recent shifts in education policy by reference to a crisis of capital accumulation. Though their theory is in itself quite wide-ranging in its scope, it has been utilized by sociologists of education in both Britain (Hextall 1980; Sarup 1982) and Australia (Freeland and Sharp 1981; Sharp 1984) to account for specific developments in education. For Holloway and Picciotto, the central dynamic of the whole social formation is provided by the 'capital relation' which enters into all features of social existence under capitalism, but in ways that give it specific forms of expression in different spheres. However, in periods of accumulation crisis, there is a tendency for the different spheres to be brought into a greater degree of correspondence than in other periods, when they can appear more or less autonomous. Attempts to gear education more closely to the needs of industry are seen as an example of the need to functionalize the state for the accumulation of capital. Holloway and Picciotto thus argue of the cuts in public expenditure:

What is significant in the present cuts in public expenditure is not so much any reduction in state activity as the attempt to functionalize the state for the accumulation of capital. . . . What is involved is the attempt to make . . . unproductive expenditure serve more closely the reproduction needs of capital . . . This reorganisation of the state is expressed not so much in the overall figures on state expenditure, not just in the shift of resources from, say, education to industrial aid – it is also reflected in the way each function performed by the state is remoulded . . . And of equal importance to the cuts in education expenditure is the attempt to gear education more closely to the needs of industry – by condemning progressive methods, encouraging industrial scholarships, etc.          (Holloway and Picciotto 1977: 96)

Other observers have fitted other developments of the type outlined earlier in this chapter into this basic pattern.

One of the strengths of Holloway and Picciotto's approach is that they stress that the outcome of crisis in any particular situation 'cannot be read off from the requirements of capital in general'. They argue that what is involved is 'a process of struggle, a struggle primarily between capital and labour, but, flowing from that, also between different capitals and fractions of the capitalist class' (Holloway and Picciotto, 1977: 93). This mode of analysis thus stresses the way in which the contradictions and tendencies of development inherent in capitalist relations of exploitation provide the limits and dynamics for class struggles throughout capitalist societies. However, at the same time, it recognizes that the actual development of those struggles can be grasped only through conceptually informed historical research. As such, it goes some way towards meeting the criticisms of a simplistic economistic Marxism as well as avoiding some of the pitfalls of an Althusserian approach.

Nevertheless, Holloway and Picciotto have not, as yet, sufficiently addressed themselves to the nature and specificities of struggles in the ideological cultural sphere. As Nowell-Smith remarks of the German theories from which Holloway and Picciotto draw much of their inspiration:

For those of us whose interest in the State concerns its regulation of cultural apparatuses, there is little to be learned from the German debate except a certain caution. . . . The steps that would take one from a general analysis of the capital form to a particular analysis of ideologies in conjuncture are many and slippery.

(Nowell-Smith 1979: 8)

Although Holloway and Picciotto introduce many caveats into their argument that distinguish it from the crudest forms of a 'logic-of-capital' thesis, it is clear that they need to pay more attention to the nature of ideological struggle, and to a lesser extent political struggle, under capitalism. Only if they do this will it be possible to develop an adequate understanding of the complex ways in which the separate dynamics of economic, political and ideological practice articulate with each other to secure or threaten capital accumulation or social reproduction.

Given that the 'needs' of capital are neither self-evident nor automatically translated into effects, one of the areas it is necessary to study in more detail is the official state discourse that seeks to persuade us of the need for change in schools. An important paper by Donald (1979) has sought to do this in the case of the 1977 Green Paper, *Education In Schools* (DES 1977). Donald's paper is suggestive not only of how this particular document 'works' to produce a new 'truth' about the curriculum and establish a consensus about what should be done, but also of how the ideological work of other such documents might be studied. His paper demonstrates the value of some of the recent theoretical and methodological developments discussed in chapter 2 and is particularly influenced by the semiology of Barthes and by Foucault's approach to discourse analysis.

Like Foucault, Donald is interested in the micro-physics of power, but still within a broadly Marxist perspective. He identifies within the text of the Green Paper a series of codes that work to construct meaning and to position human agents within ideology. He demonstrates that, although the text seeks to produce consensus, it can never entirely close off other possible readings of the situation it is trying to account for. It could therefore have become an object of ideological struggle, though in this particular case the possibilities for this were inadequately exploited, he suggests. Donald is initially concerned with the ideological effects of the text rather than its origins, but, unlike some examples of textual analysis, his paper focuses not only on the internal structure of the text but also on its relationship to the particular historical conjuncture in which it is located. He argues that the ideological work of a text only actually comes into operation as the text is circulated and consumed, and it is therefore necessary to understand the dynamics of the broader circumstances in which this takes place.

However, the disparate theoretical influences on Donald's paper create a hesitancy when it comes to dealing with the difficult issue of the precise ways in which ideological practice is related to economic practice. Donald certainly continues to display a clear interest in this issue, so that, although his major focus is upon the construction of hegemonic discourse and the way 'the state exercises and imposes its power in part through the *production* of "truth" and "knowledge" about education' (Donald 1979), his more general concern is with how the articulation of economic, political and ideological practices might work to produce a restructuring of state education on behalf of capital – or indeed other specific reproductive or transformative effects. Yet Donald's concern to avoid the language of 'base and superstructure' and 'origins and causes', together with his use of terminology such as 'articulations' and 'conjunctures', makes it difficult to get a grip on his understanding of the relationship between economic, institutional and ideological practices. Some parts of the paper would seem to be influenced by those theorists who regard official discourse, institutional practice and economic practice, and indeed all social relations, as a series of interwoven texts and discourses that construct and position human subjects in the social formation and mutually provide each other's conditions of existence. Elsewhere, however, he distinguishes between discursive, political and economic practices in ways that seem to assign primacy, and a certain amount of explanatory power, to the economic in an apparently Marxist manner. Thus, he is still exercised by the need to hold on to both ends of the chain, while stressing even more clearly than Holloway and Picciotto that the actual effects of a crisis in the economic sphere cannot be taken for granted, but are subject to relatively autonomous ideological work and potentially to ideological struggle.

A further problem with analyses that draw upon work like that of Holloway and Picciotto to explain the nature of the school curriculum or attempts to change it is that, in concentrating our attention on those aspects of schooling that can be characterized relatively easily as attempts to secure the necessary conditions of existence for a new phase of capitalism, they can often desensitize us to other aspects. Thus, as Dale (1982) points out, we should not only recognize that it is important not to confuse the functions of the state with the forms in which they are carried out, we should also beware of trying to relate everything that goes on in schools back to the functions of the state on behalf of capital. Particularly important, as we shall see when we seek to understand the dynamics of the Great Debate and the examinations controversy that I will be analysing in chapter 6, is Johnson's reminder that:

> [the] ideological conditions for a given mode [of production] . . . by no means exhaust the whole sphere of the cultural ideological in any concrete society. There are cultural elements to which capitalism is *relatively* indifferent and many which it has great difficulty in changing and which remain massively and residually present.
>
> (Johnson, 1979b: 234)

Though it is arguable that these sorts of issues are better discussed within a Weberian tradition of analysis (Collins 1977; King 1980), and it is true that a lot of Marxist writing on education is notoriously weak in its treatment of them, neither Johnson nor Donald appear to see it as necessary to make a complete break with the broader project of contemporary Marxism. As we saw in chapter 2, some formerly Marxist writers do appear to have made this break and view the practice of power and the securing of reproductive effects as entirely contingent upon the interplay of overlapping discourses, none of which is privileged in the way that economic practice is within Marxism. On the other hand, it is clear that the avoidance of vulgar economic determinism and reduction-ism, and the resurgence of interest in the specificities of ideological practice that I have noted, are not themselves without their problems.

Some commentators, including Holloway and Picciotto, have argued that, while it may be necessary to recast our understanding of the relationship between economic, political and ideological practice in new terms, it is no good simply avoiding the issue posed by Marxism. Thus, in a slightly different context, they have argued that:

> reductionist approaches [at least] have the merit of trying to provide an answer, however crude, to a real problem, the problem of how we come to a materialist understanding of political development, of how we relate political development to the contradictions of capitalist production; it is no improvement at all to simply sidestep the problem.
>
> (Holloway and Picciotto 1978: 6)

If we then substitute the term 'educational' for 'political' in this passage, we are then right back to our basic problem of developing an adequate understanding of specific developments within the educational arena, while not abandoning some of the important insights of the neo-Marxist phase of the sociology of education. This is why so many contemporary writers see it as necessary to hold on to both ends of the chain between relative autonomy and economic determination, while recognizing the importance of the specificities of political and ideological cultural practice.

Donald, who, after a brief flirtation with the approach of Holloway and Picciotto (Donald 1978), adopted the sort of approach we have just seen, has recently suggested to me yet another way forward that might help us to understand the dynamics of the Great Debate. In this case, he argues (albeit somewhat tongue-in-cheek) that perhaps a better basis for understanding lies in the idea that there was economic determination in the *first* instance rather than the *last* instance.[2] Certainly, it is clear that perceived economic needs have had a considerable impact on official policy over schooling in recent years and that this has potential implications for the curriculum. Some of these implications derive from the budgetary consequences of economic recession on the state sector, others from the sorts of demands outlined above that the curriculum should serve the needs of industry to a greater extent than it appears to do at present. What cannot be assumed, however, is that these pressures will always generate policy initiatives whose character can be derived directly from them, nor indeed is it necessarily the case that they will bring about *outcomes* that are incontrovertibly functional for capital. Much of the progress of the Great Debate in England has, for example, to be understood in terms of the peculiar political, professional and cultural character of the English educational system and the existence within it of elements to which capitalism is 'relatively indifferent' or 'has great difficulty in changing' (Johnson 1979b).

Wexler *et al.* (1981) argue that part of the difficulty capital faces within the schools derives from a contradiction between the demands of production for a new type of labour power and the continuing need for the reproduction of existing social relations which schools have always accomplished reasonably efficiently. They also recognize, but do not specifically address, the fact that schooling plays a role in reproducing the conditions necessary for production and the reproduction of capitalist social relations. They argue that, as relatively autonomous public social institutions, schools have potential dysfunctions for capital in the current context, and they suggest that, in the USA, this may potentially produce 'deschooling by default'. In the meantime, they point to the sorts of trends that the attempt to resolve the contradiction may produce in schools:

> Giving schools the central task of skills training there is no reason to burden them with the additional cost of general education, which now appears wasteful and superfluous. The risk of educating a highly skilled labor force is that there is no guarantee that the learning . . . can be restricted to purely technical uses. General education helps to develop attitudes and dispositions which do not dispose students to a later acceptance of the disciplinary requirements of the workplace. General education may engender non-cooperation or opposition to the existing social relations. [But] when the English teacher's job becomes instruction in effective letter writing (to the exclusion of expressive composition and literature), then the English class no longer offers an occasion for unwanted attitudes and dispositions. In this way, even the traditional disciplines of general education are subject to the more general process of the redefinition of the content of schooling . . .
>
> The redefinition of schooling as instruction in narrow instrumental skills is most directly promoted by the back-to-basics movement. Despite its claims for a restoration of traditional learning, the implementation of the back-to-basics-ideal results in the decomposition of more general subject matter into specific technical skills. For example, modern social studies is replaced by history and geography courses in which interpretive understanding is displaced by factual description and technical process. Geography is map-reading and government is how-a-bill-becomes-law . . .
>
> The narrowing of the content of traditional subjects has been reinforced by the political demand for public accountability. Teaching by objectives has been one response to the demand for accountability.
>
> (Wexler et al. 1981: 143–4)

It would be difficult to deny that versions of these developments are to be found on the educational agenda in Britain and Australia, as well as the USA. It is also evident that, amongst the disparate influences on schools, are those to which Wexler *et al.* point, even if there are certain dangers in attributing, as they do, 'meaning to these disparate educational changes independently of their specific historical origins and justifications'. Certainly, their implications and consequences depend on their articulation with other specific historical circumstances. It therefore remains the case that the outcomes of struggles around them are highly contingent upon the disposition of political and ideological forces in and around the educational arena, and this may differ substantially in different advanced capitalist societies. The following section explores the significance and consequences of this in the particular circumstances of English education.

## Struggles over the curriculum

We saw that Holloway and Picciotto (1977) insisted that their argument allowed for the fact that the outcomes of any crisis could not be read off from the requirements of capital but were contingent upon a process of struggle. Such struggles were 'primarily between labour and capital, but . . . also between different capitals and fractions of the capitalist class'. It is clear that the curriculum is sometimes a site of struggle but what is less clear is that it is useful to regard the groups involved in that struggle as formed in a direct relation to capital. Indeed, Bernstein (1977b, c) suggests that the groups primarily involved in determining the nature of the post-war curriculum, members of the new middle classes, are characterized in terms of an indirect relationship to the means of economic production and this is partly what constitutes education's relative autonomy. Arguably, what has been happening in the recent set of initiatives to make education more responsive to the needs of industry is an attempt by the industrial bourgeoisie to increase their direct influence on the nature of education. This has, however, been complicated not so much by resistance from the professional middle classes as by the strength of the residual cultural style of the old aristocratic and gentry classes in English society generally and in the English educational system in particular.

Williams (1965) has suggested that the style of the English secondary school curriculum is the product of an ongoing series of compromises between three groups that he terms the industrial trainers, the old humanists and the public educators. The compromise originated in the nineteenth century but has had to be periodically reworked during the present century. If the industrial training ideology dominated the mass elementary system of schooling in the nineteenth century, the old humanist approach reigned supreme within institutions of élite education. As secondary education was gradually opened to an increasing proportion of the population, however, the classical humanist curriculum of the Victorian public schools, suitably modernized in content but not generally in form, became the dominant curriculum style of the grammar schools and ultimately of the comprehensive schools. We have already seen, in chapter 1, the extent to which adoption by a mass schooling system of a curriculum based upon élite culture helped to legitimate patterns of success and failure. However, that particular style has also had consequences for the way in which both successful and unsuccessful pupils are formed ideologically within the English school system. Wiener (1981) suggests that the prevailing ethos of the high status areas of the educational system, which have a backwash effect throughout that system, is one that celebrates an 'aristocratic' style of culture which, if not directly antipathetic to industry, is at least disdainful of it. As Wiener points to the role of this cultural style in 'the decline of the industrial spirit', it is perhaps useful to see the Great Debate as one of a succession of attempts by the industrial trainers to change the balance of the curriculum compromise in their favour.

In the contemporary controversy over the need for greater relevance to industry in the curriculum, the lobby arguing that schools should teach the knowledge, skills and attitudes that are relevant to industry, and promote a positive image of industry, is the equivalent of Williams's industrial trainers. The universities, together with their associated examining boards, are amongst the heirs of Williams's old humanists, as are the public schools. In general, they support a traditional model of a liberal education based upon initiation into the academic disciplines. They are particularly concerned with academic rigour and the mainten- ance of standards amongst that section of the population deemed capable of undertaking academic studies. More generally, they see themselves as having a role in the preservation of what is 'best' in traditional English culture. Although it would be misleading to regard contemporary universities as a monolithic old humanist lobby, the activities of British universities remain, even today, far less fully integrated with those of corporate capitalism than, say, their American counterparts. This affects not only the way in which they establish priorities within the university system itself,[3] but also the priorities they support in the context of secondary education. Similarly, although inde- pendent schools have, in fact, often pioneered innovative curricula in areas like business studies and technology, this does not seem to have affected the general perception of their dominant ethos. So long as the independent schools are not seen to have changed, the state sector feels under little obligation to do so, especially when it is placed in a situation of competition with those schools.[4] The inter-personal connections of this old humanist lobby and its concern with the preservation of tra- ditional standards and values have given it considerable support in the Conservative Party, especially amongst the group that Dale (1983a) has termed the Old Tories. Thus, this section of the Conservative Party, and some of the Black Paper writers, often stress the importance of academic rigour rather more than industrial relevance.

The third of Williams's groups, the public educators, consists of the teaching profession, the labour movement and those parental pressure groups that are part of the state education lobby. Traditionally it has been concerned to extend the right to education to all groups in society. Its curriculum stance has varied, sometimes internally, but the traditional emphasis was on avoiding education becoming too narrowly vocational in orientation and on making the high-status curriculum available to all. In the post-war period there was some move away from this stance to embrace progressive ideas about a child-centred curriculum, but this tended to have more support amongst parts of the profession than within the labour movement. Nevertheless the emphasis at that time on leaving curriculum matters to the profession helped to accentuate this trend. Even so, this trend itself made relatively little impact upon the higher reaches of the school system, where the profession continued to share many of the assumptions and interests of the old humanists. In the context of the Great Debate, and the break-up of the social democratic consensus about education (CCCS 1981), there has been little in the way of a coherent public education lobby arguing for a particular curriculum style.[5] The professional wing has tended to defend the profession's right to decide such matters, while the labour movement has become thoroughly divided about the best way to proceed.

Salter and Tapper (1981) have suggested that Williams's three-fold typology of groups and positions needs to be supplemented in the contemporary context with a fourth force in curriculum decision-making, the state bureaucrats. Certainly, this group seemed to have an important role at the start of the Great Debate, when it was given a clear political lead to tip the curricular balance in favour of the industrial trainers. In the early years of the Thatcher administration, its role was less straightforward and divisions between, say, the Inspectorate and the permanent officials became more obvious. A lack of decisiveness amongst the Conservative leadership about which curriculum style, or styles, were to be sponsored, and in what institutional contexts, exacerbated this tendency. Only in 1982 did a clearer political decision begin to emerge that involved renewed sponsorship of the industrial trainers' approach. This gave the state bureaucrats renewed influence, especially through their role in the allocation of resources, but there is some evidence that it is the officials of the increasingly powerful MSC that will have the major role in this rather than those of the DES. The long-term significance of this has, of course, yet to be evaluated.

The outcomes of the Great Debate cannot, then, be plausibly represented as a straightforward translation of the effects of an accumulation crisis in the economy into curriculum changes in schools. Rather, they are contingent upon the responses of a whole variety of groups engaged in political and ideological work in and around the educational arena. In fact, of course, it is misleading to talk of outcomes, as the struggles between these groups are ongoing and no clear settlement has yet emerged from the Great Debate. What is clear is that, as yet, the balance has not been tipped decisively in the direction of the industrial trainers. Certainly, the attempt to reduce and redirect public expenditure has combined with demands for greater standardization of the curriculum to produce attempts to define and defend a core of 'central' curriculum subjects. This has meant that supposedly peripheral subjects, or what their detractors often term the 'frills', have come under scrutiny and attack. The campaign against social science education or 'modern social studies', alluded to by both Freeland and Wexler *et al.*, has also been a feature of the British scene, as we shall see in more detail when we come to chapter 7. Nevertheless, even in the changed climate in the period following the Great Debate, the effects of public expenditure cuts or of falling rolls come into play within a set of curriculum priorities that remains far more subject to professional influence than are the levels of expenditure themselves. The highly specialized and subject-oriented training of teachers in England, accentuated at the higher levels by patterns of promotion that favour candidates from a limited range of traditional subject backgrounds (Warwick 1974), has important conse-quences for the ways in which such influence is exercised. Thus, in professional eyes, what constitutes the core is often those subjects that are long-established and of high status. This has meant that not only social science but also technology, a subject with direct relevance to national needs as articulated by politicians and industrialists, has had difficulty establishing itself in a professional arena where the relevance of a subject to the world outside school can be a positive disadvantage to its development (Goodson 1983). This same feature of what gives a subject status in England means that the content of traditional subjects in the English school curriculum tends to be more resistant than American ones to the sorts of changes depicted by Wexler *et al.*, especially in the case of those parts of the curriculum examined by traditional public examinations.

Even where the traditional curriculum of a school and its mode of organization come under direct scrutiny by agents of central or local government, they are often claimed to be meeting contemporary requirements without any fundamental changes in practice becoming necessary. As the Inspectorate themselves acknowledge, their own attempts to review what the curriculum was doing in terms of 'areas of experience' rather than subjects was open to the criticism that 'the eight areas were so general that they could be used to justify any syllabus or subject'. They also noted that some subject teachers might have been tempted to engage in 'artificial exercises in justification "with subjects dredging deep to find some form of response under all eight headings" ' (HMI 1981). It does then seem that professional resistance and institutional inertia, together with the continuing influence of the old humanist tradition, has meant that large parts of the school curriculum have so far remained remarkably unchanged by the noise of the various initiatives to make education more responsive to the needs of industry. Indeed, until very recently, it seemed possible that only the marginal aspects of the education system would respond to the call rather than its 'commanding heights'. In some areas, a return to the traditional academic curriculum, at the expense of the progressive trends of the past thirty years, has been as much in evidence as the move towards greater industrial relevance.[6]

The strength of this traditional curriculum style, and the extent of the resistance to a substantial move in the direction of pre-vocational education, is indicated by the striking similarity between some of the criticisms of the curriculum made by Callaghan in his Ruskin College speech and those made by Sir Keith Joseph, Conservative Secretary of State, in launching a new initiative to help bring about what the Great Debate had signally failed to do. At the North of England Education Conference in Sheffield in January 1984, he claimed:

> The curriculum should be relevant to the real world and to the pupils' experience of it. Judged by that test, HMI reports show that much of what many pupils are asked to learn is clutter. The test means, for example, that the curriculum should contain an adequate practical element and promote practical capability for all pupils, not just for those labelled non-academic; that the technical and vocational aspect of school learning should have its proper place; and that all pupils should be introduced to the economic and other foundations of our society. (Joseph 1984: 4)

A few weeks later, he announced that a group of ministers would set about taking evidence from industry about what exactly it did require of the schools. In short, it seems as if, even in its accentuated form of the late 1970s (Cathcart and Esland 1983), the 'recurring debate' has not yet succeeded in transforming the nature of the English school system to anything like the degree envisaged. In part, this has been the result of Conservative uncertainty about the appropriate balance between restoring traditional standards in accordance with the philosophy of the old humanists and changing the form and content of the curriculum in response to the demands of the industrial trainers.

However, one recent set of developments may, in the long run, tip the balance decisively in the direction required by the industrial trainers. As Finn and Frith (1981) pointed out, the restructuring of the social relations of schooling is necessarily a long-term process, 'with contradictions and potential resistances . . . too important to be left . . . in the hands of an unreformed and "suspect" educational apparatus'. They used this argument to explain the increasing role of the MSC in youth training under the last Labour government. The Conservatives, after some initial hesitation, themselves embraced this approach and developed it into the Youth Training Scheme (YTS), potentially providing a year of training to all school leavers. Even more significant to our present concerns, however, was the decision made in 1983 to use the MSC and its vast financial resources to change the nature of the school curriculum through the TVEI.

The TVEI, originally conceived as the converse of YTS, in that it sought to make inroads not so much into the curriculum of young school leavers as into the old humanist traditions of the academic curriculum, eventually took the form of a small number of pilot projects designed to introduce technical and vocational elements into the curriculum of a range of pupils.[7] Though some commentators argue that this will only in practice produce a repetition of the usual pattern of these approaches gravitating to the lower streams leaving the high-status areas untouched, the scheme is being substantially extended in 1984. The financial incentives being offered to hard-pressed LEAs, and to teachers taking posts of responsibility within TVEI, demonstrate the seriousness of this particular attempt to transform the entrenched traditions of the profession.

It remains, however, far too early to evaluate the actual outcome of TVEI and, although it represents one of the most massive injections of resources to foster change, its outcomes cannot merely be assumed in view of the nature of the professional culture of the teaching profession and the broader cultural assumptions of British society. Unfortunately, those factors are as likely to inhibit radical interpretations of industrial relevance as they are the approach being officially sponsored. As suggested earlier, one of the considerations affecting state schools at the present time is the growing appeal of the independent sector to middle-class parents and many state schools are concerned that their curriculum offerings are of the same order. Even if it is a matter of some debate whether the high-status curriculum of the public schools has changed from the traditional model in recent years (Emms 1981; Salter and Tapper 1981), the public perception is that it has not. In the absence of clear evidence that the concept of what it is to be 'well educated' has changed in the independent sector, it is doubtful whether state schools will go it alone when the independent sector is receiving official sponsorship in its attempts to attract pupils out of the state sector (Whitty 1984). This may be one reason why Joseph has espoused a corporatist approach to changing the state school curriculum rather than relying on his preferred solution via market forces and parental choice. The strength of the old humanist tradition within British culture at large, as well as in the upper reaches of the teaching profession, suggests that market forces might just produce an outcome at variance with that being demanded by industrialists and government ministers.

In the chapter that follows, I shall explore some of these issues and their significance for recent sociological theories in considerably more detail. I shall do this with the help of some very detailed research into the origins and effects of one particular set of struggles over the school curriculum – that involved in the controversy over the future of school examinations at 16+. For a time, this controversy raged alongside the Great Debate and its aftermath. Its outcomes demonstrate, probably to an even greater degree than struggles over other curriculum issues, the continuing strength of the old humanist lobby in and around education in Britain and the problems that this poses for capital and the state.

# 6

# *The politics of*
# *public examinations*

Maclure has suggested that the external examination system is 'almost all that remains of the "public" aspect of the school curriculum' in Britain (Maclure 1975), and it is on the role of public examinations in the control of school knowledge that my discussion concentrates here. In Bernstein's terms, examining boards may be conceptualized as one of a variety of 'recontextualising contexts' located between universities engaged in the production of knowledge and schools engaged in the *re*production of knowledge (Bernstein 1982). The central function of agents and practices within the recontextualizing field is to regulate the circulation of knowledge between the primary (production) context and the secondary (reproduction) context. Traditionally, the power relations between primary, recontextualizing and secondary contexts has been unambiguously hierarchical in the case of school examining. The dominant method of examining English school leavers in the twentieth century has entailed the use of externally devised syllabuses and unseen examination papers, set and marked by examiners employed by university-based boards who have had no part in teaching the candidates. This approach was epitomized by the School Certificate system and continues in most modern General Certificate of Education (GCE) examinations.

Nevertheless, the 1960s saw some changes in the nature of the relationship between agents within the three contexts, which to varying degrees were conceived as challenges to the prevailing pattern of control over the production and distribution of knowledge (Murdock 1974; SSEC 1960). Although, in most cases, the introduction of non-university-linked Certificate of Secondary Education (CSE) boards, with a commitment to teacher involvement in the examining process, produced only minor modifications of the Mode 1 style of examining adopted by the GCE boards,[1] it did open up other possibilities. Indeed, the period 1969–78 saw a steady rise in the proportion of 16+ examinations being conducted under the alternative Mode 3 regulations, where teachers chose to set their own syllabuses and assess their own candidates subject to moderation of syllabuses, assessment instruments and standards by the various CSE and GCE examining boards. The proportion of CSE subject entries under this mode rose steadily from just over 12 per cent in 1969 to just over 26 per cent in 1978 (DES 1971–83).

However, this increase now seems to have been halted and the 1979, 1980 and 1981 examinations all witnessed small but perceptible decreases in the proportions of Mode 3 subject entries. In the GCE examinations, where the proportion of entries conducted under these boards' special syllabus regulations[2] has always been considerably smaller, it is similarly possible to detect an increased use of these in the early 1970s and a falling off towards the end of the decade. There are now those who would wish to exclude school-based assessment from the new common system of examining at 16+ altogether.[3] Whatever the outcome of their campaigns, it looks probable that, even if teachers become more fully involved in examining Mode 1 syllabuses, fully-fledged Mode 3 examinations will become a rarity. Yet, until the mid-1970s, there were still many who believed that school-based syllabuses and assessment would eventually become the norm (at least at 16+), while in other parts of the world a number of apparently similar societies have made considerable progress in this direction during the same period (Broadfoot 1979; Campbell and Campbell 1978). We need, therefore, to explore how and why it was that, in England, the apparently inexorable growth of school-based examinations at 16+ came to be checked. To do so involves us in an empirical investigation of the role of the state in the relations and movements within and between primary, secondary and recontextualizing contexts, the analysis of which Bernstein (1982) sees as a matter of some importance.

The chapter is based upon my own research into the relationships between teachers and examination boards and those between examination boards and the wider society.[4] This research was carried out through observation and interviewing in schools, examining boards and other relevant interest groups during the period 1973–83. It also involved the scrutiny of the minutes of a number of the examining boards, together with the regulations and circulars that they issued to schools in this period. Increasingly, however, the research developed an additional focus by examining in some detail the developing controversy over the proposed new system of examining at 16+, and particularly over the degree of teacher control that would be permitted under such a system. This involved the study of official pronouncements about the proposed system, the response to those pronouncements, the press coverage of the ongoing debate and interviews with key participants. The research sought to understand the effects of changes in official policy discourse on the practices of the examination boards and the implications of both for teachers within the schools. At the same time, it sought to explore the extent to which such changes in policy and practice in school examinations could be related to broader policy initiatives concerning professional autonomy, accountability and the content and relevance of the school curriculum to the needs of contemporary society, as discussed in the previous chapter. Finally, it was concerned to examine the ways in which such developments articulated with the wider economic, political and ideological climate of the period, thus exploring how far the ability 'to control others and bring sanctions to bear against others' in this particular arena could be seen to derive from 'the distribution of power and authority in the macro-structure' (Sharp and Green 1975). The intention here, then, was to utilize the research data in an interrogation of neo-Marxist perspectives in the sociology of education. In this chapter, I shall attempt just such an interrogation after outlining some of the developments in school examining during the period under consideration.

## Mode 3 as a symbol

One of the most noticeable trends during the period of the research was a reversion towards traditional Mode 1 styles of examining and an increasing tendency to place restrictions upon teachers wishing to utilize the Mode 3 regulations. Arguably, this has involved a retreat from the ideals of teacher control of examinations, and of assessment serving the needs of the curriculum (rather than vice versa), that had informed the Beloe Report (SSEC 1960) and led to the establishment of the CSE boards in the first place. Although these ideals were never fully espoused by most of the CSE boards in practice, there is little doubt that what progress has been made towards their realization has suffered a reverse in recent years. Much of this chapter focuses on the fate of Mode 3, or school-based schemes of examination, because they involve the fullest extent of devolution of power over assessment to classroom teachers that has been attempted in the history of public examinations at 16+ in England. However, it should be noted that the ideology of professional teacher control over the committee structures of curriculum agencies and examination boards (which does not in itself necessarily imply any greater involvement of classroom teachers in the examining their own pupils) has also suffered challenges to its legitimacy during the same period. Here again, the CSE boards appear to have accepted the need to make compromises in the face of opposition from the more traditional GCE boards which have never espoused this ideology with quite the same enthusiasm.[5]

In seeking to explain why the space available to teachers to develop their own courses and methods of assessment was being progressively closed down, one possibility was that restrictions upon Mode 3 developments resulted from a perception that many such schemes were subversive and permitted teachers to use their professional mandate in the interests of extremist political goals. In some cases this was seen to be achieved by their injection of radicalizing content into the curriculum; in others by undermining the legitimacy of the examination system or even, as far as the backwoodsmen of the Conservative Party were concerned, by threatening the moral fibre of the nation. Thus, despite its apparent marginality, the Mode 3 issue became during the 1970s a symbol around which broader struggles over the future content and control of the school examination system, and even society itself, could be fought out. In a radical publication that appeared in 1974, Murdock had certainly viewed the Mode 3 regulations as providing teachers with the opportunity to establish courses which:

> encourage pupils to develop and articulate their own particular sense of themselves and their situation, over and against the definitions imposed on them from outside . . . [and] by moving pupils out of their role as consumers and enabling them to become producers . . . demystify the process of authorship and cut away at the dominant definition of 'cultural' production as something separate from everyday life and best left to the experts. (Murdock 1974: 102)

To this extent, Mode 3 regulations seemed to offer the radical teacher the possibility of replacing a traditional concept of the curriculum – what Young (1977b) has termed 'curriculum as fact' – with an alternative and more liberating conception of 'curriculum as practice'. This resonated strongly with the themes of radical community politics in the late 1960s and early 1970s. There was, therefore, perhaps some basis for those on the right who took seriously the idea that Mode 3 examinations posed a threat to the sort of society that traditional forms of examination serve to uphold. Cox, for instance, argued as follows:

> In recent years Left-wing teachers have exploited a more general dissatisfaction with GCE examinations to propose that external assessment should be replaced with teacher assessment, and that the present system of O and A levels should be abandoned. Some fanatics want to abolish all external controls on the school curriculum. Examinations are said to be 'elitist', even 'fascist', an essential part of a

class-stratified, competitive society, a barrier to the emergence of a
truly popular culture.                                          (Cox 1980: 59)

On the other hand, although there undoubtedly was a small number of
teachers who did adopt Mode 3 syllabuses with radical intentions, such
motives do not appear to have been uppermost in the minds of most
teachers submitting Mode 3 proposals to the boards during the period of
the research (Whitty 1976). Rather, the rise of Mode 3s in the late 1960s
and early 1970s could be seen as part of a more general process of
curriculum development, stimulated by the Schools Council, compre-
hensivization and the raising of the school leaving age. In the early 1970s
this was fuelled by a recognition that the most effective curriculum
innovations were those which were school-based and in which curriculum and assessment objectives were in harmony. Some innovations were
presented as more in tune with the needs of pupils and of industry than
the traditional academic curriculum. Thus many of the schemes sub-
mitted to the boards were primarily concerned with providing a more
'relevant' rather than a more 'radicalizing' curriculum for the so-called
Newsom or RoSLA pupils or with extending the public examination
system beyond the 60 per cent of pupils for whom it was designed, as a
way of solving motivational and social control problems within the
school.[6] Other schemes were designed to enable parallel or mixed-ability
teaching of GCE and CSE candidates, thus allowing decisions about
which examinations pupils would enter to be postponed until their fifth
year. Little of this could be realistically construed as a challenge to the
legitimacy of the public examination system, but rather as a modification
and extension of it to meet the changing needs of the secondary school
population. In view of this, it is tempting to agree with Donald (1978) that
'it remains puzzling that Mode 3s should be regarded as subversive'.

It is therefore not immediately clear that the attack on Mode 3s as
'subversive' was in itself sufficient to bring about the changes in the
approach to Mode 3s detected during the course of the research, though
the impact of such charges is not necessarily dependent upon their
accuracy. However, such charges became effective partly because they
became articulated with certain bureaucratic concerns of the examining
boards themselves and with the much wider 'moral panic' concerning
'standards' and the use teachers were making of the autonomy granted to
them during the period of social democratic consensus of the 1960s and
early 1970s. In what follows, I trace some of the changes that have taken
place in respect of Mode 3s in the existing GCE and CSE boards and then
consider the general drift of policy in the context of the proposed 16+
reforms. I then attempt to show how these developments cannot be easily
assimilated into any uni-dimensional mode of sociological explanation,
and point to some of the political lessons that this implies.

## Examining boards and the growth of Mode 3

It is evident from a study by C. Smith (1976) that, as early as 1973, the boards were growing increasingly uneasy about certain aspects of Mode 3s. By 1976 many of them were either implementing or contemplating greater controls over Mode 3 schemes. Some of the GCE boards went as far as expressing doubts about the whole principle of internal assessment and this position was made quite explicit in a publication entitled *School Examinations and Their Function* issued by the Cambridge Syndicate in December 1976 (UCLES 1976). Though not all the examination boards entirely shared this extreme view, most operated increasingly stringent criteria for the acceptance of Mode 3 schemes by the mid-1970s.

In his 1974 survey, Smith (1976) found that generally 'GCE boards accept only those Mode 3 proposals which they are confident are fully comparable with their own Mode 1 syllabus', and he goes on to say that some GCE boards accept them only from schools they consider, from past experience, to have good standing. Even the originally more open, non-university-linked GCE board, the Associated Examining Board (AEB), began to make it increasingly difficult for new schemes to be accepted from the mid-1970s onwards and, at the same time, demanded major modification to existing ones, though not always making clear precisely what the new criteria of acceptability actually were. Another strategy favoured by GCE boards was to defuse pressure from teachers for Mode 3s by absorbing some of their demands into their main Mode 1 structures. This approach is summarized in, for example, a memorandum issued by the Joint Matriculation Board Examinations Council in October 1975, entitled *Notes on the submission of applications for specially approved syllabuses*, which instructed its subject committees as follows:

> Subject Committees are therefore instructed to follow a specific policy of guiding centres which submit proposals for specially approved syllabuses towards:
> 1 Adopting syllabuses and schemes of assessment which make use of part of the published syllabuses and examinations.
> 2 Co-operating with other centres to produce common schemes for special approval.
> 3 Co-operating with the Subject Committee to produce syllabuses which could be included in the JMB schedule as available to all centres. (JMB 1975: 4–5)

At the same time, those new schemes which continued to be accepted by GCE boards were required to be more closely linked to the nature of Mode 1 syllabuses. For example, prior to the development of national criteria, the University of London Schools Examination Board included for the first time in their 1977 revision of *Specially Approved Syllabuses (Modes 2 and 3): Notes for the Guidance of Centres* the following statement:

> In addition to . . . general criteria, Mode 2 and 3 proposals in certain subjects must also satisfy specific subject criteria. Details of the subject criteria are available on request. Criteria for integrated and interdisciplinary subjects are also available: these criteria include guidance on naming.                                    (ULSED 1977: 3)

While these subject criteria varied in the degree to which they restricted teachers' freedom in the choice of subject matter and assessment procedures, elements of Mode 1 content were quite clearly laid down in some of the criteria produced.

There is certainly a hint of worries about political extremism in a new instruction issued by one GCE board to its moderators for the first time in the mid-1970s, which required them to ensure 'that material used in the course and the content of examination papers presents a balanced view, and, in particular, avoids a one-sided and tendentious presentation of social, political, religious and other controversial questions' (AEB's instructions to moderators 1977:1). Nevertheless, this does not initially seem to have been the major issue. Rather, our discussions with board officials indicate that the boards' manifest reasons for making the changes described above, and thus applying a brake to the growth of school-based syllabuses from the mid-1970s onwards,[7] were the result of the bureaucratic difficulties Mode 3 schemes created for the boards. This was quite clearly the case with the GCE boards, where the continued expansion of Mode 3 was seen as causing considerable problems of cost and administrative load. One GCE board official, interviewed in December 1976, put the case as follows:

> this is why perhaps as a board we have tended to see Mode 3 as a means of going towards a Mode 1 examination, and perhaps not geared ourselves generally to a system of Mode 3 examinations. I mean historically we were set up for Mode 1.
>
> (fieldwork interview, 16 December 1976)

Similar difficulties were referred to in another GCE board's internal research committee paper, discussing the links between examinations and school curricula:

> The ambiguities are emphasised by its dual role [of examining body and matriculating authority] and by the structure of the committee system and the strategy which results from that structure for reaching decisions. The board seems to be well organised for producing Mode 1 examinations but is less well equipped for the consideration of specific proposals from individual schools.
>
> (GCE board internal research paper 1975: 4)

Thus the GCE boards found that elements of their structure and their historic role made it administratively difficult to deal with Mode 3s.

Constitutionally, the CSE boards had more difficulty in controlling the growth and nature of Mode 3 schemes, since strictly speaking they could only reject a submission if it was incapable of being assessed or if its title did not correctly reflect its content. They therefore tended to employ administrative devices as a way of restricting the burgeoning growth of new and disparate Mode 3 schemes. These included the listing of approved titles, the lengthening and tightening of their submission procedures and requesting considerably more detail about aims, objectives, course content and assessment procedures than had hitherto been the case, and, indeed, sometimes going far beyond that which was required for new Mode 1 syllabuses. Other changes were made to moderation procedures, while some of the boards began to consider more drastic measures such as the development of subject criteria and the insistence on the inclusion of core papers within all schemes, despite the fact that the constitutional legitimacy of such measures was open to question. Thus, although the CSE boards did not adopt identical approaches to the GCE boards, there were considerable similarities in their attempts to increase control over school-based syllabuses and assessment procedures. It is clear that these measures made definite inroads into teacher autonomy within the CSE system and, by 1982, one board official commented that 'quite frankly, there are some [CSE] boards that in my view have gone really to a GCE stance in the control of syllabuses' (fieldwork interview, 19 May 1982). Despite the fact that the CSE boards were set up specifically to cater for all modes of examination, many of them expressed similar concerns to the GCE boards, and, with the West Yorkshire and Lindsey Regional Examinations Board (TWYLREB) as the only total exception, their approaches to Mode 3 submissions increasingly came to resemble those of GCE boards. Established with centralized administrative structures (though to varying degrees) and run on a committee basis, many of these boards also became alarmed at the costs and administrative load created by Mode 3s.

Indeed, given the far greater demand for Mode 3 schemes in the CSE system, these boards often found it necessary to rationalize their submission procedures to an even greater extent than the GCE boards, some of which were able to maintain individual relationships with trusted schools. The rationalization of procedures in the CSE boards tended to draw control into an anonymous central administrative machinery, producing the perception on the part of many teachers that power was being taken away from the grass-roots teacher and the relationship of mutual trust between fellow professionals thus destroyed. Such a development was recently confirmed to us by a CSE board official in the following terms:

I think there has been a shift in what I would call the power balance
between, from the original teacher, I mean the actual grassroots teacher
who was marking scripts within the consortium to in fact, if you like,
the institutionalised teacher within the board structure and in some
senses also the LEAs and the heads have played a bigger part in the
maintenance and organisation of the system and the boards' staff
have also.                                    (fieldwork interview, 19 May 1982)

The increasing centralisation and alienation experienced by teachers
reflected a growth in the power of CSE officials and the 'institutionalised
teachers' who dominated the boards' committee structures and whose
professional concerns sometimes became more closely identified with
the organizational needs of their boards than with the educational
requirements of their colleagues on the classroom floor.

However, it would be misleading to assert that the nature and
demands of the boards' administrative structures were alone responsible
for the increasing controls over Mode 3s. There were also doubts about
the quality and comparability of many Mode 3 schemes in relation to
Mode 1s. Smith's study (C. Smith 1976) reported worries about mode
comparability and public confidence in Mode 3 standards, while many of
the board officials interviewed during 1976 and 1977 expressed concern
about the public image of Mode 3. Most felt that this supposedly poor
public image was misplaced, at least in respect of their own boards'
schemes, but nevertheless argued that it had to be taken into account. For
board officials 'public confidence' required showing that standards were
consistent from year to year and from examination to examination. In
part this requirement was translated into technical considerations of
validity, reliability and comparability. One particularly sensitive issue
for the boards was the charge that it was easier for pupils to gain high
grades on Mode 3 examinations, but, at least in terms of the crude index
of pupils gaining grade 1 passes in CSE Modes 1 and 3, the massive
discrepancies that had existed in the early years had already disappeared
by 1974 (DES 1971–83), that is prior to the major tightening up on Mode 3
submissions and moderation procedures noted here. Even the continuing evidence of small discrepancies between modes at O-level is
difficult to evaluate given the nature and size of the samples involved.

Nevertheless, it seems that at least as important as any technical
considerations of this sort in the notion of 'public confidence' is a
concern that assessment should be independently conducted by an
outside person or agency. That this in some ways could override all other
considerations is evident in the following remarks of one of the CSE
board officials that we interviewed:

At the moment, well, the whole history of CSE has shown an ever-
increasing growth of this internally assessed component, and at some

stage I think one must look at this and determine how far it can grow without destroying the validity of the examination and undermining public confidence . . . Rightly or wrongly, probably indeed wrongly in many respects . . . the public's view is that they set great store by externality which they associate with impartiality and the idea, to many people, that the teacher is in fact responsible for examining his own candidate is abhorrent.   (fieldwork interview, 5 November 1976)

There was, then, in the eyes of board officials, a tension between the growth of internal assessment and the traditional ideology of examinations, associated in most people's minds with the GCE board's external assessment procedures. This traditional ideology has a long history, as is clear from an observation in the Dyke-Acland Report of 1911 which provided the basis for the School Certificate system. Referring to the university-based examining boards, it stated, 'They possessed an academic standing and an impartiality which were above question, and they achieved a right of entry into schools where any attempt at State interference at that time would have been hotly resented . . .' (Dyke-Acland 1911), and a very similar view was expressed to us by the secretary of one of the university boards during the Great Debate when he suggested:

Now you can't give teachers complete, absolute freedom, and in this country we've restricted teachers' freedom by making the examination system the controlling element in the end . . . I think our system . . . is infinitely preferable to some dictation from on high . . . In the wrong person's hands this could be dangerous.
(fieldwork interview, 16 December 1976)

His view that the university boards were 'completely independent and impartial' agencies is widely held and the existence of such an external system, independently constituted, is frequently held to be the only guarantee of objectivity in assessment. A concern to prevent devaluation of their certification therefore led the boards to question the degree of internal assessment they should allow if they were to retain public confidence. Such concerns, together with the administrative considerations already referred to, justified the GCE boards' resistance to an extension of school-based examinations and led the CSE boards to revert towards conventional GCE-style procedures and structures, even though this sometimes conflicted with their original *raison d'être* and even, on occasions, their own assessment of what was educationally desirable.

However, the problems and doubts experienced within the boards might well have been resolved in different ways, had the issue of school-based assessment not become bound up in the late 1970s with the effects of public expenditure cuts, the 16+ reform controversy and the Great Debate. Even if the root problem had been the lack of teacher skill in syllabus construction and assessment, which clearly was very far from the whole story, the solution in a period of economic expansion might have been a massive programme of in-service training in this respect. In the context of education cuts and the general suspicion of professional autonomy regenerated by the Great Debate, this did not prove to be the preferred solution. Yet, interestingly, it was only certain elements of the Great Debate that came to influence the controversy over the reform of 16+ examinations in a significant way. While the theme that the teaching profession should be made more accountable to those outside it clearly influenced the development of the examination reform proposals, the refrain that declining standards were at the heart of the problems facing Britain increasingly took precedence over the other concern (articulated particularly by industrialists and government ministers at the start of the Great Debate) that the school curriculum was largely irrelevant to the needs of contemporary industrial society (Callaghan 1976; Weinstock 1976). Indeed, it is arguable that some of the developments within GCE and CSE examinations already discussed made it more difficult for schools to respond to the needs of industry, especially at a local level, and I shall go on to argue that the successive revisions of the 16+ reform proposals exhibited this characteristic even more clearly. Increasingly, the view of the Black Paper contributors and their supporters in the Conservative Party, that what was needed was a return to rigorous academic standards and the curbing of the influence of trendy left-wing teachers, superseded the corporatist concerns of industrialists and Labour ministers with modernizing the curriculum and enticing the 'best brains' into industry to foster economic growth. It was this development within the public and political arena that permitted the university lobby and the GCE boards to win some quite striking victories in the negotiations over the future of 16+ examining in the late 1970s and early 1980s.

## The 16+ controversy

The Schools Council's recommendations for the future of examining at 16+ were published in September 1975 (Schools Council 1975). In view of the fact that these proposals included the retention of opportunities for school-based assessment in the new common system of examining, and predicted that the proportion of candidates entered under other than Mode 1 arrangements would continue to grow, it is not surprising that they featured in the growing education debate. The newspapers over this period were continually peppered with attacks upon schools and their falling standards and on progressive teachers who had 'let our children down' (CCCS 1981). The concentration upon standards fostered by the Black Papers seems to have been further extended by a concern about internal assessment and, indeed, the two issues became fused together both within the 16+ controversy and within the Great Debate. Although by no means all the critics of the 16+ proposals accepted the claim made by the Black Paper editor Cox that 'a main aim of the reformers is that CSE Mode 3 [teacher assessed] exams will become the "norm" ', or even shared his own suspicions about their 'underlying ideological purpose' (Cox 1980), the possibility that school-based syllabuses and modes of assessment would be a significant part of any new examination arrangements did seem to provide a major source for concern for many of those commenting upon the Schools Council's recommendations. Conservative politicians, some industrialists, senior university academics, as well as the more traditional GCE boards, joined in a massive onslaught on the initial proposals. During 1975 and 1976 the press contained numerous letters, articles, and reports of speeches attacking CSE standards and the Mode 3 option and trying to ensure that such models did not come to dominate the new examination, upon whose credibility the legitimation of access to high status occupations might depend. Norman St John Stevas, Lord Belstead, Lord Annan, the Confederation of British Industry, the Committee of Vice-Chancellors and Principals, and the London and Cambridge GCE examination boards were amongst those who publicly attacked the 16+ proposals by citing the problem of school-based syllabuses, teacher assessed elements or teacher control of the system.[8] It is hardly surprising that, in the face of this sort of opposition, Shirley Williams, the then Labour Secretary of State for Education, chose, in October 1976, to delay the implementation of the Schools Council's proposals. Taking advantage of continuing doubts about the technical feasibility of a common system, she proceeded to submit them to a further round of deliberations by the Waddell Committee.

It was at this very time that, in response to the growing 'moral panic' about education, the Great Debate was being launched with the preparation of the government's Yellow Book and the speech by Prime Minister Callaghan at Ruskin College. Indeed, Hopkins has suggested that it was 'partly because of the Schools Council's injudicious exam proposals', which 'seemed to imply the most radical extension of teacher-power, with a heavy reliance on the Mode 3 principle', that 'teacher-power was one of the main targets shot at' and hence one of the central issues in the Great Debate (Hopkins 1978). Thus, if the William Tyndale affair was to provide the major pretext for the reining in of teacher autonomy (Dale 1979), Mode 3 and the issue of teacher control of examinations also played its part. An article by Christopher Rowlands in the *Daily Mail* in April 1977 (Rowlands 1977) helped to keep the issue before the public view, while the statement by Tom Howarth to a meeting at the House of Commons that 'we cannot afford to become a CSE Mode 3 nation'[9] symbolically linked the issue of teacher power and national decline and thus helped to legitimate attempts to restrict or abolish Mode 3s and to modify those parts of the Schools Council's proposals that pointed in the direction of teacher control. Yet the groups involved in this attack on the 16+ proposals were far from homogeneous and had differing motives in arguing for their abandonment or modification. What now seems to have emerged will almost certainly be of more satisfaction to some of those groups than others.

Thus, as the general political climate moved against the concept of teacher autonomy that had developed during the 1960s, it was the universities who were quick to assert their traditional role as definers of school knowledge and external arbiters of standards, even though in the early stages of the Great Debate they had been deemed almost as culpable as school teachers in Britain's economic decline, through their maintenance of élitist and over-academic curricula. Despite the fact that their own internal examination arrangements themselves constituted an extreme example of Mode 3-type procedures, they led the way in questioning the extent to which this would be an appropriate style of examining for the new 16+ examination. As already indicated, the university-based GCE boards modified their existing procedures for dealing with special syllabuses to accord with the changing climate and the formally teacher-controlled CSE boards followed suit. In addition, to the considerations discussed earlier, it was clear that in a situation where the various boards were competing for influence in the proposed new system of examining, the CSE boards were understandably reluctant to be seen to be placing too great an emphasis on school-based elements in the prevailing ideological and political climate. Particularly significant in the discussions amongst the CSE boards outside the Midlands region was a fear that high-status schools would defect to any new examining group that included the Oxbridge boards and thus create a hierarchy within the system. They therefore felt it essential to appear totally respectable in terms of the traditional criteria upon which such a hierarchy would be based. This problem was exacerbated by the formation of a strong traditionalist GCE pressure group, the Cambridge, Oxford and Southern Schools Examining Consortium (COSSEC), consisting of the three Oxbridge boards and the Southern Universities Joint Board (SUJB), and was only partially alleviated by the withdrawal of the Oxford Delegacy from this grouping. In the crucial period, the activities and pronouncements of COSSEC severely restricted the willingness of other boards and groupings of boards to consider large-scale devolution of syllabus and assessment powers to grass-roots teachers under the new system. Even if the more extreme position of the COSSEC grouping was not always accepted by the more liberal of the GCE boards (Doe 1982), the debate was effectively shifted very firmly into terrain defined by the GCE rather than the CSE boards. In addition, when it came to defining subject criteria for the new examination, the GCE boards established 'shadow' committees to ensure that their own interests and traditions were not being sacrificed in the official joint bodies that were developing these criteria.

This reassertion of the role of the universities and GCE boards also appeared to receive an increasing amount of official encouragement as the 16+ proposals went through their successive modifications. The Waddell proposals (DES 1978), in suggesting that the universities had a status different from mere 'users' of examination certificates (such as employers and non-university further and higher education) in its proposed regional supervisory bodies, seemed to legitimate their traditional role in defining knowledge and standards for schools. The GCE boards themselves seemed to be the key factor in the official acceptability of the various consortia of boards being considered, and, when the Conservative Party was returned to government in 1979, their role was further strengthened by giving them an effective veto over standards and the assessment methods to be applied to the award of the top three grades in the new system (Fairhall 1980). In eventually giving his approval to a new GCSE system, Sir Keith Joseph also announced the introduction of a new matriculation-style 'distinction certificate' (Norman 1984). At one time he was even reported to be under pressure to preserve the GCE system in its entirety (Shaw 1982) and at least to be considering confining non-traditional modes of examining to schemes eligible only for the award of the lower grades in the new system (Stevens 1982). The consequences of this increasing reassertion of the traditions and practices of the universities and their examining boards are of considerable interest in view of the sorts of criticisms being made of schools during the Great Debate. It made possible something of a resurgence of traditional GCE styles of examining at the expense of some of the innovations developed within the CSE system during the 1960s and early 1970s (Doe 1981b). These conventional modes of assessment are associated with the traditional high-status curriculum, characterized by Young (1971b) as embodying literate, abstract, differentiated and un-commonsense knowledge. This is not the knowledge demanded by corporate industry, but rather that very knowledge of the liberal academy that industrialists such as Weinstock and politicians such as Callaghan (1976) argued in 1976 was less than appropriate to contemporary needs. That this irony within the outcome of the 16+ controversy was recognized within the government and DES was hinted at in the following report from *The Times Educational Supplement* in July 1981:

> Lady Young refuses to be drawn on whether the commitment to 'maintain standards' rules out the opportunities to change the exams to fit what some see as the real demands of adult and working life. But

DES officials make it clear that the priority is to get the new exam off the ground rather than introduce all the reforms that might be considered desirable.                                                                 (Doe 1981a: 8)

It seems, then, that the universities and GCE examining boards have been able to take advantage of broader attacks on teacher autonomy to regain some of the influence over the school curriculum they had ceded to the teaching profession in the 1960s.

They have been able to do this, in the context of the 16+ reforms, by a selective utilization of the rhetoric of the Great Debate in which they have exploited the tension between the concept of 'standards' and the concept of 'relevance'. The universities and the GCE boards have been able to reassert their role as upholders of standards; in so doing they have reimposed a conformity to conceptions of school knowledge that had become increasingly under challenge in the preceding period, not only from progressive and radical teachers but also from those concerned to make the curriculum serve the needs of industry. In granting part of what was demanded in the broader, but uncoordinated, attack on schools and teachers, the university lobby appears to have stolen something of a march on some of its early allies in that attack. Not only has the growth of Mode 3 assessment in the present system been halted, and probably reversed, it seems likely that the GCE boards will continue to dominate any new system of examining that takes us into the 1990s, and, in some senses, with increased rather than diminished power. As a result, the overall pattern of changes in 16+ examinations is likely to produce outcomes considerably at variance with those initially demanded of the school system by industrial and governmental pronouncements early in the Great Debate.

Part of the reason for this lay no doubt in the emergence of Cox's co-editor of the Black Papers, Rhodes Boyson, as a junior education minister in the Conservative government and in the particular balance of forces that constituted that party at the time. Yet it also derived from the fact that the university lobby had a relatively clear view of the alternatives to teacher assessment that it offered, while the industrial lobby was much less clear or united about its own preferred alternative. Indeed, the industrial lobby seems to have become increasingly muted as the debate progressed, partly because it was unclear about the precise requirements it had of the examination system, but also because it was somewhat ambivalent about the desirability of school-based syllabuses within it. Here again we can see the tension between a concern with standards and a concern with relevance. While the influential article by Weinstock that presaged the Great Debate had been entitled 'I blame the teachers', it had also attacked the Platonic traditions of English academic life upon which the particular notion of standards embodied within the

English educational system had been built (Weinstock 1976). Certainly there is a degree of suspicion about teacher-assessed courses amongst industrial and commercial employers, and indeed some of the board officials interviewed gave this as one justification for tightening controls over Mode 3 schemes. However, our own research amongst employers showed the other side of the picture. Although these interviews did elicit various generalized criticisms of the schools and their curricula which echoed some of those voiced in the early stages of the Great Debate, they also pointed to a rather more ambivalent orientation towards Mode 3 examinations than we had anticipated from our interviews with board officials. In fact there was a considerable degree of ignorance amongst most employers about the nature of Mode 3 schemes, but, where they were reasonably well understood, concern about the difficulty of maintaining standards was often balanced with more favourable comments about the ways in which Mode 3 syllabuses were sometimes of greater industrial and vocational relevance than the typical range of Mode 1 syllabuses offered by most boards. For example, the training officer of a heavy engineering firm interviewed during our fieldwork remarked that he was 'delighted to hear the chap who was talking about this Technology Mode 3 course' because the teacher concerned had tried to involve local industrialists in its planning, to ensure that it was 'a course that *had* a relevance to local industry'. He also stated that he would 'buy Mode 3 Maths because a man can cut out a lot of old-fashioned things and keep in a lot of things that some people think are old-fashioned and damn well aren't, like imperial measure' (fieldwork interview, 14 October 1977).

It is also pertinent to note that the Rubber and Plastics Industry Training Board was making favourable public comments about the relevance of Mode 3 schemes at the very same time that the Confederation of British Industry was joining in the general criticism of school-based assessment in the context of the proposals for 16+ reform (Jackson 1976). This ambivalence is understandable given that the GCE boards' response to the industrial relevance argument seems to have largely involved cosmetic measures such as the co-option of industrialists onto committees that have no direct involvement in syllabus development. It is therefore hardly surprising that views amongst industrialists about the new system have continued to differ even after its official adoption.

## Sociological accounts

We have seen, then, that in recent years there has been something of a delegitimation of school-based schemes, even within those parts of the examination system in which they had apparently been gaining increasing acceptability in the earlier period. This can be seen as partly an effect of the particular bureaucratic structures employed by the boards, but it was also influenced by an accelerating public concern about a perceived lack of objectivity and externality in assessment at 16+. Particularly in the context of the controversy over the proposed common examination system, this led even those boards established on the basis of teacher representation and control to limit the degree of classroom teacher participation in the actual process of syllabus design and assessment. Although some of the changes that I have outlined might be interpreted as expressions of the sort of technical rationality that is often seen as serving the developing needs of corporate capitalism, others involve a reassertion of traditionalist values and approaches to examining, and seem rather less easily explicable in such terms. In view of the apparent complexity of the origins and effects of these changes in examining at 16+, it is necessary to raise some questions about the ways in which developments in examination policy have been discussed by various neo-Marxist commentators on education.

Some of these authors have attempted to explain examination reform, like other recent developments in education, in terms of a general set of requirements derived from the economic and political needs of capitalism in a period of crisis. Thus, for instance, Donald (1978) has drawn upon the work of Holloway and Picciotto (1977) to suggest that, as part of the functionalization of the state for the accumulation of capital, one would expect to find, 'examinations being made more "efficient" in terms of what they test, how the testing is done, and how the system is controlled'. In broad terms, he regards this as the thrust of the changes that have taken place in school examinations in recent years, though later in the article (and much more so in his more recent work) he does recognize that a wide range of determinations has contributed to them. More concretely, Hurford has argued that the 16+ reform proposals:

> represent a way in which the 'space' that education once had within society is being eroded, as the ruling class seeks a more direct and effective control over education than can be achieved through the Teacher Establishment. . . . The CSE boards have not been as dominated by the higher education interests as the GCE and have therefore been a less effective means of curriculum control. The new GCE [sic] boards will correct this and ensure more proper representation from 'industry'.
>
> Put in these terms it is easier to see how the 16+ will fit the new scenario where on the one hand education is more clearly seen to serve the interests of the nation/industry and on the other appear to give equality of opportunity in the shrinking job market.   (Hurford 1979: 7)

Yet, while the effects of an accumulation crisis can be seen as influences

on the developments discussed here, particularly through the impact of
public expenditure cuts on educational priorities, and in the demands of
industrialists and Labour ministers that education should serve the
needs of industry, the situation seems much less straightforward than
Hurford and even Donald imply. Both their analyses tend to over-
estimate the homogeneity of the state and the ruling class and under-
emphasize the extent to which outcomes, while influenced by the
requirements of capital, are also contingent upon a variety of concrete
historical struggles and may potentially be at variance with those
requirements.

The temptation to explain developments in terms of all-embracing, but
uni-dimensional, theories of causation is, not, however, one from which
I have been entirely immune myself. Writing in the mid-1970s about the
resistance to the idea that school-based syllabuses should be a major
element of the combined examination at 16+, I argued:

> It is, of course, the case that, in many situations, the 'various economic,
> political, bureaucratic, cultural and educational interest groups which
> make up [the dominant] order' (Young 1971b) do not share a consensus
> definition of knowledge. It may also be, however, that this is an
> instance where, faced with a common threat, business and academic
> elites combine in their resistance to it.                    (Whitty 1977: 73)

Like Hurford and Donald, and Freeland (1979) writing about similar
campaigns in Australia, I was assuming that in the context of an
accumulation crisis, there was a 'unity of purpose among the fractions of
capital and their political and ideological representatives' (Freeland
1979). Although, like Freeland, I recognized the possibility of inherent
contradictions and ideological conflict *within* the 'fractions of the ruling
class block', my emphasis, like his, was on their unity. This had the effect
not only of constructing a false sense of the ideological unity of the
dominant order in the face of the crisis but also of making the effects
of the ideological response to that crisis seem more of a foregone
conclusion than I now believe them to have been. This had unfortunate
implications for my reading of the political possibilities it offered. The
account of conflicts over Mode 3 examinations that I have developed in
this chapter has focused rather more than my earlier work on the
different positions taken up by the various groups involved in the
debate. This more detailed empirical analysis points to the way in which
my earlier position, although hardly as abstract as a crude 'logic of
capitalism' type of explanation, had served to blind me to some major
conflicts within the dominant order in this context and to the range of
outcomes that might have been possible. I now want to explore the
tension between my own empirical account and contemporary neo-
Marxist theory in greater detail.

Put at its simplest, it seems clear that the outcomes of the examinations controversy are out of step with the views of capital's requirements articulated by large sections of the industrial lobby, even if this lobby is somewhat unclear about the precise requirements it has of the examination system and about where control of the system should lie. However, to show that the industrial lobby has little direct influence over school examinations, or that recent developments are not in accord with its overt demands, does not, of course, establish that such developments fail to function effectively for capital. It is therefore necessary to give consideration to the more sophisticated argument that the exercise of control on behalf of capital is carried out largely behind our backs. Thus, for example, Bourdieu and Passeron (1977) have pointed to the way in which the apparent autonomy of the traditional academic curriculum (and its associated assessment procedures) from direct capitalist control has produced a systematic misrecognition of the vital role of the school in the reproduction of capitalist social relations. Yet, whatever the historic role of the academic curriculum, it seems questionable whether the approaches of university traditionalists and industrialists can be considered equally functional for capital at the present time. Indeed, the re-assertion of university influence in the current conjuncture in Britain can be seen as, in some respects, an attempt to resist a reorientation of the education system towards a model more in accordance with the requirements of a new phase of capitalist development. When we look at the syllabus content of existing courses and the draft subject criteria for the new system, it is certainly difficult not to be sceptical about the degree to which this aspect of education is being functionalized for capital.

Nevertheless, as we saw in chapter 2, Apple (1982b) has suggested that, rather more important than the fate of any direct attempts by industry to influence the nature of the curriculum, has been the introduction into schools of the sort of technical modes of control over the workforce that are increasingly dominant within the capitalist labour process. While Apple's own examples are based upon the large-scale introduction of teaching packages into American schools, the systematic tightening of control over British teachers, via changes in technical procedures within examination boards, would also seem to lend support to his thesis. This is particularly so in the case of those examining boards that introduced tight statistical moderation procedures to counter charges of a lack of reliability and comparability in the assessment of Mode 3 components. In view of the fact that these changes were partly a response to DES pressures for greater standardization and accountability, they would seem to offer credibility to the notion of the state functionalizing education for capital. There are problems with this argument too, however. For, even assuming that such developments within education do actually operate in the interests of capital, it has not usually been those boards most advanced in developing moderation techniques approximating to Apple's conception of technical control that have been at the forefront of the developments described in this paper. Furthermore, the technical efficacy of the traditional Mode 1 GCE style of examining, which is experiencing something of a resurgence, is highly questionable in relation to some of the newer styles of assessment developed by the CSE boards.

Such analyses, then, correctly identify some of the influences that underlie and affect contemporary state policies for education and school examinations. However, they tend to assume that particular pressures are the only ones operating and that, by and large, the needs of capital feed through to and have effects in the educational arena in relatively straightforward and unproblematic ways. In doing so, they are particularly susceptible to Nowell-Smith's charge of 'falling back into the usual banalities of British leftism of the "well-it's-all-capitalism-isn't-it?" variety' (Nowell-Smith 1979) – a form of explanation which, in fairness, is not limited merely to British leftists. This is just the sort of stance that may encourage critics to reject neo-Marxist perspectives as entirely irrelevant to an understanding of contemporary educational struggles (Lawton 1980). However, Nowell-Smith himself is rather nearer the mark than such critics when he writes:

> A full analysis of, say, the changes in the examination system *must take into account* the way the requirements of capital accumulation make themselves felt in the education sector. . . . But the ideology of examinations cannot be 'derived' in any adequate way from the logic of capital and the capitalist state.          (Nowell-Smith 1979: 8)

As we saw in chapter 5, he goes on to say that the steps from 'a general analysis of the capital form to a particular analysis of ideologies in conjuncture are many and slippery' and he adds that the arguments that are often employed in the literature are 'at best devious, at worst metaphysical'. At the very least, arguments based upon the progress of a logic of capitalism tend to obscure the historically contingent nature of the outcomes of the various policy initiatives mounted on behalf of capital. Or to put it another way, they tend to ignore what, in a more recent article on unemployment and training initiatives in Australia, Freeland (1981) terms the 'refractions' which the imperatives of capital accumulation and the demands incorporated into state policy discourse undergo in the process of implementation.

The nature of my own evidence on examinations suggests that the relationships between capitalism, the state and education are rather more complex than some neo-Marxist analyses have implied. Such analyses can have the effect of deflecting our attention from aspects of recent developments that could have important implications for the future policy and practice of those who wish to contest these developments. Certainly my account suggests that it is inappropriate to view recent developments in and around examinations purely in terms of the requirements of capital accumulation. Further, it is important not only to chronicle the fact of the subjection of teachers to greater external control, but also to detail the struggles over how that control is to be exercised and to identify the nature and goals of the various parties involved. Once again, it is useful to look at the conflict in terms of Williams's three groups: the old humanists, the industrial trainers and the public educators (Williams 1965). As we have seen, the industrial trainers, though expressing concern about the nature of school curriculum, have lacked precise and consistent prescriptions in the examination field. Meanwhile, the old humanist lobby, as represented in this controversy by the universities and the GCE examination boards, has had the advantage of a clear curriculum model and a long tradition of influencing schools, while its defence of traditional values and standards has appealed to the sort of 'golden age' mentality engendered by the 'crisis' and encouraged by some leading Conservative politicians. As for the public educators, in the particular conflict under consideration here, they were severely handicapped by the role of the Labour government and, in the aftermath of the recriminations caused by this, they lacked both the unity and common purpose necessary even for the defence of the strengths of the CSE system, let alone for the development of a more progressive alternative appropriate to the changing context.

In the particular compromise that is emerging, the old humanist lobby has exercised greater power than might have been predicted, because it has been able to organize around a coherent curriculum philosophy, an established organizational base and a considerable degree of cultural legitimacy both within education and in the wider society (Wiener 1981). It has also been able to gain the support of a powerful political constituency to take advantage of some crucial contradictions and ambiguities within contemporary discourse about education. The industrial trainers, who during at least part of the 16+ controversy seemed to have had the support of Salter and Tapper's 'fourth force' in curriculum decision-making, the state bureaucrats (Salter and Tapper 1981), have increasingly lost the initiative in the particular developments discussed here. This was especially the case in the early years of the Thatcher government where the ambiguities within Conservative education policy made it difficult for DES officials to be clear what the political priorities were.

However, the views of the industrial lobby do seem to be having more success in influencing approaches to assessment in the lower status parts of the curriculum where traditional academic interests are less firmly established. Provision for those pupils for whom the new 'common' examination system is inappropriate in all but a few subjects is more likely than that system to be substantially influenced by the recent initiatives of the MSC, though it is interesting to note how keen some of the GCE boards are to become involved in the development of graded tests, even for this group. In the case of the proposed 17+ examination, or Certificate of Pre-Vocational Education, which is increasingly becoming a major site of conflict over examination policy, it is certainly more likely that the views of the industrial trainers will predominate. Some of those most centrally involved, the Business and Technician Education Council and the City and Guilds of London Institute, have already indicated that they would like to see its approach permeate the school curriculum below the age of 16 (CGLI/BTEC 1984). It is also possible that, in the aftermath of Sir Keith Joseph's Sheffield speech (Joseph 1984), the DES and the new Secondary Examinations Council will make a more consistent commitment to the views of this lobby and seek to change the nature of the examination system by sponsoring criterion-referenced assessment and insisting that TVEI should influence the curriculum of all pupils and not just those regarded as 'non-academic'. This was to some extent the implicit message in Joseph's statement, in launching the new GCSE system, that he was keen to see in it a much bigger practical element than in existing examinations (Norman 1984). Nevertheless, the actual subject criteria developed by the boards so far and the continuing role of the university-based GCE boards, especially in the award of the new 'distinction' certificate, seem likely to give the examination a traditional academic flavour for some time to come.[10]

So far, the public educators have failed to counter the loss of public confidence described above. Indeed, some elements of the public education alliance of the post-war era, for example Labour ministers and the CSE boards, can be seen to have helped, though in different ways, to undermine the legitimacy of some of the developments that had taken place under its aegis during the 1960s and early 1970s. In addition, it is apparent that the public educators have, through their overriding concern to secure a common system of examining almost regardless of its nature, permitted key questions about the content and control of that system to be decided by the other parties involved.

In practice, this has meant that, with the relative decline of the CSE model of school examining, the teaching profession itself has effectively lost some of the control over the system it has been exercising in recent years. Meanwhile, its traditional allies in the public education lobby, the left and the Labour movement, have become increasingly divided over the best way to proceed. Initially, their stance in the 16+ debate paralleled their involvement in the development of comprehensive education itself, with the major emphasis being placed upon the achievement of a common organizational structure and the presumption that teachers should decide on the content of that structure. When the Labour government signalled its abandonment of the position that the nature of the school curriculum was an issue that could legitimately be left to the professional judgement of teachers, and seemed to place its weight behind the industrial trainers' lobby (Callaghan 1976), the left and the Labour movement lacked a clear position. Some sections of it continued to back the traditional policy of professional autonomy, others backed the parliamentary leadership, whilst still others seemed to favour the old humanist position as offering space within which socialist teachers could resist corporate encroachments into education. What was not in evidence was any attempt to develop and insert into the debates on curricula and examinations a distinctively socialist position around which to mobilize. As it became clear that conventional notions of teacher autonomy were no longer able to command widespread support, this absence was a crucial one and it allowed the issues to be contested between the old humanists and the industrial trainers, neither of whose approaches was primarily egalitarian or democratic in orientation.

## Policy implications

It is tempting, and perhaps even consoling, for those on the left to argue that a distinctively socialist policy on curricula and examinations would either be an irrelevance or doomed to failure in the face of capital's need to restructure the education system in its interests. Yet this study of the examinations controversy suggests that, although the genesis of many recent state initiatives may have been related to an attempt to secure the conditions of existence for a new phase of capitalism, the outcomes have not in any straightforward sense been a determined effect of capitalist economic imperatives. Outcomes are achieved through ideological discourse and political struggle and there is considerable scope for resisting such imperatives, as the old humanist lobby appears to have done in this particular instance. The left has a propensity to fall victim to its own theories, so that theories of tendency too often and too easily become statements of necessity which effectively obscure possibilities for contesting the terrain upon which tendencies become real outcomes. This is not to suggest that socialist alternatives can readily be established within an educational system of a capitalist society, but that mobilization around such alternatives can produce different compromises, some of which are more likely to provide secure bases for future struggles than others. Thus, it should not be assumed that a more positive intervention by the left in the examinations controversy, based upon a programme distinct from that of either the old humanists or the industrial trainers, and superseding a blind commitment to professional autonomy, would have been without significant effects. Just as the actual compromise now achieved by the intervention of the supposedly 'residual' old humanist elements within British society is decidedly different from that which might have been read off from the more economistic theories that have been used to account for recent developments in education, so a rather more progressive outcome might also have been attainable. There is therefore every reason for the left to develop a new position on curricula and examinations as part of the broader political strategy of the labour movement.

Indeed, the development of such a position can be seen to be a matter of some urgency when it is recognized just how fragile the emergent settlement discussed in this chapter actually is. I have already pointed to a number of tensions in the foregoing debates, and particularly that between 'standards' and 'relevance'. These are likely to re-emerge as the industrial lobby comes to recognize just how little impact it has had on that part of the educational system that so often defines its prevailing ethos. As we saw in the previous chapter, TVEI and Sir Keith Joseph's Sheffield speech represented an admission that many of the changes sought at the start of the Great Debate had not come to fruition. Even if the demise of the Schools Council and its replacement with separate councils for curricula and examinations represent a further blow to the professional wing of the public education lobby, the continuing tensions between academic and pre-vocational styles of education leave open the possibility that a new intervention could have some effect.

Proposals for a more genuinely democratic and responsive system of school assessment could exploit some of these tensions and gain support from some of the groups uneasy about the current settlement. Much could be learnt from the more devolved approaches to examining, such as those developed by TWYLREB in the 1960s, but devolution would need to be conceived not just as devolution to the grass-roots teacher, but devolution well beyond the bounds of the profession. By responding to criticisms of professional control, while resisting the narrow or élitist alternatives offered by the industrial trainers and the old humanists, the Labour movement might thus begin to build an alternative that could command widespread support and contribute to the realization of its political objectives.

However, it is obviously possible to argue that my detailed consideration of the debates over the 16+ proposals reveals merely an indeterminacy of outcomes in the case of struggles between different fractions of the dominant order, that is the old humanists and the industrial trainers. It might therefore tell us nothing about the real possibilities for oppositional ideological interventions in the present conjuncture, and concern only a struggle between two alternative cultural forms, both of which are entirely compatible with the successful performance by the state of the functions that it carries out on behalf of capital. Indeed, it might be argued that the differences between the industrial trainers and the old humanists in terms of the structures of curricula and assessment that they favour, as opposed to their overt content, are minimal and that my data does nothing to call into question even a relatively simplistic form of neo-Marxist theory. Alternatively, it might be suggested that, although the changes are not entirely in keeping with the demands of industrial capitalists, they will turn out to be functionally well-adapted to the needs of a British economy dominated by finance rather than industrial capital – though this argument would surely qualify for Nowell-Smith's category of 'devious' if not 'metaphysical'. Rather more plausibly, it can certainly be argued that not only does the emergent compromise between the industrial trainers and the old humanists lie well within the limits of what Kellner (1978) terms hegemonic ideology, so would any settlement that might have arisen from a more concerted intervention by the public educators into the debate.

Nevertheless, it seems implausible that all settlements within the ideological and political spheres are somehow equally functional for capital and that the differences between the possible settlements are totally irrelevant to the capacity of the state to carry out its long-term function on behalf of capital. This depends upon the relationship of any particular settlement to the outcomes of other struggles within the apparatuses of the state. Indeed, if the various possible settlements that do fall within the limits of what is appropriate for the performance of the functions of the state are the product of concrete historical struggles, so arguably is the securing of those limits. There is therefore no compelling reason to preclude the possibility that oppositional interventions in and around education might make important contributions to the nature of the settlements achieved therein, and perhaps even to broader oppositional struggles in society.

On the other hand, some people would argue that only my myopic concentration on one particular issue within education has led me to exaggerate the possibilities for change within education and even to assign to those possibilities some broader societal significance. Thus, it could be argued that, even if my claims are valid in respect of the outcome of the controversy about school examinations (and this would by no means be universally accepted), other developments in and around education can be seen to illustrate quite clearly the capacity of the state to functionalize education for capital regardless of minor setbacks in particular sectors. As we saw in the last chapter, this is essentially the argument put by Finn and Frith (1981), in respect of the role of the MSC. A similar argument has been used with regard to the control and legitimation functions of assessment to explain the rise of the DES

Assessment of Performance Unit (APU) alongside the public examination structure. Thus, Broadfoot has argued:

> The new mechanisms of control being developed around the world, such as the English APU, can be seen as the ideal answer to the current need for 'kid glove' control techniques. On the one hand, even the testing of a very small proportion of children when it is conducted on a national basis by those who hold the financial and bureaucratic power in the educational system – the DES (predictably to be emulated ere long by the local education authorities) – may well have a major impact on the educational system in allowing the State through the APU a new means of influencing educational content and standards. In this case it is conceivable that we shall soon witness a return to a more utilitarian emphasis in education . . . education geared only to basic competencies, the labour requirements of a technological society and the development of appropriate attitudes rather than free expression and personal development. On the other hand, external control of the content and practice of schooling in this form, rather than via a return to more formal control through either a nationally imposed curriculum . . . or a resurgence of Mode 1 style external examinations based on externally devised syllabuses, prevents a more direct confrontation with the powerful lobby of liberal interests supporting school and teacher autonomy. Thus teacher-developed curricula and teacher-conducted Mode III assessments . . . are rendered largely impotent as potential agents of educational 'liberation' . . . and by these unobtrusive accountability controls. We are currently witnessing an international 'shortening of the reins' to guard against any tendency of the educational system to swing too far towards the expansion of opportunity, thereby subverting its equally crucial role in the process of social reproduction. (Broadfoot 1979: 81–2)

Although I would accept parts of this assessment of the role of the APU, I would of course want to argue that there has also been a resurgence of Mode 1-style examinations. Yet the form that they have taken does not make them the equivalent of APU testing and is not likely to produce quite the narrow utilitarian emphasis that Broadfoot believes may be the outcomes of the latter. More significant here, though, is the question of whether such developments ensure that the restructuring of education required by capital will take place by one means or another, whatever resistance is forthcoming from within the educational system.

Certainly the phenomena described by Finn and Frith and by Broadfoot point to a continuing attempt to gear the educational apparatuses of the state towards the reproduction and legitimation of capitalist social relations, even while the process has encountered resistances and exhibited contradictions. It is also clear that my account of conflicts between different elements of the dominant order provides no positive evidence that oppositional interventions in the struggles over the nature of education would be potentially significant. I would want to suggest, however, that the maintenance and re-establishment of hegemonic ideologies through (among other things) education, is essentially a precarious endeavour in which resistances can, in certain circumstances, become significant for the perpetuation or interruption of tendencies towards reproduction. In the case of the MSC and the APU, the very inability of capital to produce the straightforward response in the schools, which the accumulation crisis is deemed to necessitate, has resulted in an increase in state expenditure on new modes of control without an equivalent reduction in those spheres that have produced an inadequate response. It could be argued, therefore, that the contestation of state initiatives on the content and control of the curriculum has the potential to pose problems of both 'sense' and 'value' (Dale 1981; Habermas 1976) for the state. Whether or not those problems are ultimately significant ones, however, is dependent on their articulation with similar resistances and political struggles elsewhere, and on the general disposition of political forces in relation to those struggles. This is why, to be effective, interventions by teachers in their professional contexts need to be linked more consciously with broader political movements. The importance of this will be further highlighted by the case study of social and political education contained in the next chapter, which also emphasizes the value of introducing an historical dimension into sociological studies of the contemporary curriculum.

# 7

## Continuity and change in social and political education

We have seen how, in the context of national initiatives on the curriculum and examinations, some of the expectations of industry and government have not been realized because of the continuing strength of old humanist traditions, particularly associated with the universities. We have also seen that the public educators, and especially the teaching profession, have been much less successful in sustaining their own definition of the situation at that level. However, it is important not to discount entirely the role of the teaching profession in sustaining definitions of curricular knowledge, even if it is clear that it is now less dominant than during the era of social democratic consensus, or when Eggleston (1975) claimed that 'teachers' own consciousness' was probably more significant in that process than curriculum development agencies or school examination boards. Particularly in a devolved system of education like that in England, but even in more centralized systems (Broadfoot 1983), teachers retain considerable power to resist curricular initiatives at the point of implementation. This is especially significant where professional power becomes articulated with that of a powerful interest group outside the school. Thus, one of the reasons why old humanist traditions have retained their strength in England lies in the fact that they are both closely articulated with the wider cultural values of British society (Wiener 1981) and highly influential within the professional culture of the teaching profession. In particular, such values dominate the high status sectors of the profession and, as Goodson (1983) points out, the road to status, power and resources for school subjects and their teachers conventionally involves the adoption of academic values at the expense of utilitarian or pedagogic ones. In defending their view of the curriculum, then, the old humanists have had considerable tacit support from within the teaching profession.

Thus, at least in such circumstances, professional culture at the chalk-face retains a certain capacity to be resistant to change initiated elsewhere, even if its role is often essentially defensive. This poses a problem not only for governmental and industrial attempts to give schools a more utilitarian bias, it also poses problems for those who wish to see schools as a context within which critical insights into the nature of the wider society can be developed. I now want to explore this theme further by examining the articulations between political and professional processes in the area of social and political education. In doing so, I draw upon some of the historical and ethnographic studies of social studies teaching in which I have been engaged over the past ten years (Gleeson and Whitty 1976, 1982).[1]

## The English tradition

Overt social and political education has never commanded the widespread support in England that education for citizenship appears to command in the USA and elsewhere. Although there have been successive attempts to legitimate greater curriculum provision in this field, they have often fallen foul of the considerable resistance amongst English educators to the idea that education should 'serve the needs of society' in any direct or obvious manner. The fact that practical and vocational education have always enjoyed low status within the English educational system, when compared with an education grounded in liberal humanist conceptions of culture, has tended also to militate against anything which might smack of citizenship training. As a relatively stable society, England has generally favoured implicit means of socialization into the status quo and has thus been much less overtly obsessed with the need to inculcate pupils with its dominant ideology than societies experiencing rapid social change or trying to legitimate a new political regime.

Unlike the USA, England was not faced in the early years of this century with welding together a disparate immigrant population and, unlike the Soviet Union, it was not faced with the initiation of pupils into a new political ideology. In addition, as we have seen, high status knowledge in English education has been firmly associated with the academic disciplines and hence with knowledge that tends to be literate, abstract, differentiated and unrelated to everyday life (Young 1971b). For much of this century overt state control of the school curriculum was progressively reduced and control was, especially in the period between

1945 and 1975, exercised largely through teachers' professional ideologies and a particular conception of professionalism (Grace 1978). Taken together, these features of the English educational system helped to give it an appearance of relative autonomy from its economic and political conditions of existence.

This is not, of course, to claim that even in the past education in England has been without economic and political significance. Various writers have suggested not only that such autonomy is often more limited than it appears, but also that apparently autonomous educational systems play a vital role in social and cultural reproduction (Bourdieu and Passeron 1977). Nor, indeed, has social and political education been absent from English schools. What I am pointing to here is a difference in the form in which, and perhaps in the degree to which, it has been a major feature of our schools when compared to those of many other countries. The dominant tradition of social and political education has remained that which was derived from the English public schools, in which the children of the ruling class have traditionally been educated. Here implicit socialization via the experience of the school's regime combined with the study of Ancient Greece and Rome to provide what social and political education was deemed necessary. As mass secondary education developed in this century, this high status curriculum (somewhat updated) was aped by the state grammar schools. Though academic history and geography courses grew in importance as classical studies declined, any suggestion that they were or should be vehicles for overt political education (as opposed to components of a 'liberal education') was always hotly contested. It is interesting to note, in view of my earlier remarks about social and political education being most in evidence where there was a perceived problem of social control, that what overt and explicit education for citizenship *has* always existed in English schools has been directed largely towards the children of the working class. Thus, for instance, a rather passive concept of education for citizenship, in the form of civics and similar courses, was a significant feature of the curriculum of the secondary modern schools. Yet even before these combined with the grammar schools to form comprehensives in the 1960s and 1970s, the grammar school tradition had tended to become the dominant one.

While overt education for citizenship has continued to exist in the lower streams of the comprehensive schools, it has generally been considered a low status activity amongst teachers when compared with academic history and geography teaching, and teachers of these latter subjects have consistently distanced themselves from those concerned with social studies, social education and citizenship. A Royal Geographical Society memorandum of 1950 (Royal Geographical Society 1950) deplored the growth of social studies in secondary modern schools and urged geographers to resist any further incursions by the social studies lobby, especially in the grammar schools. It claimed that social studies, even with a geographical bias, would not be as effective in producing 'intelligent and enlightened citizens' as a curriculum which included a conventional geography syllabus. It suggested that the effect of social studies on learning was similar to the effect of squeezing on a lemon – 'the juice is removed, and only the useless ring and fibres remain'. Its defence of the educational value of geography teaching was echoed by Burston's defence of traditional history teaching in an Historical Association pamphlet of 1954 (Burston 1954), though in somewhat more measured terms. Similar defences of the curricular status quo have continued ever since and these entrenched traditions have made change in this area of the curriculum difficult even in circumstances where it has been supported by powerful interests outside the educational system.

I now want to discuss three specific attempts to change the nature of social and political education within the secondary school curriculum. These attempts – by the social studies movement of the 1940s and early 1950s, the new social studies movement of the late 1960s and early 1970s, and the political education movement of the late 1970s and early 1980s – have all sought in their different ways to make explicit teaching about and/or for life in contemporary society a more central feature of the school curriculum. In looking at attempts to challenge the prevailing state of affairs, we can see something of the complexity of the influences that have sustained the mainstream curriculum model. Proponents of the three reform movements under consideration tended to see their subject as more meaningful and relevant than much of the conventional curriculum. In addition, although they differed in the particular visions of society that they espoused, they shared a view that curriculum reform in the area of social and political education could contribute to a reduction in the mismatch between their vision of the 'good society' and unacceptable aspects of society as it was or as it looked like becoming.

Yet all three have so far failed to make the impact on the school curriculum that they desired, let alone achieved the broader social ends to which they felt their respective approaches would contribute. In tackling the problem of change in different ways, the experiences of all three movements help us to recognize important elements in the dynamics of curricular continuity and change. However, it is only in bringing the three cases together that we begin to understand how it is the articulation between political and professional processes that generates reproductive or potentially transformative effects. We can then also recognize the need for any effective strategy of change to be operative at both these levels (and probably more) if it is to change the existing pattern of provision and contribute to the sorts of broader ends that the more radical proponents of these reform movements intended.

## The social studies movement

The fate of the social studies movement of the 1940s and 1950s has been chronicled many times (e.g. Cannon 1964). This rather amorphous movement was heralded with extravagant claims which have, in fact, made precious little impact upon the English educational scene. Whilst it was not a truly radical movement, since one of its major obsessions was to develop education to fit the changing demands of British capitalism and democracy after the war, it did propose significant changes in our system of schooling. It opposed the prevailing élitism of the English educational system and proposed alternatives that would open the way for a more 'healthy' society. The argument was that social studies should form a backcloth to more specialist studies and allow 'every child to feel himself [sic] to be closely associated with the past and present struggles and achievements of mankind, and to have a personal contribution to make towards future progress' (Hemming 1949). James Hemming explictly argued that pupils following courses 'broadened by Social Studies carried on with plenty of project work' were 'adventurous in outlook, approachable and articulate, eager to give their minds to new problems'. Those who followed a curriculum composed entirely of academic subject-based courses had, on the other hand, 'a marked tendency to be parochial in outlook, reserved, conditioned *against* change'. Hemming's ideas had a lot in common with the ideas of American progressivism, and there was a further parallel in the concern of two other influential writers of this time, Dray and Jordan, to ensure 'orderly change' in a society facing the dual threats of totalitarianism or anarchy (Dray and Jordan 1950). It may, of course, be argued that had the social studies movement succeeded in transforming the educational system to produce the creative, flexible and tolerant citizens Hemming envisaged, they would have bolstered British capitalism more success-fully than has in fact happened. It remains the case, however, that despite making some initial headway in secondary modern schools, this movement fell foul of the traditionalism of the British school system even before its impact on the outside world could really begin to be assessed.

The strength of 'subjects' as the central organizing category for the English school curriculum, combined with the jealous defence of the occupation of those subject slots by more traditional subjects, made the foothold of social studies increasingly tenuous as the secondary modern schools came under strong pressure to compete with the grammar schools on the latter's terms. The introduction of grammar streams into many secondary moderns, together with the eventual acceptance of the idea that they could enter pupils for academic examinations, made the struggle of a new and relatively unconventional subject to survive in the climate of the English secondary education an unequal one. There was a romantic, even epic, quality to the efforts by Hemming and his associates to transform the nature of the curriculum, efforts which, of course, they have not yet entirely abandoned (Hemming 1980). In the 1950s, however, the reforming promise of the social studies movement was certainly not fulfilled. Only the more explicitly conservative features of the tradition remained as a target for its successor, the 'new' social studies movement of the 1960s. The divisiveness by which social studies often found itself restricted to the bottom streams of secondary modern schools ultimately served only to maintain the élitism of English schools and society.

The incorporation of social education into the 'pastoral' rather than the 'academic' provision of many schools, especially for so-called Newsom pupils, also served to reinforce its low status in relation to increasingly dominant grammar school traditions. Even the limited legacy that did survive was hardly the active one Hemming envisaged, but rather a passive one in which activity and involvement did not seem to go beyond the ability to fill in an income tax form, remember the name of the local mayor or decorate an old woman's kitchen without pausing to consider why she was permitted to exist in such squalor anyway. Small wonder that their critics dismissed such courses in 'life adjustment' as 'social slops' and sought for alternatives which encouraged pupils to look critically at society rather than passively accepting their lot in a society seemingly beyond their control. The social studies movement, although it had consciously challenged the prevailing social relations of the school, had ultimately made no significant impact either there or in society at large.

It may now prove useful to consider its fate in terms of the three curricular traditions which Goodson (1983) calls academic, utilitarian and pedagogic. If we do so, we can see that, in refusing to conform to the requirements of the first of these and combining elements of the other two, the social studies movement was doomed to marginalization in a situation where the academic tradition was reasserting its dominance even in schools supposedly intended to foster the alternatives (Banks 1955). This was the case despite the fact that proponents such as Hemming (1949) and Dray and Jordan (1950) often tried to present their arguments in terms of the benefits that the new approaches would bring to society as a whole. At this time, however, political priorities for the education system were far more directed towards an expansion of the pool of educated labour than towards the precise nature of the political socialization of the workforce. The social studies movement was thus not in a position to benefit from either the professional or the political priorities of its time.

## The new social studies

It may be that the future will provide a more fertile climate than the 1950s for Hemming's attempt to challenge the hegemony of the academic subject at the heart of professional thinking, but it is clear that the first social studies movement of the post-war period of reconstruction died partly as a result of the reassertion of its hegemony at that time. On the other hand the emergent movement of the 1960s, that of the new social studies, chose to make a virtue out of what it saw as necessity. Far from challenging the central values of the English educational system, this movement sought to establish itself by celebrating at least some of those values and adapting itself to others. The problem for the new social studies movement was not so much the form of the curriculum as its content, even if it did envisage some degree of weakening in what Bernstein (1971) was later to term the classification between different contents and between school and the outside world. Even so, classification between school knowledge of the outside world and street knowledge of that world was rigidly maintained as is evident in the data of Keddie (1971) and Gleeson and Whitty (1976).

Initially, the new social studies movement in England combined an overt attack on the uncritical nature of existing social studies courses in secondary modern schools, and on the lack of rigour in Hemming's alternatives, with a rather more implicit critique of the lack of relevance in the conventional academic curriculum of the grammar schools. Thus Lawton and Dufour, in the standard reference book for the new social studies in England, mounted a dual case in support of the inclusion of social science in the school curriculum:

1 The practical need for young people to develop an awareness and understanding of their own society, illustrated by the statements made in such Reports as Crowther and Newsom that young people need to be 'less confused by' or to be able to 'find their way about' in a complex, industrial (and welfare) society.
2 The fact that our world is increasingly a social-scientific world ie that social science as a form of knowledge is increasingly important to a balanced understanding of the universe.

(Lawton and Dufour 1973: 26)

The first of these seems, in some ways, little different from the rhetoric of some of the more conservative forms of citizenship education designed to fit pupils into society as it is, while the second can be read as an appeal to the advocates of a liberal education based on initiation into 'public forms of knowledge' (Hirst and Peters 1970) not to ignore the social sciences as a form of knowledge that ought to be represented in the school curriculum. But it seems clear that many of the advocates of the new social studies saw their subject as offering a much more critical perspective on society than their public rhetoric of legitimation revealed. Rather than being committed to the fine tuning of society in terms of its traditional values and ideals, even some of the more cautious members of the new social studies movement argued on occasions that a social science based social studies should encourage 'a critical approach to the values of society' (Lawton 1968). Others implied that the exposure of pupils to the knowledge generated by the social sciences would remedy 'half-truths' and make pupils 'critically aware' of the extent to which their own common-sense ideas were distorted by bias and prejudice. The alternative firm foundation of 'true knowledge of the social structure and the social processes' (Dufour 1970), generated by the social sciences, would seemingly provide a basis for critical thinking about social reality. Social justice within education would be achieved by making the 'best' of all knowledge available to all and some supporters clearly harboured the hope that social justice might ultimately be served by the use of such knowledge as a basis for the changing world. At the very least, the teaching of the supposedly universalistic knowledge generated by the social sciences was expected to free pupils from the parochial and implicitly conservative outlook many earlier social studies courses had merely served to reinforce.

However, while the rhetoric of the movement stressed both rigour and relevance, and while some of its advocates saw it as having considerable radical potential, it was so obsessed with the need to avoid the fate of Hemming's earlier initiative that, in practice, rigour was stressed at the expense of relevance. Unlike Hemming, the advocates of the new social studies recognized quite clearly the particular role of academic subjects in English education. Most conventional subjects, and certainly those with high status, had a strong sense of continuity with subject communities in higher education. Newcomers were recruited to the profession via a narrow process of professional socialization that, for grammar school teachers, was almost exclusively subject-based. Clearly, the stress on the subject and initiation into its mysteries relates closely to prevailing patterns of segmentation within the teaching profession in England (Warwick 1974) and the new social studies movement tried to use this feature of the situation to its advantage. Recognizing that the fate of earlier social studies movements had been tied up to a lack of commitment by its teachers to a subject, and the tendency of schools to allocate to it teachers with other subject identities or none, the new social studies movement was determined to give social studies as strong a subject identity in conventional terms as possible. Most of those associated with the movement were social scientists, as was the case with the American New Social Studies Movement, but in the English case the lobby was essentially one of sociologists seeking to establish sociology in the curriculum for the first time. English historians and geographers do not regard themselves as social scientists, while at that time economists and political scientists seemed content with the rather limited place they already occupied within sixth-form academic studies. What the sociologists sought to do was both establish their own discipline at examination level and reform low status social studies courses by injecting into them the academic rigour of sociological perspectives. This was clearly recognized as providing the best route to status and resources for the subject and its teachers and hence as providing the best chance of placing what the proponents saw as a valuable educational experience on the curriculum of all pupils. In view of the ways in which other subjects had received recognition in the past (Goodson 1983), this was arguably an appropriate occupational strategy.

The thrust of the movement was, then, to establish sociology and a sociology-based social studies as a subject like any other in the school curriculum. While some of those involved would now say that this was a conscious attempt to use the space offered by the academic emphasis in English education for radical purposes, such a perspective was often lost in a quest to achieve equal status with other academic subjects. This meant that the earliest social science courses in English schools were often based on the transmission of the sort of implicitly functionalist sociology that was already beginning to be rejected by radical students in higher education as a form of conservative ideology, but which still constituted the basis of respectable academic sociology. More significantly, the social relations of social science teaching in schools were generally based on a traditional transmission model of learning, even if the methods employed often involved worksheets rather than chalk-and-talk. Above all, the emphasis on emulating other academic subjects led to the relative neglect of the dimension of relevance and thus detracted from the meaningfulness of the subject to the pupils. As Denis Gleeson and I have argued at length (Gleeson and Whitty 1976), this served to defuse most of the radical potential the movement may initially have held. Even when the earlier content was replaced with supposedly more 'critical' concepts and perspectives, it was often taught with scant regard for its meaningfulness and relevance to pupils and, in particular, to working-class pupils. The undue emphasis on teaching the concepts and structures of the social sciences as a basis for increasing critical awareness produced a social studies which was sometimes even less meaningful to pupils than earlier conservative and parochial approaches. Concepts only become tools of critical analysis and the basis of action in the real world if they are first of all recognized as meaningfully related to the world as it is experienced by pupils. Thus, social studies has to be meaningful before it can become critical in any strong sense of the term. In the absence of this, social science tends to be perceived by pupils as having little more than certification value and, as such, articulates with their 'cultural capital' in a similar way to other academic subjects, and thus performs a similar role in the process of social reproduction. In this sense, as in others, the new social studies followed what Goodson (1983) sees as a common evolutionary profile for aspiring school subjects.

It is, however, one of the ironies of the situation that the attempt to establish social science as another high status academic subject has not only militated against it being meaningful to students, and hence a possible basis for social action for change, it also seems to have failed even in its own terms. In the changing political context of the past few years there have been, as we have seen, growing demands that subjects should be 'useful' and the curriculum has once again come under scrutiny from extra-professional quarters. As I have argued earlier, this has been successfully resisted, to some extent, by defenders of the liberal humanistic conception of education, but what is noticeable is that sociology and social science-based social studies figure hardly at all either in external demands for useful subjects or in the defence by liberal humanists that certain subjects have an inalienable right to a place in the curriculum, irrespective of their immediate utility. While part of the explanation might lie in sociology's (often unwarranted) reputation for being a critical and subversive subject, it seems possible that it is as much a result of its reputation as being largely irrelevant to the real world. Even those approaches which have attempted to meet earlier criticisms of the new social studies on this score seem to have done so too late to command favour. For the present, sociology remains as a somewhat marginal examination option subject in schools, much more vulnerable to the effects of falling rolls than either history or geography, and as a significant examination subject in further education, where it is nevertheless potentially susceptible to the renewed emphasis on vocationalism in that sector. Elsewhere in the curriculum, the influence of the new social studies movement has been limited and regionally varied. Though there are now many social studies and humanities courses with some social scientific content, they have by no means replaced other approaches or succeeded in overcoming the subject's relative marginality and lack of status.

In Goodson's terms, then, we might say that, although initially the new social studies movement paid some lip-service to the alternative utilitarian and pedagogic traditions in English education, its central thrust involved the acceptance of the values of the dominant academic tradition. It therefore had to pay the price of renouncing 'practical connections and relevance to the personal and to the industrial and commercial world' (Goodson 1983). Yet, at the same time, it did not unequivocally gain the full fruits of joining that tradition in terms of resources, status, etc. Indeed, its only partial achievement of success in terms of Goodson's evolutionary profile left it vulnerable at a time when falling school rolls were putting pressure on the curriculum as a whole and when all but the most secure academic subjects were being subjected to renewed political demands that they should conform more to the utilitarian model.

## Political education

The third movement I wish to discuss here is the political education movement that rose to prominence in the late 1970s after a decade of quiet gestation. It was particularly associated with the Politics Association and the Hansard Society's Programme for Political Education, funded by the Nuffield Foundation and the Schools Council.[2] Its intention was to ensure that a particular form of political education relevant to the real world in which pupils live became part of every pupil's curricular experience. This involved developing pupils' 'political literacy', which it defined as involving 'the knowledge, skills and attitudes needed to make a person informed about politics, able to participate in public life of all kinds and to recognise and tolerate diversities of political and social values' (Crick and Porter 1978). This entailed a dual strategy of pressing for political education courses in schools while also fostering the political literacy approach in existing subjects. It also sought to get away from the over-academic approach to politics represented in most existing GCE syllabuses in the subject.

The political education approach to social and political education might thus have seemed well placed to provide meaningful starting points upon which a genuinely critical approach might be built and thus to avoid the pitfalls of the strategy of the new social studies. Indeed, there was a strand of thinking within the movement which argued that this was the case, seeing a parallel between attempts to develop the political 'literacy' of English school pupils and Paulo Freire's work in developing critical consciousness via adult literacy programmes in the Third World (Porter 1979). However, in general terms, the movement seemed more concerned to preserve rather than improve upon the basic form of society in which we lived. It was this that helped to place its ideas on the national political agenda and made it more clearly in line with 'national priorities' than either of the other movements we have been considering.

Despite the somewhat disparate nature of the educationists involved in the political education movement and even with the Programme for Political Education, many of the public statements emanating from it showed that it was far from clear that its leading members were committed to providing the context for a genuinely meaningful and critical education. The lobby's major publication, *Political Education and Political Literacy* (Crick and Porter 1978) was illustrative of the problems.

When it was published in 1978, it certainly cleared up some ambiguities about the movement's stance, but it also exposed many points of contradiction and glossed over other potential ones. While some of the work suggested in it might encourage the development of 'critical awareness', other examples might well produce the sorts of quietism or 'domestication' that were the outcome of traditional low status citizenship courses. Yet other examples seem to treat political education as another packaged commodity for pupils to consume, even though 'politics is par excellence a field to be mastered by learning by doing, by discovery through active experience' (Wright 1978). The experiential element of the featured courses consisted largely of visits, speakers, debates and simulations. Very little work was reported that was based upon active involvement in the politics of the community and the ideas of the more radical wing of the political literacy movement were certainly not in evidence in the report. However, if this left room for doubt about the central thrust of political education, the clearest indication of the movement's preferred strategy of legitimation could be seen in the way representatives described its work to the public and politicians. Here there was a clear tendency to shift the focus of the movement sharply towards a concept of political education as the production of uncritical, conforming citizens.

Thus, for example, in publicizing *Political Education and Political Literacy* in a radio interview,[3] Crick was asked whether more political education in schools would lead to demands for pupil power. He responded that, on the contrary, the pupil power movement had been the result of a *lack* of political education and then went on to make the point that, while the political education movement felt that schools should give consideration to extreme points of view, they should do so only after 'having gone through the ordinary, acceptable beliefs and institutions of society'. Even this was perhaps some advance on the academic version of Crick's ethnocentrism where he seemed to suggest that politics ceased when compromise and conciliation ceased – or, to quote Berridge's succinct statement of Crick's position, 'He offers us the politics of liberal-democracies as politics period' (Berridge 1978). Yet to argue that we should offer pupils evidence of alternatives in ways which try to predetermine their attitude towards them suggests a form of education only marginally more open than offering them no such evidence at all.

Another example came in an appendix to *Political Education and Political Literacy*. There it was suggested that the decline in public confidence in British political institutions was 'less to be associated with failings within the institutions themselves than with a failure to present . . . the broad principles and practice of Parliamentary politics to the public . . . in a systematic and purposeful way'. The writer, Chair of the Politics Association, went on to say that his association sought to end the long neglect of political education as the best long-term means of ensuring that 'the whole works' did not fall apart. It did not wish to exclude the *'consideration* of alternative ways of doing things', but it was in no doubt that schools and colleges should *'support* the principles and practice of parliamentary politics' (my emphases). In these circumstances the commitment to recognize its shortcomings and the existence of alternatives was little more than a formality. Although this position was scarcely surprising, since the Programme for Political Education was sponsored by the Hansard Society for Parliamentary Government and this particular paper was addressed to an audience of MPs, it was hardly encouraging to those who believed political education should involve a genuinely open consideration of alternatives.

The initial stimulus for the acceptance of political education onto the national political agenda lay in official anxieties about the confrontations between political groupings of the extreme right and left on the streets of London in the summer of 1977. In announcing grants for political education work by the National Association of Youth Clubs and the British Youth Council, members of the then Labour government explicitly drew attention to the drift towards extremism amongst the young and the need to win them back to the middle ground of British politics. More fundamentally, some observers have argued that the political education movement was part of an attempt to re-establish hegemony in a new phase of corporate capitalism. Explicit political education is seen in such analyses as necessitated by the collapse of the social democratic ideology in the face of contradictions in the system exposed by the re-emergence of mass unemployment (Jones 1978). Certainly the linking, in the Labour government's Green Paper on education (DES 1977), of studies of the democratic political system and studies of industry was an early indication of the intimate connection in official thinking between political education and the defence of present economic arrangements. As in a whole range of official pronouncements on economic and social policy, there was an almost Hegelian assumption that current forms of political and social organization were the ultimate end-point of human achievement and the role of education was therefore conceived in terms of defending them and extolling their virtues. Thus a senior Conservative Party spokesman on education at that time, Norman St John Stevas, demanded[4] that teachers of political education should give an undertaking to uphold the Crown and constitution, a demand clearly in conflict with recent traditions of autonomy within British education. There is then a fair amount of prima facie evidence that the success of the political education movement in mobilizing support from politicians was associated with their belief that it could assist in preserving the status quo and in bolstering respect for it in a period of economic crisis.

It therefore appears that many of those involved with the political education movement tended to seek sponsorship from those who advocated a utilitarian rather than an academic approach to curriculum planning. Certainly many of its proponents sought to distance themselves from the sorts of academic syllabuses that have traditionally constituted politics as an examination subject, though some were also concerned to revise these syllabuses in line with the new approach. In the context of the Great Debate and its aftermath, and the apparent political priorities of the period, it would thus seem that the political education movement was more clearly in tune with the ideological climate of the times than either of our other two cases. Yet, even in a situation where the traditional autonomy of the educational system has been under attack from powerful political forces, professional resistance to the introduction of political education has been remarkably strong and, at least to date, successful. Though the movement's own surveys indicate a not insubstantial amount of politics teaching in schools, much of this consists of long-standing examination courses or minor adjustments to the pastoral curriculum rather than an acceptance of the approaches of the Programme for Political Education. Indeed, in the very recent past, there seems to have been a renewed polarization between those advocating the academic study of politics and those concerned to integrate it into pastoral programmes of Personal and Social Development (David 1983).

It would therefore be wrong to infer, as might have been possible from looking at the two earlier movements, that the capacity of professional and institutional processes to resist reform is entirely contingent on the tacit agreement of hegemonic political forces in the wider society to let educationists manage their own affairs. Traditional professional values and practices remained remarkably strong and resistant to change even when educationist proponents of change were receiving overt support from powerful political interests outside the education system. Despite the undoubted value of a utilitarian rhetoric of legitimation in mobilizing the support of such external interests, such a stance still experienced considerable difficulty in countering the continuing dominance of academic values within the system. In the case of political education, resistance to change was clearly aided by the support of the wider old humanist lobby discussed earlier and by a greater ambivalence by the Conservative government towards the movement than had been shown by its Labour predecessor.[5] Yet, even before that, the portents for political education were far from good. How far and how long resistance to sustained external political pressure will be maintained in the long run remains, of course, a matter for curricular futurology. What seems certain, though, is that the conflicts will persist and possibly be heightened by initiatives such as TVEI and CPVE, outlined in previous chapters.

## Discussion

I now want to make some brief comments about the relevance of study-ing reform movements, such as those discussed in this chapter, for our understanding of the dynamics of curricular continuity and change and of the relationship between the curriculum and society. My initial comments will concern the extent to which data of the sort reported here can be related to sociological theories about the curriculum and the linkages between schooling and capitalism. I shall then consider the significance of these observations for those who wish to embark upon curriculum reform in the area of social and political education, and especially for those who regard it as a radical enterprise.

In looking just at the social studies movement and the new social studies movement, it would have been possible to infer that their impact was limited partly because (despite the claims of their proponents) their proposed reforms were out of line with the perceived political priorities of hegemonic forces within the wider society. Indeed, even regardless of the perceptions of those involved, it would be possible to argue in these cases that, although the *mechanism* of exclusion consisted of professional processes within the educational system, its *function* could best be interpreted in terms of the reproductive needs of society. Thus, the failure of these reforms, and in particular their more radical elements, could easily be understood in terms of some of the general theories adopted by sociologists to characterize the relationship between school-ing and the reproductive needs of capitalism (Althusser 1971; Bowles and Gintis 1976). It might be argued that, at the time of these reform movements, the traditional model of a grammar school curriculum was serving to reproduce the social relations of capitalism in much the same way as Bourdieu and Passeron (1977) suggest has been the case with the high status curriculum in France. In such contexts, there was little that reform groups could do to enlist the support of hegemonic interests outside the educational system to counter the internal hegemony of established professional interests within it. The reformers therefore had to face a choice between marginalization, the route taken by the earlier movement, and the acceptance of a standard evolutionary profile, for their subject, the preferred but not entirely successful solution chosen by the new social studies group.

However, even if such an interpretation were entirely sustainable in these first two cases (which, I would argue, it is not), the case for the political education movement is much less clear-cut in these terms. In this case, despite the existence of a small radical wing to the movement, its political thrust was very much in line with the expressed priorities of powerful political forces seeking to influence the educational system in the 'national interest'. This was a time when the autonomy of the education system was frequently identified in official pronouncements as a problem for British capitalism and when, in curricular terms, a 'utilitarian' approach was being officially sponsored as an alternative to the traditional academic emphasis. Yet, to date, prevailing curricular arrangements have generally been maintained in the area of social and political education. Despite the strength of political support for change, the minor adjustments that the political education movement has stimulated in the subject option system, or the pastoral curriculum, have certainly not significantly altered the curricular balance of power in such a way as to transform the ideological messages being transmitted or received. Therefore it might be argued that in this context the relative autonomy of professional processes from the direct imperatives of capital or liberal democracy was obstructing, rather than facilitating, the efficient reproduction of the sorts of social relations that would be maximally functional to capital in the present conjuncture. Any changes in the standard evolutionary profile for curricular subjects that might have been expected in the changing economic, political and ideological climate had yet to become evident. In appealing to external political forces to a much greater degree than to professional concerns, the political education movement thus underestimated the power of traditional professional values even at a time when they were under attack.

To this extent, detailed studies of curricular reform movements like these can help to make us sceptical of the cruder forms of sociological theory that regard the educational system in general, and the curriculum or professional processes in particular, as expressing in some direct manner the reproductive needs of capitalism. However, the data produced by such studies can, in no sense, be considered inconsistent with the majority of contemporary sociological theories, neo-Marxist or otherwise, which specify a general rather than a specific or constant relationship between schooling and capitalism. Those theories which see the relationship between capitalist production, the state and schooling in terms of contradictions and relative autonomies would clearly have little difficulty in accounting for the data presented here (Apple 1983; Young and Whitty 1977). Nevertheless, detailed studies in curricular history can help us to interrogate and refine those theories and this, in turn, can generate a form of theory better able to inform future studies of curricular continuity and change.

## Implications

To what extent, though, can such work be of value to curricular reformers themselves? Certainly this chapter makes it clear that social and political educators in the past have often based their strategies on an inadequate analysis of the context in which they have chosen to intervene. Thus, as we have seen, the social studies movement of the late 1940s displayed virtually no sociological understanding of the nature of the English school system and the professional values and processes associated with it. The new social studies movement of the 1960s, on the other hand, was extremely conscious of the status hierarchies of English schooling, but displayed only a limited insight into the ways in which they contributed to social and cultural reproduction. While recognizing the social significance of the existing divisive forms of curricular provision, it shared the widespread assumption that social justice would best be served by making available high status academic knowledge to all pupils. It certainly lacked the insight subsequently offered by Bourdieu and Passeron (1977) about the way in which an academic curriculum can itself be profoundly inegalitarian in its effects. It further failed to recognize the extent to which the espousal of conventional modes of professional practice would lead to co-option into an essentially conservative system, and thus to the frustration of much of the radical promise initially held by the movement. Equally, it did little to cultivate a political constituency outside the educational system that might have helped to sponsor its efforts. The dominant faction of the political education movement of the late 1970s, however, was clearly aware of the importance of mobilizing powerful political forces behind its conception of curriculum reform, though its more radical elements seemed unaware of the necessity of making links with other potentially counter-hegemonic forces, either within the professional arena or beyond it. At the same time, all wings of the movement seem to have underestimated the strength of traditional academic values and their associated professional processes.

In a sense, then, perhaps the central lesson to be drawn from all this is that curriculum reform movements should beware of studying and reacting to the fate of their immediate predecessors alone. The new social studies movement chose a strategy based on its reading of the causes of failure of the earlier one, while the political education movement was often consciously concerned to distance itself from the strategies associated with the new social studies. What the account given here certainly argues against is the drawing of strategic conclusions from such limited experience. Rather it argues for the development of historical and comparative studies of curriculum reform movements which, in a cumulative way, can contribute to the development of the sort of theory that can help us understand the complexities of past failures and their implications for new strategies of change in a new conjuncture. What the specific studies reported here demonstrate is that such understanding must embrace both professional and political processes in and around the curriculum if it is to be of value in informing the strategies of future reform movements.

For radical social and political educators, such understanding would seem to be particularly important, since it is the aspirations of this group that seem most consistently to have been thwarted in the developments discussed here. Not only do they need to define their own purposes more clearly, they must also make the fullest possible use of the available empirical and theoretical tools to understand the complex and contra-dictory nature of the professional and political context into which those purposes are inserted. If, as I have argued elsewhere (Gleeson and Whitty 1976), one of the purposes of a radical approach to social studies teaching itself is to assist students in an active exploration of why the social world resists and frustrates their wishes and how social action might focus on such constraints, then it seems only fitting that curriculum reformers in this field should themselves be engaged in such a task. The fate of past reform movements provides further justification for the claim that, for radical curriculum innovation to be potentially transformative in its effects, it requires a sociological understanding of the context within which it is being mounted, and a strategy of change that links significant elements of the teaching profession to a broader political constituency.

In substantive terms, a counter-hegemonic strategy seems likely to involve, at the present time, an approach to social and political education that is neither merely 'relevant' in a narrow sense nor merely 'academic' in its content. Rather, it would need to make sense to pupils in terms of their actual or potential experience outside the classroom but also involve critical reflection upon that experience and involvement in the development of strategies that might change it. To that extent, it would probably have something in common with the educational programmes adopted by nineteenth-century radical groups who, as we noted in chapter 3, characterized their concern as being with '*really* useful knowledge . . . concerning our conditions in life . . . [and] how to get out of our present troubles' (Johnson 1979a). It may well be that, in present circumstances, radical teachers committed to a programme of this nature would do better to take advantage of the space for such an enterprise offered by pressures for a closer relationship between school and the outside world than to defend the teaching of the social sciences *per se*. As Sharp (1982b) has remarked of work experience in schools:

> [It] throws up exciting curriculum possibilities. The class dimensions of the workplace, its sexual and ethnic divisions, its hierarchies, the social impact of technology, and the labor process itself are all easier to discuss when students have direct experience of everyday labor routines.[6]                                                                    (Sharp 1982b: 75)

Community studies and humanities programmes that link the de-velopment of critical understanding and the fostering of action skills per-haps provide the most fruitful context for the development of a genuinely meaningful and critical approach to social and political education.

Though, in the past, such programmes have had the support of only a minority within the teaching profession, in the present conjuncture conflicts between defenders of the academic model and those pushing the utilitarian alternative might well produce support for this approach from unlikely quarters within the profession and a willingness to compromise with it rather than accept the complete dominance of one of the other models.

Support for such an approach might, in addition, be found within the labour movement as an alternative either to the curricular status quo or the utilitarian model being advocated in official circles. It might, for instance, be worthwhile, in view of its current enthusiasm for the curriculum style of recent MSC initiatives, to remind the TUC that in its response to the 1977 Green Paper it not only argued that the secondary curriculum should be 'organised around relevant fields of study rather than on the basis of formal academic subject teaching', it also advocated avoiding preoccupation with the adjustment of young people to a particular set of prevailing employment and social conditions (TUC 1977). Ambiguous though that document was, it was clearly not just concerned to support generic skills training (Green 1983) nor to further the sort of course that outlawed critical forms of political education (Gleeson 1984). Rather, it warned about the danger of approaches that 'could reinforce the present assumptions about the role of labour' and argued for a critical awareness of the way standards and values are evolved. Providing, then, that such sentiments have not entirely given way to the notion that the role of education is merely to celebrate the system as it is, there is a significant political constituency there to be mobilized, just as there is amongst the large sections of the teaching profession who continue to believe that there is an important distinction to be made between education and indoctrination.

Most sociological commentators on recent curriculum trends have, however, been content to criticize the MSC's new vocationalism rather than help in the development of alternatives that might have some appeal to the labour movement. Cohen (1984) is an important exception, who has recently attempted to move on from a critique of the new vocationalism to develop with young school leavers an alternative approach to political education that differs both from conventional social studies practice and the social-and-life-skills ideology being fostered by the MSC with official TUC support. Rather like some of the Australian work discussed earlier in this book, Cohen is trying to develop a pedagogy based upon students' own styles of resistance. However, while this style of political education seeks 'to address the students' personal sense of priorities', and thus provide the meaningful element of social and political education, it also contains the critical dimension in attempting to challenge the students' tendency to accept the transition from school to un/employment as an essentially individual rather than collective phenomenon. Those involved are also attempting to develop a better understanding of what specific differences alternative practices in the field of political, social or anti-sexist and anti-racist education can make to particular groups of pupils. Despite the embryonic nature of these initiatives, their significance has been recognized by the left leadership of the Greater London Council and this suggests that there may now be some possibility that sections of the labour movement will begin to see the importance of developing new approaches to social and political education, rather than giving support to approaches that effectively serve contrary professional or political purposes. If more sociologists could, like Cohen, begin to demonstrate that the deconstruction of dominant ideologies in and around education was not an end in itself, but could also generate new modes of practice, their potential contribution to the work of radical teachers and to the broader political programme of the labour movement might gain wider recognition. In my final chapter, therefore I shall give further consideration to the possibilities of developing fruitful links between sociologists and political movements in the current context in Britain.

# 8

---

# *Sociologists and political movements: a resumé of the current issues*

I have consistently argued in this book that, in analysing the character and dynamics of ideological struggles over education and within education, it is vital to move beyond any notion that the educational apparatuses of the state respond in a mechanistic manner to the imperatives of capital or even the dominant fraction of capital. Similarly, the outcomes of crises are dependent on the disposition of political and ideological forces and are not in any simple sense necessarily functional for capital. While it would be difficult to deny that there have been some remarkable similarities between the ideological struggles fought out within and around education in advanced capitalist societies in recent years and, in particular, in those experiencing severe crises of capital accumulation, the outcomes of these struggles have varied. Thus it is understandable why, when exploring the forms in which these struggles have been played out, most contemporary sociologists have displayed something of a neurosis about following Althusser's injunction to hold on to 'both ends of the chain' between economic determination and the relative autonomy of political and ideological practice (Hall 1981). Yet, as we have seen, the temptation to emphasize one end at the expense of the other can lead to the production of simplistic accounts of the politics of the curriculum, which in turn can produce inappropriate political responses. I therefore want to consider in this final chapter the nature of an appropriate political response to the sorts of insights about the curriculum that may be derived from recent work in the sociology of school knowledge.

## Sociological and political practice

One of the important insights of the neo-Marxist phase of the new sociology of education was that the reproductive effects of schooling derived partly from the articulations between cultural forms and contents across different sites and practices within the social formation. It is for this reason that I also take the view that interventions within education can be regarded as effectively radical only when they have the potential to be linked with similar struggles elsewhere to produce transformative effects. This is why I have suggested, at various stages of this book, that professional processes alone are unlikely to bring about genuinely radical changes within the school curriculum, even when the professionals involved consider themselves to be radicals.

Though for much of the book my focus has been upon the limitations of radical professionalism amongst schoolteachers, similar considerations apply to professional sociologists of education within institutions of higher education. Too much supposedly critical scholarship assumes, rather like some of the approaches to social studies teaching discussed in chapter 7, that critical concepts have a radical effectivity regardless of the context in which they are generated and circulated. Although it would be dangerous to fall into the trap of instrumental rationality by arguing that all critical academic work should have a direct political pay-off,[1] such work can only become effectively radical if it can become meaningful within contexts of both pedagogical and political practice.

I stressed in chapter 4 that, although my own concern was with the relationship between sociological work and the pedagogical and political programmes of the radical left, this was not to deny the possibility of such work informing the policies of other political forces. Indeed, the work of O'Keeffe (1981) demonstrates that the potential exists for sociological analysis of the curriculum to be used consciously to influence the development of policy by the radical right. In addition, some observers have implied that left analyses of the curriculum have themselves been put to better use by the right than by the left. A recent editorial in the radical teachers' magazine *Teaching London Kids* noted, for instance, that:

> All Tory ministers seem to have been enlisted for the fight. Keith Joseph has tried to muzzle science teachers; Tebbitt to restrict Youth Training Schemes; Heseltine to intervene in the content of classroom resources [for peace education]. All are concerned about the social *content* of the curriculum and are trying to ensure that it never raises questions about the *status quo*. A thorough-going application of their awareness of social context, relationship and process marks out this Tory government; exploiting traditionally Left tools of analysis to further Tory aims.          (*Teaching London Kids* 1983: 2)

Even if radical journalism of this type verges upon conspiracy theory, it is true that, in the aftermath of the social democratic consensus, it has been politicians of the right rather than the left who have recognized the curriculum as a significant site of struggle. This may be evidence of the lack of an organic connection between sociologists who have been studying such issues in an academic context and the broader political movements of the left. I wish now to examine the potential for such a connection in contemporary Britain.

The cultural traditions of British academic life make the forging of such a connection particularly difficult, as do those of some of the political movements of the left. It has often been suggested that left academics within the sociology of education in the 1970s were even more guilty than others of failing to develop their work outside the academy. Indeed, as we have seen earlier in this book, it became something of an orthodoxy (Demaine 1980; Williamson 1974) that the so-called 'new sociology of education' of the early 1970s abandoned the Fabian policy-oriented tradition of the Halsey–Floud era and substituted for it a belief that the sociology of education could itself transform the world via its radical critique of the assumptions underlying the classroom and professional practice of teachers. It became a further orthodoxy that, on finding the consciousness of teachers less than easy to transform, and indeed not the root of the problem anyway, the new sociologists abandoned the world of educational practice in the mid-1970s and adopted a pseudo-revolutionary stance that refused to have any truck with the educational institutions of the capitalist state (Reynolds and Sullivan 1980) or with reformist political parties such as the Labour Party (Demaine 1980). This has led, according to some commentators, to a misguided and dangerous theoretical dogmatism on the part of neo-Marxist sociologists of education, which has sanctioned political inaction by the left and led it to neglect significant opportunities for pedagogical and policy interventions in and around state education.

Most of the writers whose work is discussed in this book espouse oppositional ideals, in the sense that they share a general assumption that it would be desirable to replace the prevailing systems of social relations in advanced capitalist societies with more democratic, egalitarian and equitable ones. However, they do differ in their views of what this change might involve in practice, and the best means of attaining it. They also differ in their assessment of the role of education within such a programme of social transformation. On the one hand, there are those who regard radical school reform as an appropriate gradualist means of achieving a fairer and more humane society, while, on the other hand, there are those who adopt the sort of revolutionary socialist perspective that regards all desirable change as predicated upon the prior overthrow of the capitalist mode of production. However, as we have seen, most contemporary analysts take a position somewhere between these two extremes and take the view that oppositional interventions in and around education can, in the current context, play a significant, albeit probably minor, role in social transformation when consciously linked with other policies committed to similar ends in other spheres. The question of what broader political movements oppositional struggles in education might be linked with is clearly one which will be answered differently in different situations, though I have suggested that Williams's (1973) distinction between alternative and oppositional aspirations might offer one source of criteria upon which decisions might be made.[2] At the same time, as Apple (1982c, 1983) has pointed out, there are occasions when alliances with liberal forces can usefully be entered into by the radical left so long as the basis and limitations of these alliances are recognized. I argued in chapter 4 that it had certainly never been part of my own analysis that particular arenas could be decisively written off as sites for oppositional struggle by theoretical fiat, and also pointed out that I did not take the view that either state education or the British Labour Party, let alone the wider labour movement, could be regarded as irrelevant sites of struggle in the current conjuncture.

Indeed, on the contrary, I regard the Labour Party and its affiliated organizations as amongst the most relevant political movements with which left sociologists of the curriculum concerned to bring about educational and social change should become involved. This view derives, of course, from my belief that existing patterns of class, race and gender relations should be radically transformed into socialist ones, but even those who agree with me that such a change is desirable may question the relevance of the Labour Party to such an aspiration. My view does not, however, rest upon the belief that the Labour Party is, by any means, an unambiguously oppositional party. It does, on the other hand, seem to me that, at the present time, it is one of the few contexts in which disparate forms of resistance to existing forms of social relations might become consciously articulated together into a coherent oppositional programme around which mass support might be mobilized. Certainly, those who oppose capitalism rather than wishing to see it preserved in an alternative form may currently be in a minority within the party, but it is a growing and far from insignificant one. Their presence within the party, alongside others who may be won to such a programme in the future, provides a base for further struggles far more secure than any likely to be found in disparate professional contexts or single-issue cultural movements. When we recall the difficulties left academics in America face in linking critical scholarship to broader forms of oppositional struggle, it is worth remembering that in

Britain we at least have a major political party that is constitutionally committed:

> To secure for the workers by hand or by brain the full fruits of their industry and the most equitable distribution thereof that may be possible upon the basis of the common ownership of the means of production, distribution and exchange, and the best obtainable system of popular administration and control of each industry or service.[3]

It may also be worth remembering that, when the Labour Party last returned to government after a period in opposition, it was on a manifesto committed to 'a fundamental and irreversible shift in the balance of power and wealth in favour of working people and their families'.[4] Whatever the limitations of the terminology employed in that commitment, it is arguable that it was the government's retreat from it, rather than any attempt to implement it, that helped to generate popular enthusiasm for the policies of the radical right.

If the Labour Party is, then, one of the contexts within which radical educational practices can become articulated with broader socialist policies, what role might sociologists committed to that end play in the process? I have suggested in chapter 4 that their role needs to be organic to the movement rather than imposed from outside. Indeed, it has been part of my argument that the failure of the sort of social democratic policy espoused by the Labour Party in the past has resulted not only from its content but also from the form in which it has been generated. The generation of future education policy should certainly not be the preserve of sociologists, teachers or professional politicians alone. Like Johnson (1981), I regard the handing down of policies by experts as inappropriate, but this is not to say that the contribution of such experts to the democratic policy-making process should be denied on the basis of a spurious populism (Ahier 1983). It may therefore be fitting to end this book with a resumé of some of the important insights that the sort of sociology of the curriculum I am advocating here might bring to a Labour Party in search of an education policy consistent with a political commitment to the transformation of the social relations of British society. This is not, I must stress, a blueprint for education in a socialist society, or even a transitional programme. Rather, it is an attempt to set out some of the curriculum issues that need to be given greater consider-ation by socialists within the labour movement than they have been given hitherto. To suggest that sociologists have a role in generating discussion of them is not to dichotomize the role of intellectuals in giving the party 'political knowledge' and the task of 'raising the activity of the masses of the workers' (Lenin 1975). It is to see them both as parts of an ongoing educative process, essential to a movement that seeks to transform the nature of economic, political and ideological/cultural relations.

## Issues facing the left

We have seen that the Labour Party leadership tended, even during the introduction of comprehensive secondary education, to argue that the traditional grammar school curriculum should be made available to all. It then seemed to switch much of its allegiance during the Great Debate to a version of the pre-vocational curriculum model. What it has rarely questioned is the view that these are the only alternatives and it has therefore done little to further the development of a curriculum specifically designed to foster the interests of the groups that it claims to represent. Even many of those in the Labour Party who have had doubts about this approach by the leadership have often argued that questions about curricula, pedagogy and assessment can only be sorted out when we have finally achieved a completely comprehensive institutional structure. This has left us in recent years with a system of secondary education that most people believe to be comprehensive but whose curriculum in no sense deserves that label. What exists in many comprehensive schools is an uneasy compromise between academic and pre-vocational models of education that satisfies no one and breeds the sort of dissatisfaction the right can mobilize in support of their reactionary policies. It is partly this failing that has given a certain amount of legitimacy to the idea of renewed institutional separation between different forms of schooling and even to proposals for the deconstruction of a common system of state education via an extension of privatization.

The analyses of curricular policy and practice carried out by sociologists over the past decade, which make the dangers of traditional social democratic policies abundantly clear, have clearly not made the necessary impact either amongst the leadership of the Labour Party or amongst the large numbers of parents of all classes who are persuaded that the Conservative analysis is the correct one (CCCS 1981). Yet, when we look at both the form and content of prevailing curriculum models, it is clear that neither the academic nor the pre-vocational approach as currently conceived serves the interests that the labour movement ought to be promoting. David Hargreaves (1982) points, for instance, to one aspect of the problem in a way that resonates with much of the analysis of the contemporary curriculum presented in the second part of this book. In his own book *The Challenge for the Comprehensive School*, Hargreaves comments:

> It is one of the saddest ironies of our age that the comprehensive school

should become so dominated by the academic, grammar-school curriculum, when . . . it is least suited to the needs of our time and least likely to pay occupational dividends to that section of working class pupils who have the capacity to master it.          (D. Hargreaves 1982: 71)

At the same time, Cohen (1984) points to both the inadequacies and the appeal of the alternative pre-vocational style of curriculum in claiming that: 'The unpleasant fact is that popular support for MSC initiatives . . . stems from the way they exploit *real* deficiencies in secondary schooling, while doing nothing to remedy them' (Cohen 1984: 161).

When one considers the wealth of sociological work that documents the social bases of these curriculum models, it is scarcely surprising that working-class groups, blacks and women have gained so little of value from exposure to such curricula. The academic curriculum reflects what Williams (1965) called a 'selective tradition' and much of it still represents the traditional culture of an élite as the only worthwhile knowledge. White upper- and middle-class male exploits dominate school history even today, while other groups are relegated to the sidelines and are seen to take a relatively passive part in events. Similarly, individual achievements continue to be granted more legitimacy than collective struggles within both the content and the form of much of the curriculum. Recent limited moves towards a greater emphasis on labour history, women's history and black history are now being condemned by conservative critics as diluting and distorting 'our' cultural heritage! So much of the academic curriculum still derives from the cultural experience of a ruling minority that vast numbers of pupils find little meaningful within it to relate to. Its very emphasis on separate academic subjects, apparently divorced from each other and from the world outside school, makes it difficult for pupils to use this curriculum to gain a critical purchase on the world in which they live. Such a curriculum thus helps, at least by default, to maintain existing social arrangements and their attendant inequalities and injustices.

But the pre-vocational model that is gaining increasing legitimacy in the lower status parts of our further education colleges and comprehensive schools, and is now being promoted by the MSC, should not be accepted as the answer either. Not only does it still remain a 'second best' for those adjudged to be failures in terms of academic criteria, it too encourages acceptance of the status quo. Many courses have the effect of making existing forms of work and work discipline appear natural rather than demonstrating the extent to which they are the product of a fundamentally unjust and inegalitarian system. Though such courses sometimes seem more meaningful to pupils than the academic alternatives, they are predominantly in the business of social control rather than social criticism. Many of the special courses now being introduced to cope with rising youth unemployment contain the implicit message that unemployment is the fault of individuals rather than the system that creates it.

Thus, in this curriculum again, favoured solutions to present difficulties are presented in individualistic rather than collective terms, thus posing no threat to the prevailing structure of social relations. Yet, the very term pre-vocational has a cruelly ironic, even cynical, ring to it at a time when there is mass unemployment and when many previously skilled crafts are being deskilled or even destroyed (Gleeson 1983). For girls, the domesticating function of courses in this part of the curriculum is often particularly stark as they still find themselves guided towards options that prepare them for work in the home and only for traditionally 'female' jobs outside it. Though socialists and feminists sometimes take heart from evidence of growing pupil resistance to such courses, this cannot of itself be regarded as an adequate substitute for the development of a coherent collective strategy to change them.

As is clear from the research reported in chapter 6 of this book, the potential for a renewal and consolidation of the division between academic and pre-vocational approaches to schooling can be seen especially clearly in the way policy on public examinations has developed under the Conservative government. For all the rhetoric about new forms of curriculum control and accountability we have heard in recent years, the examination system remains the single most important means of controlling the curriculum of English secondary schools. In current plans for the future of 16+ examinations, it still seems probable that the universities and the traditional model of academic education they espouse will continue to dominate that part of the curriculum that leads to such examinations. If so, it is unlikely that, whether or not there are any formal restrictions, the 'common' system will cater adequately for more than the 60 per cent of pupils for which the present system was designed, and it might conceivably cater for even less. This, in turn, would allow the government, aided by the MSC, to sponsor a much narrower instrumental and pre-vocational approach for the remaining 40 per cent. Similarly, in 16–19 education, the extremely narrow but academically oriented A-level system is to be retained (even if 'broadened' by equally academic Advanced Supplementary examinations), while the lower-level 17+ examination is to be dominated by vocational interest groups. Though there are those on the left who would have no truck with the examination system at all because of its individualistic and system-serving nature, there is a strong argument for contesting the nature of any system that does exist to try to make it a genuinely common one, based on a meaningful and critical curriculum, and with scope for collective as well as individual modes of assessment.

The lack of developed thinking on these matters does, however, make it tempting for the labour movement to collude with one or other of the prevailing curriculum models. As we saw in chapter 7, some trade unionists have tried to argue that the only way of resolving the continuing divisiveness represented in the curriculum, and of helping the recovery of British industry in the process, is to espouse the cause of pre-vocational education for all as an alternative to academic education for all. This was, of course, also the view held by the industrialists, who argued during the Great Debate that much of the failure of British industry was to be put at the door of the élitist and irrelevant education to which its future managers are subjected, a form of education which, they argued, had turned away from industry many of those people who in other countries might be attracted to it. Even Thatcherism, arguably less attached to traditional ruling-class culture than earlier forms of conservatism, has yet to grasp this nettle in a decisive manner, and it remains to be seen whether TVEI does have any impact on the high status as well as the low status curriculum. Be that as it may, it is clear that for the left, the concern should not be to revive and celebrate industry in its present form but to transform it so that it serves the interests of those it currently exploits. If the attraction of pre-vocational education lies in its appeal to relevance and meaningfulness in education, its disadvantage lies in its uncritical approach to the status quo. On the other hand, the elements of critique and rigour which some people argue are central to the academic curriculum are rarely actually used to probe the assumed merits of current social arrangements.

It is therefore vital for the labour movement to recognize that neither of the prevailing curriculum models will adequately serve the needs of the disadvantaged groups within our society. A genuinely comprehensive curriculum needs to be both meaningful *and* critical, and to ensure that its definitions of relevance and rigour are not ones that relate only to the culture and interests of those who at root support an inegalitarian society. The academic tradition has its roots in the curriculum of nineteenth-century public schools, designed to perpetuate an élite; the pre-vocational model is in some respects a modern equivalent of the nineteenth-century elementary tradition designed to control rather than emancipate the masses. Yet even socialist support for mass access to elementary education in the nineteenth century, and to secondary education in the twentieth, has often been accompanied by an uncritical attitude towards the sort of education pupils are to gain access to. Despite the fact that there were alternative traditions, including some interesting socialist educational alternatives outside the state system, these traditions have rarely informed the labour movement's policy on the content and control of state provision. Important as it is to defend state education as something from which disadvantaged groups can potentially gain, it is equally important not to defend the indefensible. Present approaches to curricula, pedagogy and assessment too often fall into this category. They must now be subjected to critical scrutiny and, where found inappropriate, contested. This is not to suggest that all aspects of existing curricular arrangements should be written off because of their social origin. It is to suggest that the value of many of them to working-class students and their current relevance to the political aspirations of the movements that claim to represent their interests has too often been taken for granted by the left.

One of the reasons why the left has given so little thought to the nature of the curriculum is that it has often held the view, at least in the post-war period, that such matters are best left to teachers. As we have seen, the Great Debate and subsequent attacks on teacher control over curricula and examinations have helped to put under strain the tacit understandings that existed about this between the teaching profession and the labour movement. Yet this need not necessarily have been an entirely reactionary development. It has effectively become that because the left has made no distinctive contribution to the debates about alternatives to conventional notions of teacher professionalism. While other groups in the community have been quick to make their own claims upon the school curriculum, the left has failed to develop, in conjunction with the political constituencies whose interests it claims to represent, a sense of a present-day equivalent of what nineteenth-century radicals dubbed '*really* useful knowledge'. This would presumably include an exploration of ways in which social injustices and inequalities could be investigated, questioned and eventually transformed (Ozolins 1979). The development of such a curriculum would surely have benefited from the insights generated by sociological analyses of the curriculum, and one might have expected socialist sociologists of education to be actively involved in such a process. Yet, despite Warwick's claim (Warwick 1974), few were involved even in the progressive and radical curriculum innovations of the 1960s and early 1970s, some of which espoused similar aims. Partly because of its lack of an adequate theoretical underpinning or a recognition of the need for a broader political base outside the profession, such work was easily marginalized and discredited by right-wing politicians and the media. In any future alliance between radical teachers and the labour movement, curriculum issues need to be matters of open discussion and collaboration from the start and sociologists of education could have a significant role to play in such a development.

## Possibilities and problems

Of course, one of the things that sociologists would almost certainly bring to such discussions would be a degree of caution, derived partly from the sort of study of past attempts at innovation that I offered in chapter 7. They would also be concerned to explore the possible conflicts between innovations designed to counter various types of disadvantage, whether of class, race or gender (Culley and Demaine 1983). More generally, they would be sceptical about the degree to which the development of a distinctive but popular socialist position on the curriculum could be established as the mainstream curriculum of the state educational system. Nevertheless, they would almost certainly suggest that, if the left were to develop and mobilize around a clearer view of an appropriate curriculum than it has espoused hitherto, it would at least have a chance of influencing the outcomes of current debates on the issue. Whatever may have been true of the neo-Marxist contributions of the mid-1970s, there is little within contemporary sociological studies of the curriculum to suggest that such interventions are either impossible or irrelevant to the political programme of the left. Rather, they tend to suggest that for the left to give uncritical support to any of the existing views of the curriculum, either actively or by default, is likely to help ensure that the system never even begins to serve the interests of those ill-served by existing arrangements.

Indeed, there are even some aspects of the analysis offered in this book that suggest that today's generally bleak educational scene gives certain grounds for a cautious optimism about the effects that a coherent intervention from the left might have. The idea that it is possible to create a form of curriculum that combines rigour and relevance is at least as appealing as the idea that the solution to disillusion with the current situation is greater division between them. The concern from both sides of industry about the nature and effects of existing academic curricula could lead to more support for such a development than might initially be expected. In addition, the effect of falling school rolls on school curricula is likely to be devastating in the next few years. In some schools, the very idea of a curriculum based upon discrete subjects may not remain viable for much longer and multi-disciplinary and integrated programmes may thus become a necessity. Whatever the failings of some of these programmes in the past, at their best they can offer considerably more space than conventional curricular arrangements for examining the nature of the disciplines and using them to explore meaningful issues in a systematic and critical way (Gleeson and Whitty 1976). In this situation, the choice between rigour and relevance can be exposed as an unnecessary one and one that no longer needs to bedevil discussion of the context and organization of the curriculum.

Indeed, if discussions about a core curriculum involved major rethinking along these lines, rather than just identifying which existing subjects should be in or out, then they could be a potentially progressive development. Yet the potential in all such situations has to be activated and this is why the left needs to develop and mobilize around policies on these issues, both professionally and politically. The same is true of other recent initiatives such as political education, multi-racial education and equal opportunities policies. Though increasingly treated with suspicion by conservatives as they gain confidence to pursue even more reactionary policies, these initiatives have ironically themselves often been conservative in their effects. Yet they need not inevitably be so. Here again, the experience of individual teachers and groups of teachers in developing critical consciousness and in fostering anti-sexist and anti-racist policies within their schools demonstrates the radical possibilities inherent within such attempts to change the curriculum (Green 1982). The recent initiatives by authorities like the Inner London Education Authority (ILEA) on class, gender and race and on political education take this process one stage further, and make it more difficult for teachers to avoid confronting these important issues. Nevertheless, the nature and progress of the ILEA curricular initiatives to date and the responses to them demonstrate just how entrenched conventional views of the curriculum are, and how much change is going to be necessary if constructive new working relationships are to be developed between Labour politicians, educational professionals and those sections of the wider community that have traditionally been excluded from curriculum decision-making.[5]

Another step recently taken by the ILEA is also worthy of comment in this context. At a time when sociologists are somewhat removed from the policy-making context, ILEA has appointed one of the most prolific sociologists of education, David Hargreaves of Oxford University, to chair a major enquiry into the curriculum of its secondary schools. Subsequently, the authority has appointed him as its chief inspector. In some respects, both the findings of his survey and his subsequent appointment seem in line with the arguments presented in this book. For example, one of the strongly held views of his committee of enquiry was that the 'conceptual dichotomy between academic and practical learning must be challenged and overcome' (D. Hargreaves *et al.* 1984). The practical involvement of a sociologist such as Hargreaves in the day-to-day implementation of the curriculum policies of a progressive authority could also be a welcome move. On the other hand, there are aspects of the report and the nature of Hargreave's involvement in developing policy and practice that are more questionable. Both the strengths and the weaknesses of the initiative, in terms of the arguments presented in this book, were neatly summarized in a profile of Hargreaves recently published in *New Society*:

[Hargreaves] recently irritated some fellow academics at the annual Westhill conference on the sociology of education, by suggesting that unless they became more involved in politics and policy making, their work would become increasingly irrelevant. 'He discounted the way that many people are involved,' said one academic who was there. 'People are on local education committees, working with schools and local groups and the women's movement: it was as if he was only really referring to a mandarin style of policy making. He admitted he was joining the establishment, but he said it wouldn't make him less radical.' We'll have to wait and see.                    (St John-Brooks 1984:28)

Certainly the appointment of Hargreaves at a time of major curriculum initiatives alongside political and financial tensions within the authority will require considerable sensitivity to the conflicts between professional and political interests and between the local and national state. It is therefore to be hoped that Hargreaves's recent tendency to move outside purely interactionist modes of sociology into a serious consideration of the contributions of other perspectives will be maintained (D. Hargreaves 1982).

## Concluding remarks

Part of the argument of this book has been that such perspectives demonstrate that the roots of social and educational inequality cannot be addressed solely in terms of everyday professional practice as implied by the new sociologists of education in the early 1970s. In so far as they need to be understood in terms of the broader social relations of our particular capitalist society, it is difficult to shrink from the recognition that effective strategies of change will necessarily involve us in oppositional politics. Those sociologists who wish their work to have radical effects will need therefore to be more actively involved in collective political movements at *all* levels. For left sociologists of the curriculum, as for other socialist teachers, this suggests that they need to make their project part of a broader programme of political reconstruction on the left. This will involve abandoning old conceptions of professionalism and developing new ways of working with what are sometimes called the popular constituencies – the labour movement, the women's movement and black movements (CCCS 1981).

The responsibility of the whole of the left in the years ahead is to develop and fight for policies that genuinely relate to the broader concerns of those groups that the selective tradition in education, as well as fundamental aspects of the structure of British society, have never begun to serve. Though it is clear that there are aspects of state education that are less than functional for capitalism, it is also the case that amongst the greatest beneficiaries of the 'swollen state' of the 1950s and 1960s were white, middle-class education and welfare professionals, including many sociologists of education. It is partly this that the new right has been able to capitalize upon in seeking popular support for policies of privatization which are even less likely to serve the interests of those currently excluded from wealth and power (Whitty 1984). Such policies threaten, even more than the current curriculum trends outlined above, the notion that collective struggle, rather than the individual exercise of supposedly free choice in an unequal society, can produce human betterment. To this extent, it is necessary to defend state education, but to occupy the space it offers with the most politically progressive forms of practice that are feasible within the present conjuncture and mobilize around them. It is important to remember that, in Cohen's words, even if 'state schooling has never been popular amongst sizeable sections of the working class . . . it does not follow that it is not a potential site for constructing a popular educational practice' (Cohen 1984: 161).

If there is any truth in the charge that left sociologists of education failed the labour movement in the 1970s (Demaine 1980) through their over-deterministic and monolithic views of the capitalist state, both the current state of the discipline and the contemporary political context offer us ample scope for remedying any such failing. In doing so, it is possible that we could retrieve the radical promise of a sociology of the curriculum, which was briefly, but quite inadequately, glimpsed in the early 1970s.

# Notes

## Chapter 1

1 In pointing to the radical potential of placing science in its social context, Hine's paper perhaps helps us to understand the recent concern on the part of Secretary of State Sir Keith Joseph to exclude such considerations from examinations in physics in the new 16+ examinations. See *The Sunday Times*, 18 September 1983.

2 There is some parallel here with the anomaly between the views of Willis (1977), on the one hand, and Bowles and Gintiš (1976), on the other, about how working-class pupils respond to the values and attitudes embraced by the education system. In one case the emphasis is on resistance, in the other on conformity.

## Chapter 2

1 A much clearer indication of the distinctiveness and significance of work influenced by post-structuralism and by Foucault can be gleaned from a book that unfortunately only became available just as the present volume was going to press. See Henriques *et al.* (1984). In an attempt to transcend the various versions of the individual–society dualism, the book discusses the formation of human subjects in terms of a 'power–knowledge–subject' complex, which permits the exploration of the concept of 'contradictory subjects/subjectivities', and tries to advance a new theorization of subjectivity vital to a politics of social transformation.

2 It is interesting to note in this connection that, in a review of Smart's *Foucault, Marxism and Critique* (1983), Glyn Williams comments that 'it seems to be a peculiarly British concern to seek to relate [Foucault's work] to Marxism' (*Sociology*, 18 (1), February 1984).

3 Although, as argued elsewhere (Arnot and Whitty 1982), there are some aspects of the work of these writers which make it distinctive from that of other

traditions, there are also significant differences amongst them which make it somewhat misleading to regard them as constituting a single school of thought. I am particularly grateful to Madeleine Arnot for her help in developing the analysis contained in this section of the chapter, which owes much to the joint-authored paper referred to here.

4 Acker (1981) has also pointed out that, at least until recently, women have been under-represented in the sociology of education particularly in terms of publications in the field. My own edited collections with Michael Young (Whitty and Young 1976; Young and Whitty 1977) are unfortunate examples of sexism in this respect and, indeed, in terms of some of the language employed in them. I am grateful to Jean Anyon for being the first (of many) to bring this latter point to my attention.

5 For a discussion of some of the theoretical issues involved, see Kuhn and Wolpe (1978). At the levels of both theory and strategy, there continue to be considerable disagreements between liberal feminists, radical feminists and socialist/Marxist feminists about the best way to proceed.

6 Other writers have pointed to the need to develop analyses sufficiently complex to encompass the separate dynamics of religion (Popkewitz 1981; White 1982) and age/generation (Hood-Williams and Fitz 1983; White 1982).

7 For recent attempts to develop analyses of class, race and gender along these lines, see various contributions to Barton and Walker (1983) and Walker and Barton (1983).

## Chapter 3

1 Lawton's colleagues at the Institute of Education have included Bill Gibby, Peter Gordon, Maggie Ing and Richard Pring, but their work, and his work in collaboration with them, is not discussed here. Denis Lawton himself has subsequently been appointed Deputy Director, and now Director, of the Institute.

2 Those associated with the Centre for Applied Research in Education at East Anglia include Clem Adelman, John Elliott, David Jenkins, Barry MacDonald, Jean Ruddock and Rob Walker.

## Chapter 4

1 This section of the chapter again owes much to work carried out jointly with Madeleine Arnot, and originally published in Arnot and Whitty (1982).

2 At least one radical educator in the USA has, however, presented this lack of an entrenched socialist tradition as a positive virtue. See Sklar (1978).

3 I am grateful to Bob Connell, Rob Gilbert, Peter Gronn, Ken Johnston, Jim Walker and Bruce Wilson for assisting me, in various ways, in the preparation of this section of the chapter.

## Chapter 5

1 The myth that curriculum control via professional autonomy is a tradition that has prevailed throughout the history of state education in Britain is not, of course, one that can be sustained.

2 It will be clear from what I have said earlier that Donald's own analysis is much more sophisticated than this rather stark comment may seem to imply. A recent Open University unit by Donald (1984) gives a much clearer indication of the complexity of his considered position.

3 For example, the restructuring exercise undertaken by the University Grants Committee in the early 1980s has been seen by some commentators as an example of the frustration by an entrenched 'liberal arts academic establishment' of industrial and governmental efforts to make the universities more relevant to the needs of contemporary industry. It is worth noting that, although the left is often critical of the élitism of the old humanist tradition, it has also sometimes used its model of supposedly disinterested learning as a convenient buffer in the face of corporate encroachments.

4 The Assisted Places Scheme, introduced by the Conservative government in 1981, may have helped increase the sense of direct competition between state and independent schools. See Whitty and Edwards (1984).

5 There has, however, been somewhat more coherence within this group in its opposition to cuts in public expenditure, at least during the period of Conservative government. Even here, the role of Labour-controlled LEAs in implementing those cuts in some areas has complicated the issue.

6 The latest DES curriculum paper (DES 1984), which was issued as this book was going to press, itself illustrates some of the problems involved in changing conventional views of the curriculum. Even while indicating some of the limitations of the traditional subject curriculum, it still uses subjects as the central organizing device for its discussion of the secondary phase. Thus, the new developments favoured by the Secretary of State appear as afterthoughts, some of which are admitted to be difficult to implement.

7 The idea that part of the original plan was to develop élite technical education on the European model has been put to me by three different observers involved in the early negotiations about the scheme. The prevailing assumption has, however, been that the scheme as now conceived will not make major inroads into the area of the curriculum now dominated by academic public examinations. See, for example, a leading article in *The Times Higher Education Supplement*, 19 November 1982.

## Chapter 6

1 In Mode 1, the examination board provides the syllabus, sets the examination and carries out the assessment; in Mode 2, the school provides the syllabus but the board carries out the assessment procedures; in Mode 3, the school provides the syllabus and carries out its own assessment procedures subject to moderation by the board. Methods of assessment are not restricted to particular modes of examination, but in practice traditional unseen papers remain the standard method of assessment in the vast majority of Mode 1 syllabuses, whilst continuous assessment and coursework are often favoured within Mode 3 schemes, though usually in combination with formal examination papers.

2 Although the term Mode 3 derives from the regulations governing the CSE, it has subsequently been applied to the procedures carried out under the special syllabus regulations of the GCE boards.

3 The new system will be called the General Certificate of Secondary Education (GCSE). It will be run by regional consortia of existing GCE and CSE boards and be based on a set of agreed 'national criteria'. The final decision to go ahead with a 'common' system from 1988 was announced by Sir Keith Joseph on 20 June 1984, just as this book was going to press.

4 I am grateful to the University of Bath research fund for its support of this work between 1976 and 1978 and to Richard Bowe for his assistance with it

184 Sociology and School Knowledge

and with parts of this chapter. For a discussion of some of the early findings of the research, see Whitty (1976).

5 It is impossible to do justice to the complexity of the constitutions of the various boards here. The GCE Ordinary level examinations (which super-seded the old School Certificate system in 1951) are administered by examination boards which, in all but one case, have strong university links. Although only the London board remains fully incorporated within its parent university, the appointments procedures employed by all the university-linked GCE boards effectively ensure that they retain a university-oriented ethos. The CSE system has been administered by regional boards dominated by senior members of the teaching profession and local authority representatives.

6 Initially, GCE O-level was deemed suitable for the top 20 per cent of each age-cohort and CSE for the next 40 per cent, though in practice they have often been extended beyond these limits anyway.

7 Because of the time involved in negotiating revisions in the syllabuses, and then in teaching them, this did not have a marked effect on subject entries until the end of the decade.

8 See *The Guardian*, 24 November 1975 and *The Times Educational Supplement* 9 January, 16 January, 27 February, 19 March, 9 April, 26 May 1976.

9 See *The Times Educational Supplement*, 20 May 1977.

10 There remains considerable doubt about how far Sir Keith Joseph's calls for a greater practical element in 16+ examinations can anyway be implemented without additional funding. The GCE boards were quick to point to this problem and to various other practical difficulties in Sir Keith's proposals. See *The Times Educational Supplement*, 31 August 1984.

## Chapter 7

1 I am grateful to Denis Gleeson with whom some of the analysis presented in the first part of this chapter was first developed.

2 The major funding was from the Nuffield Foundation from 1974–7. There was Schools Council funding for a study of how the Programme's conclusions could be diffused. Related work has been funded by the Leverhulme Trust and by the Department of Education and Science.

3 'The world this weekend', BBC Radio 4, 16 July 1978.

4 See *The Times Educational Supplement*, 27 January 1978.

5 It was, for instance, clear that there was some disagreement on the issue between the Secretary of State, Sir Keith Joseph, and his junior minister, Rhodes Boyson. This can be related to the ambiguities and contradictions in Conservative policy discussed in chapters 5 and 6.

6 Sharp's quotation continues with the words already quoted in chapter 4 about the failure of sociologists to follow up their analyses 'either with practical and concrete suggestions which could guide teachers in the mass schooling system or with the production of well-worked out curriculum materials'. The work of Cohen (1984), mentioned at the end of this chapter, is an early attempt to remedy this deficiency.

## Chapter 8

1 I am grateful to Stanley Aronowitz for pointing out this danger.

2 I am again drawing here on Williams's (1973) distinction between alternative and oppositional forms, the nature of which I outlined briefly in chapter 4.

Here the distinction is between those who want to 'make capitalism accept-able' and those who wish to replace it with socialist social relations. This is a somewhat different distinction than the conventional one between reformist and revolutionary *means* of achieving the transformation to socialism. Those with oppositional aspirations may espouse either or both of these means.

3 This quotation, from Clause IV(4) of the Labour Party constitution, appears on the membership cards of all members of the party and is the only clause to do so.

4 These words are taken from the manifesto upon which the Labour Party fought the February 1974 election.

5 For a discussion of some of the difficulties, see an article in *The Guardian* at the time of public consultation over the authority's policies on multi-ethnic education during 1983 (O'Connor 1983).

# References

Acker, S. (1981) 'No-woman's-land: British sociology of education 1960–1979', *Sociological Review*, 29(1).

Aggleton, P. and Whitty, G. (1985) 'Rebels without a cause: Socialization and subcultural style amongst the children of the new middle classes', *Sociology of Education*, 58(1).

Ahier, J. (1977) 'Philosophers, sociologists and knowledge in education' in M. Young and G. Whitty (eds) *Society, State and Schooling*, Lewes, Falmer Press.

Ahier, J. (1983) 'History and sociology of education policy' in J. Ahier and M. Flude (eds), *Contemporary Education Policy*, London, Croom Helm.

Althusser, L. (1971) 'Ideology and ideological state apparatuses' in *Lenin and Philosophy and Other Essays*, London, New Left Books.

Alvarado, M. & Ferguson, B. (1983) 'The curriculum, media studies and discursivity', *Screen*, 24(3).

Anderson, D. (1980) 'Have the supersaver sociologists asked for it?', *The Times Educational Supplement*, 14 March.

Anderson, P. (1968) 'Components of the national culture' in A. Cockburn & R. Blackburn (eds) *Student Power*, Harmondsworth, Penguin Books.

Anyon, J. (1978) 'Elementary social studies textbooks and legitimating knowledge', *Theory and Research in Social Education*, 6(3).

Anyon, J. (1979) 'Ideology and United States history textbooks', *Harvard Educational Review*, 49(3).

Anyon, J. (1980) 'Social class and the hidden curriculum of work', *Journal of Education*, 162(1).

Anyon, J. (1981a) 'Social class and school knowledge', *Curriculum Inquiry*, 11(1).

Anyon, J. (1981b) 'Elementary schooling and distinctions of social class', *Interchange*, 12(2/3).

Anyon, J. (1983) 'Intersections of gender and class' in S. Walker & L. Barton (eds) *Gender, Class and Education*, Lewes, Falmer Press.

Apple, M. W. (1971) 'The hidden curriculum and the nature of conflict', *Interchange*, 2(4).

Apple, M. W. (1977) 'Power and school knowledge', *Review of Education*, 3(1).

Apple, M. W. (1979) *Ideology and Curriculum*, London, Routledge & Kegan Paul.

Apple, M. W. (1980) 'The other side of the hidden curriculum: correspondence theories and the labour process', *Journal of Education*, 162(1).

Apple, M. W. (1981) 'Social structure, ideology and curriculum' in M. Lawn and L. Barton (eds) *Rethinking Curriculum Studies*, London, Croom Helm.

Apple, M. W. (ed.) (1982a) *Cultural and Economic Reproduction in Education*, London, Routledge & Kegan Paul.

Apple, M. W. (1982b) 'Curricular form and the logic of technical control' in M. W. Apple (ed) *Cultural and Economic Reproduction in Education*, London, Routledge & Kegan Paul.

Apple, M. W. (1982c) 'Education and cultural reproduction: a critical assessment of programs of choice' in R. Everhart (ed.) *The Public School Monopoly*, Boston, Ballinger Press.

Apple, M. W. (1983) *Education and Power*, London, Routledge & Kegan Paul.

Apple, M. W. (1984) 'The political economy of text publishing', *Educational Theory*, 34.

Apple, M. W. and King, N. (1977) 'What do schools teach?', *Curriculum Inquiry*, 6 (4).

Arnot, M. (1981) 'Culture and political economy: dual perspectives in the sociology of women's education', *Educational Analysis*, 3(1).

Arnot, M. and Whitty, G. (1982) 'From reproduction to transformation', *British Journal of Sociology of Education*, 3(1).

Aronowitz, S. (1983) 'Socialism and beyond', *Socialist Review*, 69.

Ashenden, D. (1979) 'Australian education: problems of a Marxist practice', *Arena*, 54.

Ashenden, D., Blackburn, J., Hannan, B. and White, D. (1984) 'Manifesto for a democratic curriculum', *The Australian Teacher*, 7.

Banks, O. (1955) *Parity and Prestige in English Secondary Education*, London, Routledge & Kegan Paul.

Banks, O. (1974) 'The "new" sociology of education', *Forum*, 17(1).

Bantock, G. (1968) *Culture, Industrialisation and Education*, London, Routledge & Kegan Paul.

Bantock, G. (1973) 'Are we in the wrong struggle?', *The Times Educational Supplement*, 5 October.

Barrett, M., Corrigan, P., Kuhn, A., and Wolff, J. (eds) (1979) *Ideology and Cultural Production*, London, Croom Helm.

Bartholomew, J. (1974) 'Sustaining hierarchy through teaching and research' in M. Flude and J. Ahier (eds) *Educability, Schools and Ideology*, London, Croom Helm.

Barton, L. and Lawn, M. (1980) 'Exploring the mists of ambiguity – a curriculum case study', unpublished mimeo.

Barton, L. and Walker, S. (eds) (1983) *Race, Class and Education*, London, Croom Helm.

Bates, R. (1980) 'New developments in the new sociology of education', *British Journal of Sociology of Education*, 1(1).

Bates, R. (1981) 'What can the new sociology of education do for teachers?', *Discourse*, 1(2).

Beck, J., Jenks, C., Keddie, N. and Young, M. F. D. (eds) (1976) *Worlds Apart*, London, Collier-Macmillan.

Ben-Tovim, G. and Gabriel, J. (1979) 'The sociology of race – time to change course?', *The Social Science Teacher*, 8(4).

Berger, P. and Luckmann, T. (1967) *The Social Construction of Reality*, Harmonds-worth, Allen Lane.

Bernbaum, G. (1977) *Knowledge and Ideology in the Sociology of Education*, London, Macmillan.

Bernstein, B. (1971) 'On the classification and framing of educational knowledge' in M. F. D. Young (ed.) *Knowledge and Control*, London, Collier-Macmillan.

Bernstein, B. (1977a) *Class, Codes and Control*, vol. 3, London, Routledge & Kegan Paul.

Bernstein, B. (1977b) 'Class and pedagogies – visible and invisible' in B. Bernstein, *Class, Codes and Control*, vol. 3, London, Routledge & Kegan Paul.

Bernstein, B. (1977c) 'Aspects of the relations between education and production' in B. Bernstein, *Class, Codes and Control*, vol. 3, London, Routledge & Kegan Paul.

Bernstein, B. (1982) 'Codes, modalities and the process of cultural reproduction: a model' in M. Apple (ed.) *Cultural and Economic Reproduction in Education*, London, Routledge & Kegan Paul.

Berridge, G. (1978) 'Crick and the curriculum', *Teaching Politics*, 7(3).

Best, R. (1976) 'New direction? Some comments on the "new sociology of education" ', *Radical Education*, 5.

Bleiman, B. and Burt, S. (1981) 'Beyond the comprehensive ideal', *Socialism and Education*, 8(1).

Bourdieu, P. (1971a) 'Intellectual field and creative project' in M. F. D. Young (ed), *Knowledge and Control*, London, Collier-Macmillan.

Bourdieu, P. (1971b) 'Systems of education and systems of thought' in M. F. D. Young (ed) *Knowledge and Control*, London, Collier-Macmillan.

Bourdieu, P. (1976) 'The school as a conservative force' in R. Dale *et al.* (eds) *Schooling and Capitalism*, London, Routledge & Kegan Paul.

Bourdieu, P. and Passeron, J-C. (1977) *Reproduction in Education, Society and Culture*, London, Sage Publications.

Bowles, S. (1976) 'Unequal education and the reproduction of the social division of labor' in R. Dale *et al.* (eds), *Schooling and Capitalism*, London, Routledge & Kegan Paul.

Bowles, S. and Gintis, H. (1976) *Schooling in Capitalist America*, London, Routledge & Kegan Paul.

Boyson, R. (1975) 'Maps, chaps and your hundred best books', *The Times Educational Supplement*, 17 October.

Broadfoot, P. (1979) *Assessment, Schools and Society*, London, Methuen.

Broadfoot, P. (1983) 'Assessment constraints on curriculum practice' in M. Hammersley and A. Hargreaves (eds) *Curriculum Practice*, Lewes, Falmer Press.

Burston, W. H. (1954) *Social Studies and the History Teacher*, London, Historical Association.

Callaghan, J. (1976) 'Towards a national debate', *Education*, 148 (17).

Campbell, W. J. and Campbell, E. M. (1978) *School-Based Assessment: Aspirations and Achievements of the Radford Scheme in Queensland*, Canberra, Australian Government Publishing Service.

Cannon, C. (1964) 'Social studies in secondary schools', *Educational Review*, 17.

Carby, H. (1980) 'Multi-culture', *Screen Education*, 34.

Carr, E. H. (1961) *What Is History?* London, Macmillan.

Cathcart, H. and Esland, G. (1983) 'Schooling and industry: some recent contributions', *British Journal of Sociology of Education*, 4(3).

CCCS (Centre for Contemporary Cultural Studies) (1981) *Unpopular Education*, London, Hutchinson.

CCCS (Centre for Contemporary Cultural Studies) (1982) *The Empire Strikes Back*, London, Hutchinson.

CGLI/BTEC (City and Guilds of London Institute/Business and Technician Education Council) (1984) *The Certificate of Pre-Vocational Education*, London, CGLI/BTEC Joint Board for Pre-Vocational Education.

Clarke, J., Critcher, C. and Johnson, R. (eds) (1979) *Working Class Culture*, London, Hutchinson.

Cohen, P. (1984) 'Against the new vocationalism' in I. Bates *et al.*, *Schooling for the Dole?*, London, Macmillan.

Collins, R. (1977) 'Some comparative principles of educational stratification', *Harvard Educational Review*, 47 (1).

Connell, R. W., Ashenden, D. J., Kessler, S. and Dowsett, G. W. (1982) *Making the Difference*, Sydney, Allen & Unwin.

Connell, R. W., Ashenden, D. J., Kessler, S. and Dowsett, G. W. (1983) 'In defence of *Making the Difference*', *Arena*, 62.

Cooper, B. (1983) 'On explaining change in school subjects', *British Journal of Sociology of Education*, 4(3).

Cotgrove, S. (1958) *Technical Education and Social Change*, London, Routledge & Kegan Paul.

Cox, C. B. (1980) 'How education fails Britain's children', *Now!*, 52.

Cox, C. B. and Boyson, R. (eds) (1975) *Black Paper 5: The Fight for Education*, London, Dent.

Cox, C. B. and Dyson, A. E. (eds) (1969) *Fight for Education: A Black Paper*, London, Critical Quarterly Society.

Craft, M. (ed.) (1970) *Family, Class and Education*, London, Longman.

Crick, B. and Porter, A. (eds) (1978) *Political Education and Political Literacy*, London, Longman.

Culley, L. and Demaine, J. (1983) 'Social theory, social relations and education' in S. Walker and L. Barton (eds) *Gender, Class and Education*, Lewes, Falmer Press.

Cutler, A., Hindess, B., Hirst, P. and Hussain, A. (1977/8) *Marx's 'Capital' and Capitalism Today*, London, Routledge & Kegan Paul, 2 vols.

Dale, R. (1979) 'Control, accountability and William Tyndale' in L. Barton and R. Meighan (eds) *Schools, Pupils and Deviance*, Driffield, Nafferton Books.

Dale, R. (1981) 'The state and education: some theoretical approaches' in Society, Education and the State Course Team *The State and the Politics of Education*, part 2, Milton Keynes, Open University Press.

Dale, R. (1982) 'Education and the capitalist state: contributions and contradictions' in M. W. Apple (ed.) *Cultural and Economic Reproduction in Education*, London, Routledge & Kegan Paul.

Dale, R. (1983a) 'Thatcherism and education' in J. Ahier and M. Flude (eds) *Contemporary Educational Policy*, London, Croom Helm.

Dale, R. (1983b) 'The Political Sociology of Education', review essay, *British Journal of Sociology of Education*, 4(2).

Dale, R., Esland, G. and MacDonald, M. (eds) (1976) *Schooling and Capitalism*, London, Routledge & Kegan Paul.

Daunt, P. E. (1975) *Comprehensive Values*, London, Heinemann.

David, K. (1983) *Personal and Social Education in Secondary Schools*, York, Longman/Schools Council.

Deem, R. (1978) *Women and Schooling*, London, Routledge & Kegan Paul.

Delamont, S. (1978) *Interaction in the Classroom*, London, Methuen.

Delamont, S. (1983) 'The conservative school?' in S. Walker and L. Barton (eds), *Gender, Class and Education*, Lewes, Falmer Press.

Demaine, J. (1980) 'Sociology of education, politics and the left in Britain', *British Journal of Sociology of Education*, 1(1).

Demaine, J. (1981) *Contemporary Theories in the Sociology of Education*, London, Macmillan.

DES (Department of Education and Science) (1971–83) *Statistics of Education*, vol. 2, published annually, London, HMSO (1971–81), DES (1982–3).

DES (1977) *Education in Schools. A Consultative Document*, London, HMSO.

DES (1978) *School Examinations*, Part 1, London, HMSO.

DES (1979) *A Framework for the School Curriculum*, London, HMSO.

DES (1980) *The School Curriculum*, London, HMSO.

DES (1984) *The Organisation and Content of the 5–16 Curriculum*, London, Department of Education and Science.

Doe, B. (1981a) 'Fears grow on eve of 16 plus exam preview', *The Times Educational Supplement*, 3 July.

Doe, B. (1981b) 'Alarm spreads over proposals for new 16 plus exams', *The Times Educational Supplement*, 20 November.

Doe, B. (1982) 'Cambridge plan for 16 plus rejected by GCE boards', *The Times Educational Supplement*, 5 March.

Donald, J. (1978) 'Examinations and strategies', *Screen Education*, 26.

Donald, J. (1979) 'Green Paper: noise of crisis', *Screen Education*, 30.

Donald, J. (1984) *Education Policy and Ideology*, Unit 29 of 'Conflict and change in education', Milton Keynes, Open University Press.

Dray, J. and Jordan, D. (1950) *A Handbook of Social Studies*, London, Methuen.

Dufour, B. (1970) 'Society in the school', *Education and Social Science*, 1.

Dwyer, P., Wilson, B., and Woock, R. (1984) *Confronting School and Work*, Sydney, Allen & Unwin.

Dyke-Acland, A. H. (1911) *Examinations in Secondary Schools*, Report of the Consultative Committee, London, HMSO.

Eagleton, T. (1976) *Marxism and Literary Criticism*, London, Methuen.

Edwards, R. (1979) *Contested Terrain: The Transformation of the Workplace in the 20th Century*, New York, Basic Books.

Eggleston, J. (1975) 'Conflicting curriculum decisions', *Educational Studies*, 1(1).

Elliott, J. (1980) 'Who should monitor performance in schools?', in H. Sockett (ed.) *Accountability in the English Educational System*, London, Hodder & Stoughton.

Elliott, J. (1983) *Legitimation Crisis and the Growth of Educational Action-Research*, Cambridge, Institute of Education.

Elliott, J. and Adelman, C. (1976) 'Innovation at the classroom level', Unit 28 of Open University Course E203, Milton Keynes, Open University Press.

Emms, D. (1981) *HMC Schools and British Industry: A Personal Enquiry*, London, Headmasters' Conference.

Entwistle, H. (1978) *Class, Culture and Education*, London, Methuen.

Entwistle, H. (1979) *Antonio Gramsci*, London, Routledge & Kegan Paul.

Erben, M. and Gleeson, D. (1977) 'Education as Reproduction' in M. Young and G. Whitty (eds) *Society, State and Schooling*, Lewes, Falmer Press.

Esland, G. (1971) 'Teaching and learning as the organization of knowledge' in M. F. D. Young (ed.) *Knowledge and Control*, London, Collier-Macmillan.

Fairhall, J. (1980) 'Single exam system to replace O-level, CSE', *The Guardian*, 20 February.

Filmer, P., Phillipson, M., Silverman, D. and Walsh, D. (1972) *New Directions in Sociological Theory*, London, Collier-Macmillan.

Finn, D. and Frith, S. (1981) 'Education and the labour market' in Society, Education and the State Course Team *The State and the Politics of Education*, part 2, Milton Keynes, Open University Press.

Finn, D., Grant, N. and Johnson, R. (1977) 'Social democracy, education and the crisis', *Working Papers in Cultural Studies*, 10.

Flew, A. (1976) *Sociology, Equality and Education*, London, Macmillan.

Foucault, M. (1979) *Discipline and Punish*, Harmondsworth, Penguin Books.

Foucault, M. (1981) 'The order of discourse' in R. Young (ed.) *Untying the Text*, London, Routledge & Kegan Paul.

Freeland, J. (1979) 'Class struggle in schooling – MACOS and SEMP in Queensland', *Intervention*, 12.

Freeland, J. (1981) 'Where do they go after school: youth unemployment, legitimation and schooling', *The Australian Quarterly*, 53 (3).

Freeland, J. (1982) 'Learning from the Community Youth Support Scheme Campaign', unpublished conference paper.

Freeland, J. and Sharp, R. (1981) 'The Williams Report on Education, Training and Employment – the decline and fall of Karmelot', *Intervention*, 14.

Giddens, A. (1979) *Central Problems in Social Theory*, London, Macmillan.

Gilbert, R. (1983) *Practising the English Ideology*, mimeo, James Cook University of North Queensland.

Gintis, H. and Bowles, S. (1981) 'Contradiction and reproduction in educational theory' in R. Dale *et al.* (eds) *Education and the State*, vol. 1, Lewes, Falmer Press.

Giroux, H. (1981a) *Ideology, Culture and the Process of Schooling*, Lewes, Falmer Press.

Giroux, H. (1981b) 'Hegemony, resistance and the paradox of educational reform', *Interchange*, 12 (2/3).

Giroux, H. (1981c) 'Schooling and the myth of objectivity: stalking the politics of the hidden curriculum', *McGill Journal of Education*, 17(3).

Giroux, H. (1983) *Theory and Resistance in Education: A Pedagogy for the Opposition*, London, Heinemann Educational Books.

Giroux, H. and Penna, A. (1979) 'Social education in the classroom: the dynamics of the hidden curriculum', *Theory and Research in Social Education*, 7 (1).

Gleeson, D. (ed.) (1983) *Youth Training and the Search for Work*, London, Routledge & Kegan Paul.

Gleeson, D. (1984) 'Someone else's children: the new vocationalism in further education and training' in L. Barton and S. Walker (eds) *Social Crisis and Educational Research*, London, Croom Helm.

Gleeson, D. and Whitty, G. (1976) *Developments in Social Studies Teaching*, London, Open Books.

Gleeson, D. and Whitty, G. (1982) 'The sociological imagination and the reality of schooling', *The Social Science Teacher*, 12 (1).

Golding, P. and Murdock, G. (1979) 'Ideology and the mass media: the question of determination' in M. Barrett *et al.*, *Ideology and Cultural Production*, London, Croom Helm.

Goodson, I. (1983) *School Subjects and Curriculum Change*, London, Croom Helm.

Goodson, I. (ed.) (1985) *Social Histories of the Secondary Curriculum*, Lewes, Falmer Press.

Gorbutt, D. (1972) 'The new sociology of education', *Education for Teaching*, 89.

Gould, J. (1977) *The Attack on Higher Education – Marxist and Radical Penetration*, London, Institute for the Study of Conflict.

Gouldner, A. (1972) *The Coming Crisis of Western Sociology*, London, Heinemann Educational Books.

Grace, G. (1978) *Teachers, Ideology and Control*, London, Routledge & Kegan Paul.

Gramsci, A. (1971) *Selections from the Prison Notebooks of Antonio Gramsci* (eds), Q. Hoare and G. Nowell-Smith, London, Lawrence & Wishart.

Green, A. (1982) 'In defence of anti-racist teaching', *Multi-Racial Education*, 10 (2).

Green, A. (1983) 'Education and training: under new masters' in A. M. Wolpe and J. Donald (eds), *Is There Anyone Here from Education?* London, Pluto Press.

Habermas, J. (1976) *Legitimation Crisis,* London, Heinemann Educational Books.

Hall, S. (1977) 'The hinterland of science: ideology and the "sociology of knowledge" ', *Working Papers in Cultural Studies,* 10.

Hall, S. (1981) 'Schooling, state and society' in R. Dale *et al.* (eds) *Education and the State,* vol. 1, Lewes, Falmer Press.

Halsey, A. H., Heath, A. F. and Ridge, J. M. (1980) *Origins and Destinations,* Oxford, Clarendon Press.

Hammersley, M. and Hargreaves, A. (eds) (1983) *Curriculum Practice: Some Sociological Case Studies,* Lewes, Falmer Press.

Hand, N. (1976) 'What *is* English?' in G. Whitty and M. Young (eds) *Explorations in the Politics of School Knowledge,* Driffield, Nafferton Books.

Hargreaves, A. (1980) 'Synthesis and the study of strategies' in P. Woods (ed.), *Pupil Strategies,* London, Croom Helm.

Hargreaves, A. (1982) 'Resistance and relative autonomy theories: problems of distortion and incoherence in recent Marxist analyses of education', *British Journal of Sociology of Education,* 3 (2).

Hargreaves, D. (1967) *Social Relations in a Secondary School,* London, Routledge & Kegan Paul.

Hargreaves, D. (1982) *The Challenge for the Comprehensive School,* London, Routledge & Kegan Paul.

Hargreaves, D. *et al.* (1984) *Improving Secondary Schools,* Report of the Committee on the Curriculum and Organisation of Secondary Schools, London, Inner London Education Authority.

Harris, K. (1979) *Education and Knowledge,* London, Routledge & Kegan Paul.

Hatcher, R. and Shallice, J. (1983) 'The politics of anti-racist education', *Multi-racial Education,* 12 (1).

Hemming, J. (1949) *The Teaching of Social Studies in Secondary Schools,* London, Longman.

Hemming, J. (1980) *The Betrayal of Youth: Secondary Education Must Be Changed,* London, Marian Boyars.

Henriques, J., Holloway, W., Urwin, C., Venn, C. and Walkerdine, V. (1984) *Changing the Subject,* London, Methuen.

Herndon, J. (1970) *The Way It Spozed to Be,* London, Pitman.

Hextall, I. (1980) 'Up against the wall: restructuring state education' in M. Cole and B. Skelton (eds), *Blind Alley,* Ormskirk, Hesketh.

Hextall, I. (1984) 'Rendering accounts: a critical analysis of the APU' in P. Broadfoot (ed.), *Selection, Certification and Control,* Lewes, Falmer Press.

Hindess, B. (1977) 'The concept of class in Marxist theory and Marxist politics' in J. Bloomfield (ed.) *Class, Hegemony and Party,* London, Lawrence & Wishart.

Hindess, B. (1983) 'Power, interests and the outcomes of struggles', *Sociology,* 16.

Hine, R. J. (1975) 'Political bias in school physics', *Hard Cheese,* 4/5

Hirst, P. Q. (1979) *On Law and Ideology,* London, Macmillan.

Hirst, P. H. and Peters, R. S. (1970) *The Logic of Education,* London, Routledge & Kegan Paul.

HMI (Her Majesty's Inspectorate of Schools) (1977) *Curriculum 11–16,* London, Department of Education and Science.

HMI (1978) *A Survey of Primary Education,* London, HMSO.

HMI (1979) *Aspects of Secondary Education,* London, HMSO.

HMI (1980) *A View of the Curriculum,* London, HMSO.

HMI (1981) *Curriculum 11–16. A Review of Progress,* London, HMSO.

Hogan, D. (1981) 'Capitalism, liberalism and schooling' in R. Dale *et al.* (eds), *Education and the State*, vol. 1, Lewes, Falmer Press.

Holloway, J. and Picciotto, S. (1977) 'Capital, crisis and the state', *Capital and Class*, 2.

Holloway, J. and Picciotto, S. (eds) (1978) *State and Capital: a Marxist Debate*, London, Edward Arnold.

Hood-Williams, J. and Fitz, J. (1983) 'Sociology of childhood: a review essay', *British Journal of Sociology of Education*, 4 (1).

Hopkins, A. (1978) *The School Debate*, Harmondsworth, Penguin Books.

Hurford, J. (1979) 'Testing times', *Rank and File Teacher*, 64.

Illich, I. (1971) *Deschooling Society*, London, Calder & Boyars.

Jackson, M. (1976) 'Sniped at now from all sides', *The Times Educational Supplement*, 3 December.

Jessop, B. (1982) *The Capitalist State*, Oxford, Martin Robertson.

Jevons, F. (1975) 'But some kinds of knowledge are more equal than others', *Studies in Science Education*, 2.

Johnson, R. (1979a) '*Really* useful knowledge' in J. Clarke *et al.* (eds), *Working Class Culture: Studies in History and Theory*, London, Hutchinson.

Johnson, R. (1979b) 'Three problematics: elements of a theory of working class culture' in J. Clarke, C. Critcher and R. Johnson (eds), *Working Class Culture: Studies in History and Theory*, London, Hutchinson.

Johnson, R. (1981) 'Socialism and popular education', *Socialism and Education*, 8 (1).

Jones, P. (1978) 'The politics of political literacy', unpublished MA dissertation, University of London Institute of Education.

Joseph, K. (1984) 'View from the top', *The Times Educational Supplement*, 13 January.

JMB (Joint Matriculation Board) (1975) *Notes on the Submission of Applications for Specially Approved Syllabuses*, Manchester, Joint Matriculation Board.

Keddie, N. (1971) 'Classroom knowledge' in M. F. D. Young (ed.), *Knowledge and Control*, London, Collier-Macmillan.

Keddie, N. (ed.) (1973) *Tinker, Tailor . . . The Myth of Cultural Deprivation*, Harmondsworth, Penguin Books.

Kellner, D. (1978) 'Ideology, Marxism and advanced capitalism', *Socialist Review*, 42.

Kelly, A. (ed.) (1981) *The Missing Half: Girls and Science Education*, Manchester, Manchester University Press.

Kelly, G. and Nihlen, A. (1982) 'Schooling and the reproduction of patriarchy' in M. W. Apple (ed.) *Cultural and Economic Reproduction in Education*, London, Routledge & Kegan Paul.

Kemmis, S., Cole, P. and Suggett, D. (1983) *Orientations to Curriculum and Transition: towards the socially-critical school*, Melbourne, Victorian Institute of Secondary Education.

King, R. (1980) 'Weberian perspectives and the study of education', *British Journal of Sociology of Education*, 1 (1).

Kogan, M. (1971) *The Politics of Education*, Harmondsworth, Penguin Books.

Kuhn, A. (1978) 'Ideology, structure and knowledge', *Screen Education*, 28.

Kuhn, A. and Wolpe, A. M. (1978) (eds) *Feminism and Materialism*, London, Routledge & Kegan Paul.

Lacey, C. (1970) *Hightown Grammar*, Manchester, Manchester University Press.

Lawton, D. (1968), Report of an address, *Association for the Teaching of the Social Sciences Newsletter*, 9.

Lawton, D. (1973) *Social Change, Educational Theory and Curriculum Planning*, London, Hodder & Stoughton.
Lawton, D. (1975a) *Investigating Society*, London, Hodder & Stoughton.
Lawton, D. (1975b) *Class, Culture, and the Curriculum*, London, Routledge & Kegan Paul.
Lawton, D. (1977) *Education and Social Justice*, London, Sage Publications.
Lawton, D. (1979) *Beyond the Secret Garden*, London, University of London Institute of Education.
Lawton, D. (1980) *The Politics of the School Curriculum*, London, Routledge & Kegan Paul.
Lawton, D. (1983) *Curriculum Studies and Educational Planning*, London, Hodder & Stoughton.
Lawton, D. (1984) 'Curriculum control', *Forum*, 26 (3).
Lawton, D. and Dufour, B. (1973) *The New Social Studies*, London, Heinemann Educational Books.
Layton, D. (1973) *Science for the People*, London, Allen & Unwin.
Lenin, V. I. (1975) *What Is To Be Done?* Peking, Foreign Language Press.
MacDonald, B. (1979) 'Hard times: educational accountability in England', *Educational Analysis*, 1 (1).
MacDonald, M. (1977) *The Curriculum and Cultural Reproduction*, units 18–19 of 'Schooling and Society', Milton Keynes, Open University Press.
MacDonald, M. (1981) 'Schooling and the reproduction of class and gender relations' in R. Dale *et al.* (eds) *Education and the State*, vol. 1, Lewes, Falmer Press.
MacLure, S. (1975) 'The Schools Council and examinations' in R. Bell and W. Prescott (eds) *The Schools Council: A Second Look*, London, Ward Lock.
McNeil, L. (1981a) 'On the possibility of teachers as the source of an emancipatory pedagogy – a response to Henry Giroux', *Curriculum Inquiry*, 11 (3).
McNeil, L. (1981b) 'Negotiating classroom knowledge: beyond achievement and socialization', *Journal of Curriculum Studies*, 13 (4).
McRobbie, A. (1978) 'Working class girls and the culture of femininity' in Centre for Contemporary Cultural Studies, *Women Take Issue*, London, Hutchinson.
Mardle, G. (1977) Review of *Explorations in the Politics of School Knowledge*, *The Times Educational Supplement*, 26 August.
Milner, D. (1975) *Children and Race*, Harmondsworth, Penguin.
Milner, D. (1983) *Children and Race: Ten Years On*, London, Ward Lock Educational.
Moore, T. (1974) *Educational Theory*, London, Routledge & Kegan Paul.
Mullard, C. (1981) 'The social context and meaning of multi-cultural education', *Educational Analysis*, 3 (1).
Murdock, G. (1974) 'The politics of culture' in D. Holly (ed.) *Education or Domination?*, London, Arrow Books.
Musgrave, P. (1967) *Technical Change, the Labour Force and Education*, Oxford, Pergamon Press.
Musgrave, P. (1973) *Knowledge, Curriculum and Change*, London, Angus & Robertson.
Musgrave, P. (1979) *Society and the Curriculum in Australia*, Sydney, Allen & Unwin.
Musgrove, F. (1968) 'The contribution of sociology to the study of the curriculum' in J. F. Kerr (ed.) *Changing the Curriculum*, London, University of London Press.
Musgrove, F. (1969) 'Curriculum objectives', *Journal of Curriculum Studies*, 1 (1).
Musgrove, F. (1979) *School and the Social Order*, Chichester, John Wiley.
Nava, M. (1980) 'Sexual divisions and education', review article, *Schooling and Culture*, 7.

Norman, M. (1984) 'New 16-plus exam in four years', *Daily Telegraph*, 21 June.

Nowell-Smith, G. (1979) 'In a State', *Screen Education*, 30.

O'Connor, M. (1983) 'A Morrell Dilemma,' *The Guardian*, 3 May.

Offe, C. (1984) *Contradictions of the Welfare State*, London, Hutchinson.

O'Keeffe, D. (1981) 'Labour in vain: truancy, industry and the school' in A. Flew *et al.*, *The Pied Pipers of Education*, London, The Social Affairs Unit.

Open University (1976) *Curriculum Design and Development*, Course E203, Milton Keynes, Open University Press.

Open University (1977) *Schooling and Society*, Course E202, Milton Keynes, Open University Press.

Open University (1983) *Purpose and Planning in the Curriculum*, Milton Keynes, Open University Press.

Ozolins, U. (1979) 'Lawton's "refutation" of a working class curriculum', *Melbourne Working Papers 1979*.

Pollard, A. (1984) 'Ethnography and Social Policy for Classroom Practice' in L. Barton and S. Walker (eds) *Social Crisis and Educational Research*, London, Croom Helm.

Popkewitz, T. S. (1977) 'The latent values of the discipline-centred curriculum', *Theory and Research in Social Education*, 5 (1).

Popkewitz, T. S. (1981) 'The social contexts of schooling, change and educational research', *Journal of Curriculum Studies*, 13 (3).

Porter, A. (1979) 'The Programme for Political Education – a guide for beginners', *Social Science Teacher*, 8 (3).

Poulantzas, N. (1973) *Political Power and Social Classes*, London, New Left Books.

Pring, R. (1972) 'Knowledge out of control', *Education for Teaching*, 89.

Radical Education Dossier (1984) 'Schooling: What future? Which direction?' *Radical Education Dossier*, 22.

Ramsay, P. (1983) 'Fresh perspectives on the school transformation–reproduction debate', *Curriculum Inquiry*, 13 (3).

Reeder, D. (1979) 'A recurring debate: education and industry' in G. Bernbaum (ed.) *Schooling in Decline*, London, Macmillan.

Reimer, E. (1972) *School Is Dead*, Harmondsworth, Penguin Books.

Reynolds, D. (1984) 'Relative autonomy reconstructed' in L. Barton and S. Walker (eds), *Social Crisis and Educational Research*, London, Croom Helm.

Reynolds, D. and Sullivan, M. (1980) 'Towards a new socialist sociology of education' in L. Barton, R. Meighan and S. Walker (eds), *Schooling, Ideology and the Curriculum*, Lewes, Falmer Press.

Roderick, G. and Stephens, M. (eds) (1981) *Where Did We Go Wrong?* Lewes, Falmer Press.

Roderick, G. and Stephens, M. (eds) (1982) *The British Malaise*, Lewes, Falmer Press.

Rowlands, C. (1977) 'How the teaching cheats brand our children', *Daily Mail*, 5 April.

Royal Geographical Society (1950) 'Geography and "social studies" in schools', Memorandum from the Education Committee to Council, June.

St John-Brooks, C. (1980) 'Sociologists and education', *New Society*, 4 September.

St John-Brooks, C. (1984) 'Taking ideas to school', *New Society*, 5 April.

Salter, B . and Tapper, T. (1981) *Education, Politics and the State*, London, Grant MacIntyre.

Sarup, M. (1982) *Education, State and Crisis*, London, Routledge & Kegan Paul.

Sarup, M. (1983) *Marxism/Structuralism/Education*, Lewes, Falmer Press.

Saunders, P. (1981) *Social Theory and the Urban Question*, London, Hutchinson.

Schools Council (1975) *Examinations at 16-plus: Proposals for the Future*, London, Schools Council.

Schools Council (1981) *The Practical Curriculum*, Schools Council Working Paper 70, London, Methuen Educational.

SSEC (Secondary Schools Examinations Council) (1960) *Secondary School Examinations Other than the GCE*, London, HMSO.

Sharp, R. (1980) *Knowledge, Ideology and the Politics of Schooling*, London, Routledge & Kegan Paul.

Sharp, R. (1982a) 'Self-contained ethnography or a science of phenomenal forms and inner relations'. *Journal of Education*, 164 (1).

Sharp, R. (1982b) 'Response to Wexler', *Interchange*, 13 (3).

Sharp, R. (1984) 'Urban education and the current crisis' in G. Grace (ed.) *Education and the City*, London, Routledge & Kegan Paul.

Sharp, R. and Green, A. (1975) *Education and Social Control*, London, Routledge & Kegan Paul.

Shaw, D. (1982) 'Forget single 16-plus exam, says MP', *The Standard*, 4 February.

Shepherd, J. and Vulliamy, G. (1983) 'A comparative sociology of school knowledge', *British Journal of Sociology of Education*, 4 (1).

Silver, H. (ed.) (1973) *Equal Opportunity in Education*, London, Methuen.

Simon, J. (1974) ' "New direction" sociology and comprehensive schooling', *Forum*, 17 (1).

Sivanandan, A. (1982) *A Different Hunger*, London, Pluto Press.

Sklar, M. (1978) 'Some remarks on Ollman's "On teaching Marxism" ' in T. M. Norton and B. Ollman (eds) *Studies in Socialist Pedagogy*, New York, Monthly Review Press.

Smart, B. (1983) *Foucault, Marxism and Critique*, London, Routledge & Kegan Paul.

Smith, C. (1976) *Mode III Examinations in the CSE and GCE*, Schools Council Examinations Bulletin 34, London, Evans/Methuen.

Smith, R. and Knight, J. (1978) 'MACOS in Queensland: the politics of educational knowledge', *Australian Journal of Education*, 22.

Smith, R. and Knight, J. (1982) 'Liberal ideology, radical critiques and change in education', *British Journal of Sociology of Education*, 3 (3).

Sockett, H. (ed.) (1980) *Accountability in the English Educational System*, London, Hodder & Stoughton.

Spender, D. (1982) *Invisible Women: The Schooling Scandal*, London, Writers & Readers Publishing Cooperative.

Steed, D. (1974) 'History as school knowledge', unpublished MA dissertation, University of London Institute of Education.

Stenhouse, L. (1975) *An Introduction to Curriculum Research and Development*, London, Heinemann Educational Books.

Stevens, A. (1982) 'O-levels face a test', *The Observer*, 14 February.

Stone, M. (1980) *The Education of the Black Child in Britain*, London, Fontana.

Sumner, C. (1979) *Reading Ideologies*, London, Academic Press.

Taxel, J. (1979) 'Justice and cultural conflict: racism, sexism and instructional materials', *Interchange*, 9 (1).

Taxel, J. (1980) 'The depiction of the American Revolution in children's fiction', unpublished doctoral thesis, University of Wisconsin-Madison.

Taxel, J. (1981) 'The outsiders of the American Revolution: the selective tradition in children's fiction', *Interchange*, 12 (2/3).

Taxel, J. (1983) 'The American Revolution: an analysis of literary content, form and ideology' in M. W. Apple and L. Weis (eds) *Ideology and Practice in Schooling*, Philadelphia, Temple University Press.

Taylor, W. (1978) 'Power and the curriculum' in C. Richards (ed.), *Power and the Curriculum*, Driffield, Nafferton Books.

Teaching London Kids (1983) 'Fighting the siege mentality', editorial, *Teaching London Kids*, 21.

Thompson, E. P. (1978) *The Poverty of Theory and Other Essays*, London, Merlin Press.

TUC (Trades Union Congress) (1977) *Response to the Green Paper: 'Education in Schools'*, London, Trades Union Congress.

Toomey, D. (1983) Review of *Making the Difference, Discourse*, 3(2).

UCLES (University of Cambridge Local Examinations Syndicate) (1976) *School Examinations and Their Function*, Cambridge, University of Cambridge Local Examinations Syndicate.

ULSED (University of London School Examinations Department) (1977) *Specially Approved Syllabuses (Modes 2 and 3): Notes for the Guidance of Centres*, University of London School Examinations Department.

VSTA (Victorian Secondary Teachers Association) (1976) *Secondary Curriculum: Reprints from 'The Secondary Teacher'*, Melbourne, Victorian Teachers Association.

Vulliamy, G. (1972) 'Music education in secondary schools – some sociological observations', unpublished MA dissertation, University of London Institute of Education.

Vulliamy, G. (1976) 'What counts as school music?' in G. Whitty and M. Young (eds) *Explorations in the Politics of School Knowledge*, Driffield, Nafferton Books.

Vulliamy, G. (1977) 'School music as a case study in the new sociology of education' in J. Shepherd *et al.* (eds) *Whose Music? A Sociology of Musical Languages*, London, Latimer New Dimensions.

Walker, J. (1983) 'Ideology, educational change and epistemological holism', *Access*, 2 (1).

Walker, R. and MacDonald, B. (1976) *Curriculum Innovation at School Level*, Unit 27 of 'Curriculum Design and Development', Milton Keynes, Open University Press.

Walker, S. and Barton, L. (eds) (1983) *Gender, Class and Education*, Lewes, Falmer Press.

Warwick, D. (1974) 'Ideologies, integration and conflicts of meaning' in M. Flude and J. Ahier (eds), *Educability, Schools and Ideology*, London, Croom Helm.

Weinstock, A. (1976) 'I blame the teachers', *The Times Educational Supplement*, 23 January.

Weis, L. (1983) 'Schooling and cultural production: a comparison of black and white lived experience' in M. W. Apple and L. Weis (eds), *Ideology and Pratice in Schooling*, Philadelphia, Temple University Press.

Wexler, P. (1982a) 'Structure, text and subject: a critical sociology of school knowledge' in M. W. Apple (ed.) *Cultural and Economic Reproduction in Education*, London, Routledge & Kegan Paul.

Wexler, P. (1982b) 'Ideology and education: from critique to class action', *Interchange*, 13 (3).

Wexler, P., Whitson, T., Moskowitz, E. (1981) 'Deschooling by default: the changing social functions of public schooling', *Interchange*, 12 (2/3).

White, D. (1982) Review article on *Making the Difference, Arena*, 61.

Whitty, G. (1974) 'Sociology and the problem of radical educational change' in M. Flude and J. Ahier (eds), *Educability, Schools and Ideology*, London, Croom Helm.

Whitty, G. (1976) 'Teachers and examiners' in G. Whitty and M. Young (eds), *Explorations in the Politics of School Knowledge*, Driffield, Nafferton Books.

Whitty, G. (1977) *School Knowledge and Social Control*, Units 14/15 of 'Schooling and society', Milton Keynes, Open University Press.

Whitty, G. (1984) 'The "privatization" of education', *Educational Leadership*, 41 (7).

Whitty, G. and Edwards, A. (1984) 'Evaluating policy change: the assisted places scheme' in G. Walford (ed.), *British Public Schools: Policy and Practice*, Lewes, Falmer Press.

Whitty, G. and Young, M. (eds) (1976) *Explorations in the Politics of School Knowledge*, Driffield, Nafferton Books.

Wiener, M. (1981) *English Culture and the Decline of the Industrial 1850–1980*, Cambridge, Cambridge University Press.

Willeman, P. (1978) 'Notes on subjectivity – on reading "Subjectivity under Siege" ', *Screen*, 19 (1).

Williams, R. (1965) *The Long Revolution*, Harmondsworth, Penguin.

Williams, R. (1973) 'Base and Superstructure in Marxist cultural theory', *New Left Review*, 82.

Williams, R. (1977) Review of *Reproduction* and *Society, State and Schooling*, *New Society*, 5 May.

Williamson, B. (1974) 'Continuities and discontinuities in the sociology of education' in M. Flude and J. Ahier (eds) *Educability, Schools and Ideology*, London, Croom Helm.

Willis, P. (1977) *Learning to Labour: How Working Class Kids Get Working Class Jobs*, Farnborough, Saxon House.

Willis, P. (1979) 'Shop-floor culture, masculinity and the wage form' in J. Clarke, C. Critcher and R. Johnson (eds), *Working Class Culture: Studies in History and Theory*, London, Hutchinson.

Willis, P. (1981) 'Cultural production is different from cultural reproduction is different from social reproduction is different from reproduction', *Interchange*, 12 (2/3).

Woods, P. (ed.) (1980a) *Teacher Strategies*, London, Croom Helm.

Woods, P. (ed.) (1980b) *Pupil Strategies*, London, Croom Helm.

Wright, N. (1978) 'One man's mainstream . . .', *The Times Educational Supplement*, 27 January.

Wright, W. (1975) *Sixguns and Society*, Berkeley, University of California Press.

Wynn, B. (1977) 'Domestic subjects and the sexual division of labour' in G. Whitty, *School Knowledge and Social Control*, Milton Keynes, Open University Press.

Young, M. F. D. (ed.) (1971a) *Knowledge and Control: New Directions for the Sociology of Education*, London, Collier-Macmillan.

Young, M. F. D. (1971b) 'An approach to the study of curricula as socially organised knowledge' in M. F. D. Young (ed.) *Knowledge and Control*, London, Collier-Macmillan.

Young, M. F. D. (1972) 'On the politics of educational knowledge', *Economy and Society*, 1.

Young, M. F. D. (1973a) 'Curricula and the social organisation of knowledge' in R. Brown (ed.), *Knowledge, Education and Cultural Change*, London, Tavistock.

Young, M. F. D. (1973b) 'Taking sides against the probable', *Educational Review*, 25 (3).

Young, M. F. D. (1977a) 'School science – innovations or alienation?' in P. Woods and M. Hammersley (eds), *School Experience*, London, Croom Helm.

Young, M. F. D. (1977b) 'Curriculum change – limits and possibilities' in M. Young and G. Whitty (eds) *Society, State and Schooling*, Lewes, Falmer Press.

Young, M. and Whitty, G. (eds) (1977) *Society, State and Schooling*, Lewes, Falmer Press.

# Name index

# Subject index